Mythology

Other titles in
Chambers Compact Reference

To be published in 1993

Mythology

Fernand Comte

Chambers

EDINBURGH   NEW YORK   TORONTO

Published 1991 by W & R Chambers Ltd,
43–45 Annandale Street, Edinburgh EH7 4AZ
95 Madison Avenue, New York N.Y. 10016

First published in France as *Les grandes figures des mythologies*
© Bordas, Paris 1988
© English text edition W & R Chambers 1991

Library of Congress Cataloging-in-Publication Data applied for

ISBN 0 550 17000 6

Cover design Blue Peach Design Consultants Ltd
Typeset by Hewer Text Composition Services, Edinburgh
Printed in England by Clays Ltd, St Ives plc

Acknowledgements

Translated from the French by Alison Goring

Adapted for the English edition by Gillian Ferguson
Min Lee
Mary Lorenz

Chambers Compact Reference Series Editor   Min Lee

Illustration credits

Page

Half-title © Bibliothèque nationale/
Archives Photeb
24 © Rijksmuseum, Amsterdam/Photeb
27 © by courtesy of the Oriental
Institute of the University of
Chicago/Photeb
29 © Shogakukan/Artephot
43 © Staatliche Museen zu Berlin/
Archives Photeb
45 © G. Dagli Orti
48 © L. Von Matt
53 © British Museum, London/
Archives Photeb
56 © G. Dagli Orti
63 © J.L. Nou
70 © Bibliothèque nationale/Photeb
72 © Musée de l'Homme, Paris/Photeb
73 © J.L. Nou
76 © für Kunst und Geshichte, Berlin
77 © J.L. Nou/Photeb
79 © British Museum, London/
Archives Photeb
83 © Bibliothèque nationale/Photeb
84 © Alinari-Viollet/Archives Photeb
86 © ATA Photeb
87 © Bibliothèque nationale/Archives
Photeb
93 © J.L. Nou
94 © Staatliche Museen zu Berlin/
Photeb
98 © Museum of Fine Arts,
Boston/Archives Photeb
102 © Anderson-Viollet/Archives
Photeb
104 © L. von Matt
111 © J.L. Nou/Photeb

Page

114 © Musée Borely, Marseille/Photeb
116 © Bibliothèque nationale/Photeb
119 © J.L. Nou
120 © J.L. Nou/Photeb
121 © J.C. Fauchon-Ana
131 © G. Dagli Orti
138 © Ashmolean Museum, Oxford/
Photeb
142 © L. von Matt
149 © Bibliothèque nationale/Photeb
151 © Archives Photeb
151 © Bibliothèque nationale/Archives
Photeb
151 © Lauros-Giraudon/Photeb
154 © G. Dagli Orti
154 © G. Dagli Orti
157 © Musées nationaux/Photeb
162 © Anderson-Giraudon/Archives
Photeb
165 © Lauros-Giraudon/Archives
Photeb
169 © Musée des Beaux-Arts,
Strasbourg/Photeb
173 © Musée de l'Homme, Paris/Photeb
180 © J.L. Nou/Photeb
181 © J.C. Fauchon-Ana
182 © Archives Photeb
185 © Musées nationaux/Photeb
189 © Archives Photeb
196 © Giraudon/Photeb – D.R.
198 © Nationalmuseet, Copenhagen/
Photeb
204 © Anderson-Viollet/Archives
Photeb
221 © J.L. Nou/Photeb
224 © G. Dagli Orti

Front cover (Poseidon, from the temple of Artemis, Athens) © Explorer
Spine (Horus) © Explorer

Contents

Equivalents or analogies between Greek and Latin myths are shown
in brackets. Gods and heroes are placed alphabetically under their
Greek name.

Civilizations:
Their Gods and Heroes

Introduction

There are countless gods, heroes and demons. They are to be found in literature, painting and sculpture as well as in religious practices and daily customs and have quietly influenced the decisions and actions of men. The wars undertaken by the Hebrews were only the more obvious manifestation of an altogether more important battle in which Yahweh was pitted against the gods of other peoples, and the Romans succeeded in conquering the world only because they knew how to take over the gods of other nations.

Of course this is ancient history, but it reveals the society of the time. Indeed, the ancient peoples cannot be understood *without* understanding their mythology. The gods represented, expressed and gave form to that which, for these people, constituted the sacred: the essential and tangible. They perhaps existed more in the hearts of men than in reality, but they expressed the needs, desires and aspirations of men and represented something beyond the mundane nature of their lives, the limits of their actions and the dangers of their undertakings.

Thus the legends of mythology defy the conditions of the material world and the limits of time and space. They are, in every sense, 'marvellous,' and in order to understand them we must abandon our rationality and logic. They appeal to another part of us which, although not entirely unconnected to our everyday experience, rises far above it. These myths have not come about by chance, or without reason.

It is not insignificant that the ancient Greeks made gods of Love (Eros), War (Ares) and Retribution (Nemesis), but not a god of the word (the logos). This occurred even though an important part of the influence of their civilisation came from the 'logos' of Socrates, Plato and the philosophers. In opposition to this, Christianity made God one with the word and wiped out the others. Rather than compare the beliefs of ancient Greece with those of the gospel, it is important to note the link between myth and the civilisation from which it comes.

To allow freedom of thought, there are few interpretations in this book. It gives only an *account* of the main mythological stories which run through the history of humanity. This is primarily because some of the essential characteristics of myth are its ability to captivate, to be the source of many diverse faiths, to awaken dreams and provoke thought. It can also bear witness to history and show links both between generations and perhaps regions of the world.

Myths are found in every country. It seems, therefore, that all peoples have had to adopt this kind of framework to strengthen their origins, unite their communities and, indeed, to affirm their identity. Each of these peoples has a body of myths which may sometimes seem very strange to a reader who is part of a remote civilisation. But it also allows the reader to depart from his usual mental territory.

This journey through the myths enables us to visit the great civilisations and, to some extent, enter the private lives of those who lived in them. The Greek gods, who are perhaps closest to us, have been explored, as well as other mythologies: Egyptian, Mesopotamian, Norse, Slavonic, Indian, Chinese and so on.

However, this book rarely deals with the characters of the great universal religions. What is myth for one person is reality for another. These major religions have made their mark on modern civilisation, being more or less imprinted on each person's mind. Here it is not a question of beliefs, but simply of wonderful tales.

Frequently the many alternative versions of a myth have been omitted. The importance of a myth lies in its relation to the situation which gave birth to it and the circumstances which made it endure. The best-known versions — that is, the ones which have lasted longest and travelled farthest — are presented.

The enduring nature of myths is witnessed in the personalities of the characters who populate them. When circumstances differ, and even when the sudden changes of fortune in an adventure are altered, the characters remain the same. From the time of their conception, through the trials and tribulations attributed to them, the gods, demons and heroes possess a certain outward appearance, clearly delineated character traits and a specific moral quality.

This book is a dictionary of the principal mythological characters from all areas and from all over the world. It contains accounts of their adventures as they have come down to us through literature, the visual arts and the rites revealed by archaeology.

Universal Myths

Myths of Creation

'In the beginning . . .' — such is the introduction to many accounts of creation. These myths aim to go back to the very beginning of time, when nothing existed . . . or almost nothing, for it is difficult to imagine something born out of nothing. Throughout history and in different countries we find a great many tales of creation. Each has its own originality and is specific to the people who conceived it. Yet even within this great diversity, there are elements which are repeated as if they revealed a common thread through human development. A journey through these myths can seem like a strange probe into the beliefs of humanity.

The creator

'How could Being be born from Non-Being? Oh, my dear one, Being alone existed in the beginning, Being unique, second to none.' (*Chândogya Upanishad*, VI, 2)

In Israel, the creator is called *Yahweh* or *Elohim*, while in Egypt he was *Ptah, Ra,* or *Amen-Ra, Atum* or *Khepri*. The Bantus of Kenya call him *Wele*; to the Canaanites he was *El*; to the Javanese he is *Tunggal* or 'he who masters the universe'; to the Akkadians he was known as *Anu, Apsu* or *Marduk*; *Amma* to the Dogons; *Mangala* to the Malinka and Bambara, and so on.

He is the supreme god, but occasionally, through the course of time, he loses his supremacy. He is always responsible for creation but is not necessarily the active agent who determines the course of events.

According to the Zulus, the eternal spirit commanded the goddess-mother to create herself and then to create the stars, sun and earth.

According to the Delaware Indians of North America, *Tirawa*, the creator, gave most of his powers to the stars, and from their union with each other were born the people who would inhabit the earth. (R.

Linton, 'The Sacrifice of the Morning Star by the Skidi Pawnee', in *Field Museum of Natural History*, Chicago, 1922)

Primitive chaos

'In the beginning of creation, when God made heaven and earth, the earth was without form and void, with darkness over the face of the abyss, and a mighty wind that swept over the surface of the waters.' (*Genesis* 1, 1–5)

Primitive chaos is that which existed before existence. The ancient Egyptians called it *Nun*; for them it was a kind of anterior world, an expanse of water which contained the seeds of all future life.

'The world was nothing but a great confused and undefined mas which is called the Great Beginning,' wrote *Houai-nan tseu*, a Chinese writer of the 2nd century BC. 'At the time when Heaven and Earth did not yet exist there reigned a great formless mist: what darkness! What still and silent immensity and no one could say from where it came!' (Ch. 7)

The Tibetans say, 'There was no intermediary space between Heaven and Earth. There was nothing tangible: no reality, no sign. Since this world possessed neither the nature of existence nor that of non-existence, it was called a potential world and all that exists and is visible came from it.' (M. Tucci, *Tibetan Painted Scrolls*, Rome, 1949)

The first creation

'From the primitive waters, where Elivagor formed the Yawning Void or Ginnungagap, emerged a life, created by the contact between heat and cold, which took human form.' (*Gylfaginning*, 4, 6)

The first movement, the first act, of creation has no cause. It is a spontaneous genesis, as if chaos operated upon itself. It swells, enlarges, becomes enormous; it heats itself by friction and by this action diversifies, cracks, separates, disperses, becomes distinguishable as several entities, multiplies itself to infinity, organises itself and arranges itself into a hierarchy. Thus are born fire, light, life, spirit and all that goes to make up the universe of men.

The *Traibhumikatha* ('The Book of Three Worlds', AD 1345), by King Lut'ai of Thailand, explains: 'The four winds blow on the water, stirring up the waves and transforming the surface into a kind of muddy foam. This surface is then transformed into *Kalala*, like the water used to boil rice. Then the Kalala changes into *Ambuda*, which is like boiled rice, then the Ambuda is changed into *Pesi*, the muddy Pesi . . . becoming land once more.'

According to the Bambara of West Africa, the original void began to wind itself into two spirals turning in opposite directions, and so it gave birth to four worlds. A heavy mass fell and became the Earth; a light element rose and became the Heavens, which spread over the Earth in the form of water and created the conditions for the birth of life. Thereafter, grass and aquatic life appeared. (André Akoun, *Mythes et croyances du monde entier* (Worldwide Myths and Beliefs), Paris, 1985; t. III, p. 35)

The cosmogonic egg

'A large egg emerged from the five primordial elements. On the outside, the white rock of the gods formed on the shell of the egg. Inside, a white lake, like a conch, swirled around clearly in the liquid of the egg. In the centre the beings of the six categories made their appearance on one part of the egg and eighteen eggs came from the yolk of this egg.' (*Po ti bse ru*, Tibetan writing)

Chaos often resembles an egg. Heaven and Earth (in Japanese myth called *Izanagi* and *Izanami*) are not separate but joined, as the male and female principles are joined. (Izanagi is a male god and Izanami is a female one.) The egg is the primordial entity: a perfect totality without distinction or difference. It is sufficient unto itself, smooth, colourless and amorphous.

According to the Egyptians, the egg came out of Nun. 'Ptah is its creator. He poured his seed on it, and within it the Eight (ancestors from the first, earlier times) came into existence' (inscription from the Ptolemic era). In India, a golden egg was formed in the first waters and floated on its surface (*Catapathabrahmana*, XI, 1–6). It is a golden egg, 'clothed in the brilliance of the sun with a thousand rays' (*Manavadharmaçâstras*, Ch. 1).

In certain Siberian myths, the supreme being took the form of a bird so it could lay, on the primordial waters, the egg from which the world would emerge. The cosmogonic egg is fullness as yet untouched. Time begins with its hatching. The universe begins to exist when Chusor, the master craftsman of gods, opens the egg, divides it into two, lifts out one half and makes the Heavens from it, and brings down the second half and makes it into the earth (Damascius, *Problems and solutions regarding the first principles*, Ch. 125).

The separation of the two halves of the egg also represents the separation of male and female. Hesiod, the Greek, tells us how Uranus (Heaven) and Gaea (Earth) were so closely bound that they were unable to let their children rise towards the light. The break was effected by Cronus, who castrated his father. (*Theogony*, 132–138)

Birth of the gods

'Erebus and black Night were born of Chaos. Night in its turn gave birth to Air and Light. Gaea, the Earth, first of all gave birth to a being equal to herself, capable of covering her completely. This was Uranus (Heaven), whose duty was to offer the gods a perpetually firm foundation. Gaea also gave the world the high mountains [. . .]. She gave birth, too, to the barren, raging and swollen sea.' (Hesiod, *Theogony*, 123–132)

The first god to appear was to emerge by his own strength from a kind of sleep, a latent state, in order to create himself, become aware of his existence and begin to work. Ptah, the Egyptian creator-god, is the one 'who gave the beginning to existence, being alone, without any other; he was born of himself and fashioned himself at the beginning, without father or mother to create his body; alone and single, he made the gods, but he himself had not been created.' (*The Tenure of Ptah*, taken from the temple of Edyou, Ostracon, from the museum of Cairo, 3rd–1st cent. BC)

According to the Akkadians, the first gods appeared as if by a miracle: 'When the heavens above were as yet unnamed, and the earth below had no name, when even primordial Apsu, begetter of the gods and Mummu Tiamat, who gave birth to them, mingled their waters, when the fragments of the reeds were not yet gathered together and their growing place as yet unseen, when no god had yet appeared, been named or been subject to his destiny, then, from the bosom of Apsu and Tiamat were born the gods Lakhmu and Lakhamu. They came forth and were named. The ages grew and lengthened . . .' (*Enuma Elish*, tablet I, 1–10)

Of the Wallis Isles it is said, 'Ta'aroa grew by himself in his solitude. He was his own parent, having neither father nor mother [. . .]. The forms of Ta'aroa were countless but there was only one Ta'aroa above, below, and in the night.' (Bonnefoy, *Dictionnaire des mythologies* (Dictionary of mythology), Paris, 1981)

The processes of creation

'Atum-Khepri spat out Shu, the father of the gods; he spat out a jet of saliva which was Tefnut, from whom were born Geb, the Earth, and Nut, the Heavens.' (*Texts of the Pyramids*, Section 1652)

All processes appear to have been used to achieve creation. Ra 'joined himself with his own body in such a way that they (the gods) came out of myself after [. . .] which my dream was fulfilled by my hand' (*Bremmer Rhind Papyrus*, XXVIII, 20 ff.). Khnum-Re shaped men on a potter's wheel and modelled all kinds of livestock; he formed all things on his wheel (*temple of Esna*, text no. 319). Apsu of the Akkadians is only an ordinary procreator: he engendered the other gods by sexual union with Tiamat (*Enuma Elish*, tablet I, 1).

The Bantus of Zaîre say that the god

Nzambi, having experienced severe stomach pains, vomited forth the sun, the moon and the stars and then sandbanks, plants, animals and men (André Akoun, *Mythes et croyances du monde entier* (Worldwide myths and beliefs), Paris, 1985).

According to the Manavu of Mindanao in the Philippines, the first man, Manama, the only being in existence in the world, created the Earth by moulding the dirt which he took from under his fingernails. This dirt swelled up and became inorganic earth, without any vegetation.

The Rwanda Bantus say that the supreme god Imaana created from nothing by the strength of his word, just as Yahweh in the Bible created by forming a wish which was immediately realized: '"Let there be light," and there was light' (*Genesis* 1, 2). In the same way *Io*, a Polynesian god, shaped the universe by his words alone.

Creation is of no interest to the Buddhists, Confuscianists and Taoists. However, putting the world in order is the work of spirits: 'The first is he who listed the grains of sand, the second is he who baled out the Earth, the third is he who counted the stars, the fourth he who dug out the rivers, the fifth he who planted the trees, the sixth created the forests, the seventh built the pillar of the Heavens (popular song from the Nghê Tinh region of Vietnam).

The dismembered giant

'The Earth was fashioned from the flesh of Ymir, the mountains from his bones, the Heavens from the skull of the giant who was as cold as ice, and from his blood the sea.' (*Vafthrudhrismal*, verse 21)

The first being came from the primitive egg. The Chinese tell this story: 'At the time when Heaven and Earth were a chaos resembling an egg, P'an Ku was born in this egg and lived there for eighteen thousand years. And when Heaven and Earth were made, the pure elements *Yang* formed the Heavens, and the base elements *Yin* formed the Earth. And P'an Ku, who was in the middle, changed his form nine times a day, sometimes into a god in Heaven and sometimes into a saint on Earth' (quoted in *La naissance du monde* (The birth of the World), Paris, 1959).

The narrative continues by telling how P'an Ku became the ancestor of the ten thousand beings of the universe: 'When P'an Ku died, his head became a sacred peak, his eyes became the sun and moon, his fat became rivers and seas, his hair became trees and other forms of vegetation' (*Chu yi ki*, gathered in the 6th cent. AD).

The *Vishnu-purana* says that Prajapati, the master of all creatures, 'pulled cattle from his belly and sides, horses and elephants [. . .] from his two feet. From the hair of his body grew plants, fruits and roots' (I, 47–48).

The universe is nothing but the limbs and body of a sacrificed supernatural being; Prajapati is the inventor of sacrifice, he is sacrifice personified (*Rig Veda*, X, 90). The natives of ancient Germany believed that the giant Ymir was dismembered to make up all the parts of the universe. According to the Chinese, P'an Ku pulled out of his body animals, vegetables, minerals and everything that goes to make up the world.

The plunge into the waters

'God was flying around. A man too was flying around [. . .]. God said: "Dive to the bottom of the sea and bring me clay." The man did this and God threw the clay onto the surface of the sea and commanded: "Let this be the earth. Thus the earth was born." (Radlov, *Proben der Volkslitteratur der türkischen Stämme Südsibiriens*, Saint Petersburg, 1866)

All creation comes from water; thus, according to the Tungus of Siberia, it was God himself, called *Eskeri*, who plunged into the vastness of the water and brought back the mud from which he would mould the Earth. For the Modoc from the north-west coast of North America, it was the creator, Qumoqums, who plunged again and again into the waters of Lake Tule. The fifth time he reached the bottom and took a handful of mud, laid it beside the lake and spread it until it covered the whole surface of the lake. He then formed the mountains and rivers, and pulled the trees and plants out of the earth (Claude Lévi-Strauss, *Les mythologiques* (Mythologies), Paris, 1964–71).

In India it is a boar who dives and brings up the Earth from the depths of the waters. In Chota Nagpur, the Birhor say it was the tortoise who was first commanded to dive, and then the crab, but both lost the silt as they came back to the surface. Eventually, it was the leech who finally succeeded by swallowing the earth and spitting it back out when he returned to the surface.

The forces of evil

'A black man, as tall as a spear, was created. Because this man was the master of non-existence, of instability, of killing and destruction, he was given the name "black Hell". He made the sun and the moon die and assigned demons to the planets and harmed the stars [. . .]; he made the rain fall at the most inopportune times.' (G. Tucci, *Tibetan Painted Scrolls*, Rome, 1949).

There are often two principles which battle each other. For the Germanic people, for example, there was, in the north, a world of darkness and cold, *Niflheimr* and in the south, a world of fire, *Muspellsheimr*. *Ymir*, hybrid and ancestor of the giants, was born of the confrontation between the two. The various parts of Ymir's murdered body went to make up the world.

This explained why the world was not perfect. The Georgian mountain people found another solution: in the beginning there was a couple because God had a sister. She became angry with her brother and, when he created the sky in the form of a vast net, she created rats and mice to gnaw through the mesh. When he created the vine, the demon created the goat to nibble it, and so on.

The *Avesta* of Mazdaism refers to two primordial spirits, 'who, as twin rulers, have declared their nature, the better and the wicked . . . And when the two Spirits came together, they first created Life and Non-life.' (*Yasna*, 30, 2–3)

The Flood and the Fear

'At first the cloud will bring snow from the highest mountains to the deepest valleys . . . Water will flow in great torrents, and those places where even now you can see sheep tracks will become impassable!' (*Avesta, Videvdat*, 2)

'This race of men whom I have created, I will wipe them off the face of the earth — man and beast, reptiles and birds. I am sorry that I ever made them.' (*Genesis* 6, 7). These were Yahweh's words on seeing the wickedness of men. And 'The flood continued upon the earth for forty days . . . More and more the waters increaased over the earth until they covered all the high mountains everywhere under heaven.' (*Genesis* 7, 17–19)

The myth of the flood is almost universally known: in Sumer in the *Epic of Gilgamesh* (tablet XI); in India in the *Satapatha-Brahmana* (I; VII, 1) and the *Bhagavata-purana* (VIII; XXIV, 7 ff.); in Iran (*Avesta, Videvdat*, Ch. 2); in Greece (Apollodorus, (*Bibliotheca*, I; VII, 2); in South-East Asia, Melanesia, and Polynesia; in the tribes of South America, Central America and North America.

Re-creation

The cataclysm which came to pass was usually followed by the creation of the world. Noah in the Bible, invited by God himself to build a boat which would float on the water and thus survive, is called *Ziusudra* in the Sumerian version, *Utnapishtim* in the Akkadian version and *Manu* in the Indian version. In Iran, Ahura Mazda himself tells Yima, the first man, of the catastrophe to come, and Prometheus warns his son, Deucalion, of Zeus's decision to destroy humanity.

Each time a small group is saved. Noah took with him a pair of animals of each species. Utnapishtim discovered, to his surprise, that the human race had not been completely wiped out. Manu was saved by the fish identified in the *Mahabharata* (III, 187) as Brahma, and Deucalion escaped with his family in an ark.

Variations on the same theme

'The flood continued upon the earth for forty days, and the waters swelled and lifted up the ark so that it rose high above the ground. They swelled and increased over the earth, and the ark floated on the surface of the waters. More and more the waters increased over the earth until they covered all the high mountains everywhere under heaven. The waters increased and the mountains were covered to a depth of fifteen cubits. Every living creature that moves on earth perished.' (*Genesis* 7, 17–21)

In Australia there was a giant frog. It drank up all the water and dried up the whole earth, and so the parched animals decided to do something about it. In front of the frog, the eel performed contortions which made the frog laugh and, unable to hold in the water, he spat it all out at once and thus caused the flood. The frog is a symbol of the moon, whose relationship with water is well-known.

In South America, it is one of the original twins who, by tapping his foot on the earth, made streams gush forth whose waters flooded the earth.

According to the Quichés, the Mayan people of Guatemala, the two creators, Tepeu and Gucumatz succeeded, after several attempts, to make beings 'capable of saying their names'. Unfortunately, they had neither memory nor reason and so they decided to drown them in a flood. (A. Recinos, *Popol Vuh. Las antiguas historias del Quiché*, Fondo de Cultura Economica, Mexico, 1952)

Kabunian is the supreme god of the Ifugao of the Philippines. He too decided to kill humanity because it did not make sacrifices to the gods. However, a brother and sister, the children of Kabigat, were warned and took refuge at the summit of a high mountain.

The Indochinese Sre believe that the flood originated in the sea. All was destroyed except a brother and sister who had hidden in a barrel; when the waters began to recede, it was left on Mount Yang-La.

In Thailand, it was only the genii, who survived the flood by making a vessel which, when the waters rose, took them up to heaven. The King of Heaven, however, welcomed them and then sent them back to the world of men, having first made them a gift of a buffalo.

In China, Yu is the hero who managed to master the waters: 'Vast waters rose to the sky; an immense expanse of water surrounded the mountains and submerged the hills.' At first it was Kouen who was charged with the task of quelling the flood; he set out to build sea walls using the 'swelling earth', but failed. He was followed by Yu, who succeeded in draining the water by means of outlets. This took him thirteen years. (*Chouking*, Ch. 'Yu Kong: the tribute of Yu')

In India, the flood lasts for one hundred years and is preceded by a cosmic fire. Everything is destroyed. It is the return of the world to initial chaos in which Vishnu lies, asleep, the gathering place for all creatures.

Meaning

'Man did not listen to the thên (gods). In spite of three warnings, man disobeyed them. Consequently, the thên started a flood which submerged the world from below and destroyed everything; sand flew up to the heavens, all men disappeared. Pu Lang S'oeung and Khun K'an understood that the thên were furious with them.' (*Manuscript E 11*, Prakeo Library, Vientiane, Laos)

The memory of a natural disaster is doubtless at the root of all these myths about a flood. One explanation is that Babylon was situated between two very strong rivers, the Tigris and the Euphrates. Both were liable to terrible flooding which spread over a vast area. At some point the flood came from both sides of the town simultaneously, leaving no refuge for the inhabitants. It was perhaps natural, then, to imagine a cosmic cataclysm capable of destroying the whole earth.

This popular heritage has been transformed into a mythical tale with a religious and moral lesson. It is the divinity who brings about the flood; the reason for it is the sins of men or the decay of the world—ultimately, the failure of creation. God repents of having created the world, and he brings about a return to the primal waters which constituted original chaos.

'When the Lord saw that man had done much evil on earth and that his thoughts and inclinations were always evil, he was sorry that he had made man on earth, and he was grieved at heart. (*Genesis* 6, 5)

The flood became an expression of fear: the fear of men unable to control their environment; the fear of not living up to that for which they were created; the fear that despite themselves they would be dragged down into failure and destruction.

However, hope is never lost and there is always a little something in reserve—namely, a couple who will give birth to a new humanity. The flood illustrates the ability to start afresh, for the divinity just as much as for humanity. The flood can become hope, the beginnings of a new era, the beginnings of the golden age.

In this way, the flood is both life and death, destruction and purification. It marks the end of one phase, of an age of the world, and the beginning of another. The Hindus give the name *Kalpa* to these cosmic periods, which follow one after the other. Each lasts about twelve million years.

This cyclical theory of the history of the universe appears in many countries. It can be found in Heraclitus in the 5th century BC and with the Stoics.

The Beyond: Heaven and Hell

'I tell you this: today you shall be with me in Paradise.' (*Luke* 23, 43) These were the words of Jesus to the thief who had repented of his crimes. Heaven, hell, the beyond and life after death have been the subject of many myths throughout history.

Whether as a myth of hope or of fear of the unknown, man has always imagined another world, even if he feels that the great 'beyond' is more a state than a place. Nonetheless, the images conveyed by this myth, while they are clumsy or awkward, occasionally poetic and always emotionally charged, do represent a reality perceived to exist beyond death.

The story generally begins with the approach of the unknown. Death is a long process which is not over at the end of earthly life but, on the contrary, takes on a surreal dimension.

The steep path

'And so, a woman who is beautiful, strong, well-built, blooming [. . .] gifted and virtuous comes. She throws down the sinful souls of wicked men into the darkness. The souls of the just she helps to cross the Chinvat bridge.' (*Avesta*, XIX, 26 ff.)

The dwelling place of the dead is not easily accessible. The North Asian shamans know that obstacles must be overcome during their trances, so that they can guide the souls of the dead to their new resting place.

The Mesoamericans actually describe the path. One must climb up steep mountains which clash against each other, cross inhospitable deserts, confront poisonous snakes, endure the 'obsidian' winds which cut like razors, and cross the nine rivers of hell.

According to the Persians, the dead person must cross the Chinvat or 'grading' bridge, which is as wide as nine spears laid end to end for the just and as narrow as a razor blade for the wicked.

The Greek hell, or Hades, is separated from the world of the living by four rivers: Ocean, Acheron, Phlegethon and Cocytus (Plato, *Phaedo*). Charon ferries souls in his boat to the other bank of the Acheron, which is a chaotic mixture of fire and glacial, Stygian water (*The Odyssey*).

Two hounds guard the entrance to this domain: 'your two guard dogs, O Yuma, four eyes to guard the way and watch over men' (*Rig Veda*, X, 14, 11). For the Greeks it was Cerberus who guarded the gates to Hell.

The other world

'. . . The numberless guilty are stripped of their clothes, which are then hung from a tree. How loud is the moaning of these numberless voices! The unfortunate ones are uncertain where to go; they spin around, move about restlessly, and, clutching one another, hold their head in their hands and wail.' (*Pien-wen*, discovered in Touen-houang, China)

Tartarus is in the very depths of the universe, 'as far below Hades as the Heavens are above the Earth' (*Iliad*, VIII, 13–16). It was described as the cosmic centre from which all waters flow (Plato, *Phaedo*, 112–113); a cave (Hesiod, *Theogony*, 301); the realm of darkness of Erebus (*Iliad*, XVI, 327); humid and musty (*Iliad*, X, 512); and a quagmire reserved for the uninitiated and the damned (Aristophanes, *The Frogs*).

It is separated from the world of the living by an abyss (the *ba-Ila* of Zimbabwe) and is situated either in the East — the departed travel in the opposite direction to the sun — or in the South, like the land of Yama, the Indian king of the dead. It might also be in the West, as in Egypt, where the dead are called 'those of the West'. Mexicans, on the other hand, called it 'the place where the sun sleeps'.

The Finno-Ugrians (*Kalevala*) call the

dwelling place of the dead *Tuonela*, and the Turks and Mongols call it *Tamu/tamuk.*

In the beginning it was thought that this 'beyond' consisted of a life similar to the one we know, a sort of double of our world with the dead continuing to live in a familiar landscape, taking part in the same activities. This belief is quite common in Africa, among the Hopi Indians, in Birmani, and in New Guinea.

In New Caledonia, the inhabitants of the other world eat lizards as meat, bamboo instead of sugar-cane and excrement instead of vegetables.

The people of North Asia see the world of the dead as a world which is inverse to our own, with their day corresponding to our night, their summer to our winter, and, when there is poverty in our world, there is plenty in theirs. When something is broken in our world it is intact in theirs, and vice versa. Our right is their left, high is low and so on.

Hades was a vast cavern inside the earth where there was no distinction made between the good and the wicked. Hades was preferable, however, to the wanderings of those who had had no burial. The agonies of Tantalus, Tityus and Sisyphus give us a picture of what this suffering was like.

The story according to the Persians was that a young girl and her double, *Daena*, came to meet the deceased. If the dead person's actions had been good, his guide would be young, pretty, elegant, bedecked with jewels and smell sweetly of perfume. If he had been wicked, she would be like an old witch: sinister, foul-smelling, filthy and in rags. The pretty one helped the *Fravarti* (the soul of the dead person) to cross the bridge, while the horrible, wicked old witch hurled it down into the ravine.

Paradise

'O Soma, who is made clear in this inexhaustible abode of the immortals, let me settle where perpetual light shines, in this same world where the sun had its place! [. . .] There in the fold of Heaven where the waters are eternally young, make me an immortal there, O Soma!' (*Rig Veda*, IX, 113)

It was usual for the dead to go to heaven, but sometimes this was reserved for certain privileged persons. In Egypt, at first only the Pharoah and his family had the right to go there, but later this privilege was granted to everyone. In the world of the dead the hierarchy existing in the world of the living was copied. A certain stage of evolution had to be reached before paradise became the reward for a virtuous life.

The *Mahabharata*, the *Ramayana* and the *Puranas* describe the heavens of the five great Indian gods. Indra's heaven was peopled with dancers and musicians, Vishnu's was made of gold and scattered with pools covered in lotuses and in Brahma's heaven the dead enjoyed the company of celestial nymphs. The main elements of these heavens were gold, gardens, song, dance and pretty girls.

In the 'western paradise', the 'pure earth' was linked with Amitabha: 'there is no physical pain or mental anguish. The sources of joy are innumerable. This is why this land is called the happy land . . . Around it are seven overlapping vaults, seven rows of precious veils and seven rows of noisy villages. It is embellished with seven great terraces, seven rows of palm trees with seven lakes covered in lotus blossoms of every colour, which are as big as chariot wheels . . . Every possible kind of bird sings praises to the law. Everywhere precious stones glitter and the sound of bells rings out . . . Amitayas lives there surrounded by his faithful followers, too numerous to count' (*Ashtasakasrita*, XV).

'Even the air,' says the *Apocalypse of Peter*, a 1st century Christian apocryphal text, 'is lit up by the rays of the sun and the earth abounds with spices and with plants which do not perish, whose beautiful flowers never wither and which bear blessed fruit . . . Those who dwell in this place wear the same clothing as the stuff which makes the angels shine, and their country is like their clothes.' 'The city is made of gold,' says the *Apocalypse of Paul*, 'and four rivers flow through it: rivers of milk, honey, wine and oil. On their banks grow trees with ten thousand branches bearing ten thousand clusters of fruit, and the country is bathed in light so bright it shines seven times more brightly than silver.'

For the Mesoamerican Indians, the paradise of the god Tlaloc is called *Tlalocan*, and it is above all for warriors killed in combat. There they have a procession to the sun. For the North American Indians, paradise is 'land rich in game' where they spend their time tracking vast herds of buffalo, and salmon abounds in the fisherman's net.

Among the Celts, the other world, known as the *Sid* or *Tir na nOg* (Land of the Young), *Tir na mBéo* (Land of the Living), Tir ma mBan (Land of the Women), or *Mag Meld* (Plain of Pleasure), is a world where milk, honey, beer and wine flow freely. There are always feasts in the palaces which are built of gold, silver, bronze and crystal. They are surrounded by young women of unforgettable beauty and lively intelligence. They know no illness there, nor old age, and sin does not exist there.

The land of the blest is, for Pindar (*Threnoi*), the land of the nocturnal sun; for the Romans, it is the wealthy islands where heroes are taken; and for the Hebrews, the 'bosom of Abraham'—a paradise for the elect.

Hell

'At dawn, after the third night has passed, the wicked man's soul finds itself in the middle of a desert, and it has the sensation of breathing foul air. It feels a wind blow from the north, from the northern countries, a wind which stinks, more foul-smelling than the other winds. The soul of the wicked man breathes this wind in through his nostrils.' (*Hadôkht*, II)

There is also another world of the dead which is gloomy, cold, dark and peopled with ghosts: 'Their food is dust, and they eat mud . . . they are like swine who roll in filth. They are in darkness and will never see the light.' (*Epic of Gilgamesh*)

For the Mesopotamians it is the kingdom of the god Nergal, and the goddess Ereshkigal, an underground place whose infernal deities, demons and hideous monsters eternally destroy each other. 'Those who enter here are deprived of light and their bread is made from clay [. . .] The door and bolt of this realm are covered in dust.' (*The Descent into Hell of the Goddess Ishtar*)

'If I told you,' said Nergal to Gilgamesh, 'about the law of the underworld, I know that I would see you sit down and cry.' (*Epic of Gilgamesh*, IV, 1–5)

In India the *Isha Upanishad* speaks of 'these worlds which are designated sunless, since they are completely in impenetrable darkness: those who have killed, their souls go there after death.' The Hindus imagined twenty-one hells where sinners suffer hunger and thirst, are devoured by wild beasts, roasted, sawn into pieces, boiled in oil and crushed to pulp. Buddha continues, 'they are harnessed to enormous carts and made to walk long distances through flames; others are forced to plunge their heads into a cauldron of boiling water; others are thrown into great fires.' Hell is only temporary for Buddhists, but it can last 576 million years. (*Majjimanikaya*)

There are eight hells of heat and eight hells of cold, and each group is surrounded by sixteen lesser hells. It is here that the damned tear off each other's skin with metal claws, and iron elephants crush their victims and so on. (*Mahayana*)

The *Apocalypse of Paul* describes, in its own way, the sufferings of hell for the early Christians: He talks of enormous worms with two heads, three feet long, which gnaw at the entrails of the damned; of burning wheels which turn a thousand times in a day; of white hot razors; of a pestilential abyss where those who have not been baptized must rot. It is the fiery gehenna of which the Bible speaks, which will be the punishment for the wicked at the end of the world.

In Northern Europe, where cold is the worst thing, hell takes on this aspect; it is called *gwern* (swamp), or *oer, oerfel* or *rhew* (cold or icy).

The Function of Myths

Myths do not die, they change. In the course of their development they are altered by the shifting beliefs of humanity. They resist extreme change and adapt to the new circumstances, reinterpreting their characters and transforming their structures. They still manage to retain their prestige, however, even if there remain only traces of the civilisation which conceived of them. Sometimes, myths even become entangled with each other and their contents overlap, making it difficult to challenge them by direct means. For this reason, it would be better, perhaps, to consult them than to try and destroy them.

The Roman gods

'It is through religion that we have conquered the world.' (Cicero)

The Romans had a very elevated idea of what divinity was and would not dedicate a cult to a god until he had shown himself to them. The way in which the Etruscan god Juno came to Rome is a good example of this. For ten years the Roman army had been laying seige to Veii. After certain wonders had occurred, like the waters of Lake Alba rising for no apparent reason, they chose a leader. The new leader not only gave military orders but also spoke to the divine protectress of Veii in these words: 'Queen Juno, who at present dwells in Veii, I beg you to follow us, after our victory, to Rome which will soon be your city; there we will build a temple worthy of your greatness.' (Livy V, 21, 3) Thus the Roman Pantheon was built.

However, they soon discovered in foreign gods similarities with their own deities. The Consul Lucius Junius immediately recognized that Aphrodite of Mount Eryx was the same as Venus, whom the Romans had long worshipped; and so, by successive assimilations, Zeus became Jupiter for them, Hera was called Juno, Artemis was merged with Diana, and so on.

When Caesar crossed Gaul, he renamed the cults and indigenous gods he came across with Roman names. Thus a kind of intercommunication of myths between different civilisations was achieved.

Brigit and Saint Bride

'Brigit, that is to say, the daughter of Dagda, is Brigit the poetess or, alternatively, she is Brigit the goddess worshipped by the poet, because of the great and renowned protection they received from her. There were three sisters of the same name other than Brigit the *file* (poet). There was a second Brigit who practised medicine and a third who was a smith. All three were daughters of Dagda and all three were goddesses, and in Ireland the name of the goddess Brigit signifies all of them. (*Glossary of Cormac*, 900)

Brigit was a great Irish goddess. Her name means 'greatness'. She was the goddess of Fire, Fertility and Poetry, and the daughter of Dagda. In *De bello Gallica* (VI, 17, 2), Caesar called her Minerva and considered her the goddess of work and the arts. The Brigantia, the people of the North of England, made her their national goddess.

Saint Bride, mother of eight children, was the founder and abbess of the monastery at Vadsténa, an ancient hermitage established on a druidic sanctuary kept by women who undertook to keep an everlasting fire alight. The Irish made her their patron saint, equal to Saint Patrick.

Brigit disappeared and Saint Bride took her place. However, within this new figure there remained a symbol, a presence, a protective force which was hitherto called Brigit. In fact, the two characters have been blended together and it is no longer clear what in the legend refers to which.

The parable of Odysseus

'If Odysseus could be held back by the Lotus-eaters because of the sweetness of their fruit; if the gardens of Alcinous were able to delay him; and if, finally, the Sirens, luring him by their charms, almost succeeded in bringing about his shipwreck by sensual pleasures; and if he had to fight against the enchantment of their melodious voices, how much more should religious men be captivated by the wonder of celestial deeds! And, it is not merely a question of ascertaining the sweetness of the berries, but the bread which has fallen from Heaven.' (Saint Ambrose of Milan, *Exposition of the Gospel according to Saint Luke*, IV, 2–3)

Thus myths change and sometimes are consciously changed. From the 2nd century onwards, Christians made use of mythologies which did not come from the same source as their faith. Odysseus, for example, seduced by the Sirens' voices, becomes the Christian who is attracted by worldly pleasures. When Odysseus stops the ears of his companions with wax he shows how the faithful must remain deaf to the deceptive propaganda of paganism or the heresies which would lead to their downfall. When he ties himself to the mast he is the image of Christ, and of the believer, on the Cross, and it is his being hanged there that allows him to regain his homeland.

Even though these commentators do say, and repeat, that the myths taken from other ages and cultures are manifestly false, and even if they declare that they are only using them as illustrations, this usage would seem to prove that they are somehow bearers of truth. They bring to life certain attitudes and explain behaviour in a particular way.

Universal myths

'At the age of nine, they were nine cubits wide and nine fathoms tall, and they threatened the Immortals by bringing the tumult of spirited war to Olympus. They wanted to pile Mount Ossa onto Olympus and Mount Pelion with the restless leaves onto Mount Ossa in order to mount their assault on Heaven.' (*Odyssey*, XI, 305–320)

There are certain myths which are found in many different civilisations. This can be easily understood as far as creation, the afterlife, the beginning and the end are concerned, but the numerous tales of the flood are more difficult to explain. And the way in which the story about Tower of Babel (*Genesis*, 11, 109) resembles the Aloeids' ladder to Heaven (*Odyssey*, XI, 305–320), or the destruction of Sodom and Gomorrah is like the adventure of Phaethon (Euripedes, *Hippolytus*, 735 ff.), and the way in which Niobe can be compared to, if not assimilated in Lot's wife (*Genesis*, 19, 26), and the prophet Joseph to Bellorophon, Saint George to Hercules and Samson to Heracles, reveal similarities which are indicative of some extraordinary coincidences.

To a greater or lesser extent myths are interpreted in the light of the beliefs of each epoch. By virtue of their being recorded in history, they constitute a kind of fundamental basis for humanity. They are sustained by such power that each new faith and new civilisation has had to make do with their imagery — without, of course, acknowledging it.

To a great extent Freud used mythologies to explain the mechanics of human psychology, and we have become aware that individuals may live out, in their own way, the adventures of Oedipus or the drama of Antigone.

Whether mythology is transcendent or merely an embellished story, it cannot leave *homo religiosus* indifferent. It questions him, pushes him around and makes him stumble, but it also sometimes enlightens him, sets him in front of his choices and coerces him into making decisions and commitments. This is perhaps the primary function of myth.

Modern Myths

'Myth takes on the outward appearance of an ardent belief with all the features of greatness. From close up the belief is shown to be a prejudice which has no control over its sources, conditions or claims.' (Emmanuel Mounier, *Révolution personnaliste at communautaire* (Individual and communal revolution), Paris, 1935)

So, what of myths today? This is the age of reason and science. The only things considered true are those which have been rationally legitimized or scientifically tested. Everything else is nothing but nonsense: a fairy tale, artistic exuberance or toys for children. Myths are easily relegated into the past; they have lost their credibility and are nothing but a pious memory.

But two examples, amongst many, serve to show that modern society has not done away with all myths. On the contrary, it exudes, invents and manipulates them. Myth is still a driving force in life just as it was in ancient societies.

The myth of science

The pursuit of science 'is just as irrational and emotional in its motives and just as intolerant in its daily practices as any of the traditional religions it has taken over from . . . It is not enough for it that it claims that its myths alone are true; it is the only religion which has the arrogance to claim that it is not based on any myth at all but on Reason alone, and whose particular mixture of intolerance and amorality is presented as tolerance.' (*Survivre* no. 9, August/September 1971)

Man has built himself wonderful instruments of discovery. He has refined his reasoning and exercised it rigorously, and found the most reliable methods for devising the most practical theories. In this way, he has extended his sphere of influence, taken into his own hands certain means of control which were hitherto unknown, exercised control over the world and transformed his own life. Science has imposed itself on the universe like some kind of latter-day *deus ex machina*, possessing all the knowledge of the past and all that can be predicted about the future.

Weaknesses in this phenomenal progress, however, have appeared. Even the most rigorous stringency is never without its flaws. Reason is incapable of eliminating all contradiction and has proved unable to achieve the consistency which was supposedly inherent in its nature. The coexistence of certain differing philosophical systems is proof of this. But, above all, science has come to realize that the principle of non-contradiction which is at the heart of its development is more a requirement of its methods than a characteristic of reality. Science often, particularly when it reaches extremes — the infinitely large or the infinitely small — finds itself up against something irrational which calls its methods and experiments into question and renders their conclusions somewhat doubtful. Its logic is applicable only in the short term and under certain conditions.

Science and technology, engendered by the human mind, advance inexorably. They are always pushing back the limits of their domain without ever tackling a complete explanation, which would be beyond the ability and even the ambition of scientists. They challenge every approach to the natural world which is unfamiliar to them; Science seems to be a terrible god who drives away his rivals and makes draconian demands.

The fact is that science and technology are a long way from testing everything and finding an explanation for it. There is a very great area which remains outwith the sphere of science and technology, and their claim to lay down the law has been greatly challenged. It seems that they have neither the knowledge nor the ability to go beyond the scientific domain, whose limits become more apparent every day. Science often conflicts with ethics, whose purpose is to protect, not govern, what science does. Science also seems unable to give a clear direction for the development of ethics.

Presented as fact and with methods whose efficacy grows more impressive every day, and an obvious factor in the incredible acceleration of material civilisation, science still does not provide that breakthrough into the unknown which classic mythology endeavours to reveal. It shows only one side of things, only one aspect of problems. Science deals with the invisible only to restrict it, to make it act like the visible. However, it starts off with practical and limited applications and moves, without apparently even being aware of it, towards a claim of being universal truth. It presents itself as Truth, other than which there is none; it denies everything which cannot be encompassed within its sphere. The only justification for this exclusion is subjective. It is not founded on reason, it is irrational. It does, in fact, display a mythological nature.

Like the classical myth, 'scientism' has its images: the ideal society where everything is listed, counted and measured (Aldous Huxley, *Brave New World*). Like the classical myth, it is separated from the man of today by time (past or future); like the classical myth, it is full of social rites, churches, and clergy; like the classical myth it is sustained by faith, sometimes even by fanaticism. In short, it has created a new form of myth.

The star

According to André Malraux, 'the star is a person with a minimum of dramatic talent whose face expresses, symbolizes, and embodies a collective instinct. Marlene Dietrich is not an actress like Sarah Bernhardt, she is a myth like Phryne.' *Esquisse d'une psychologie du cinema* (Sketches from a psychology of the cinema)

The development of the media has meant that people have been, in some ways, brought closer together. They can see what is happening in other lives, in other places. But the divide between the privileged and the common man still exists. Instead of the privileges of class and power which have traditionally occupied the interest, the focus is now on the conspicuous privilege of 'stars'. They possess, or are supposed to possess, riches and fame; they are beautiful and happy; they are known everywhere.

Their public imagine they are not bothered by the trivial things of everyday life, but like the gods of Olympus they do share the passions of humanity, and like the gods are exceptional in the powers of persuasion and seduction. Their followers flock to see them or their images and collect 'relics' connected with their idols; they adopt the same modes of dress, gestures, habits and are grief-stricken should anything happen to their chosen 'god'.

There are many 'religions' which have given rise to a particular mythology — politics, sport, rock, cinema, television — all a reflection of the age in which we live.

Gods and Heroes

Achilles

Greek hero

An impassioned man

He was almost invulnerable as a warrior: if he was sullen, defeat was inevitable; but if he fought, victory was certain.

Achilles was the seventh son of Peleus, king of Phthia, and the goddess Thetis. To make her children immortal, Thetis covered them with ambrosia during the day and thrust them into the fire at night. Achilles was the only one to escape this, thanks to his father snatching him from his mother's hands just in time (*Apollodorus*, III, 13, 6). Only Achilles's lips and right ankle bone were burned, and Cheiron, the centaur, replaced his ankle bone with one taken from the giant Damysos who was a particularly fast runner. Achilles therefore inherited this attribute and was given the nickname, Achilles the light-footed.

According to other sources, Thetis, in order to make the child invulnerable, dipped him in the water of the Styx, the infernal river. Only his heel, since she held him by it, remained vulnerable — the famous heel which became Achilles's only weak point. (*Fulqence*, III, 7)

The Trojan Wars

Two texts tell of Achilles's departure for Troy. One says that he was warned by an oracle that if he went he would have a short

but glorious life, and if he stayed he would have a long but unremarkable one. Achilles obviously chose the more noble course of action (*The Iliad*, IX, 14). According to the other text, his parents were warned that he would die in Troy and hid him, disguised, among the daughters of Lycomedes, the king of Scyros. Achilles was unmasked, however, by the wily Ulysses who ordered a trumpet-blast. Achilles, responding to his warrior's instincts, seized the weapons which were there . . . by chance (*Apollodorus*, III, 13, 6).

The Iliad is all about the wrath of Achilles when Agamemnon stole Briseis, a young girl whom Achilles had received as booty from him. Our hero did not want to go to war until she had been returned. And since it was he, and he alone who inspired terror in the Trojans, the Greeks went from one defeat to the next. Ambassadors were sent to beg him to take up arms again. One day, in order to deceive the Trojans, he agreed to lend his own armour to his friend Patrocles so that the Trojans would think Achilles was in the battle. The ruse, however, did not last long and Patrocles was killed. Achilles flew into a terrible rage and ran to revenge his friend's death. He killed Hector and led the Greeks to victory (*The Iliad*, XVII, 855 ff).

Achilles was killed by Paris — or by Apollo himself — by an arrow in his heel, the only vulnerable part of his body (*The Iliad*, XIX, 417; XXII, 278, 359). Thetis took his remains to the Isle of Achillea on the Danube, where sailors heard the clash of weapons and the hubbub of a banquet (*Pomponius Mela*, II, 7, 208).

Achilles had a cenotaph at Sparta and another at Olympia (*Pausanias*, III, 30, 8; VI, 23, 2) and a temple was built in his honour on the promontory at Sigeum (*Strabon*, XII).

The Styx

One of the rivers of Hell; its waters had magical properties.

Adapa

Akkadian hero

The wise one

A paragon of intelligence, he was one of the seven Apkallu, the extraordinary envoys of Ea/Enki, the divine creator of men and a civilizing influence.

Adapa was wise because the god whom he served was wise himself and taught Adapa everything he knew. Adapa became an instrument of progress and civilisation in the land of the Akkadians, 3000 years BC. What is remembered most about him is his obedience, bound hand and foot, to his master. He lost his opportunity for immortality by such obedience.

He was Ea's chief representative at his temple at Eridu, and from time to time he liked to go fish in the Bitter River. One day when Adapa had sailed out a long way from the shore, Shutu, the south wind, rushed straight towards him, rocking his boat and finally capsizing it. Adapa escaped from the wreck, however, and, seized by a great rage, attacked Shutu and cut off his wings. Shutu, like all gods of the wind, had the form of a bird — and for a whole week the south wind was not heard.

Anu, the god of Heaven at this time, was surprised by the silence and asked to know the reason for it. When he had been told, he demanded that the guilty person appear before his tribunal. Just as Adapa was going, Ea warned him, 'Make friends with the keepers of the doors of Heaven and when you are in the presence of Anu do not touch the food and drink which you will be offered. It is the food and drink of death. You will also be offered clothing which you should put on, and oil with which you should annoint yourself.'

Adapa did as he was told; he got on so well with Tammuz and Nin Gishzida, the two keepers of the doors of Heaven, that he was received, not before a tribunal, but at the table of Anu. Anu offered Adapa the food and drink of eternity. He refused and so lost his chance of immortality. The god of Heaven then ordered that the ungrateful Adapa should be chased out of his sight, making Adapa the definitive victim of disagreements between gods.

The Apkallu

It is said that there were seven, eight or sixteen Apkallu. They were beings of great brilliance, skill and genius, expert in every field. They were regarded by sovereigns, gods and men as deputies, viziers who were completely submissive to their masters. They brought knowledge to these masters and were instruments in their power. Ea was the patron of Apkallu and used them to introduce the comforts of life and civilization to men. He himself was the Apkallu of the gods.

In the Seleucidic Era (from the 6th–1st century BC) they were called *Ummanu*. One of them wrote *The Epic of Erra* and another wrote *The Epic of Gilgamesh*.

The revenge of Anu

There is another version of the story in which Anu says, 'Since Adapa, a human being, has by his own means broken the wings of Shutu, let it be thus: whatever illness Shutu has put into the bodies of men, Ninkarak (goddess of Health and Cure) can, with him, ease them and the illness will depart. But without him, let there remain an icy fever and let the ill person be held in a gentle drowsiness from which there is no respite.'

The 'Bitter River'

The name given to the Euphrates, which was unpredictable and capricious.

Aditi

Indian goddess

The kindly one

The Vedic hymns celebrate her as the goddess of all plants and animals and as the mother of all beings.

A mother-goddess, Aditi gave birth to the Adityas, originally serpents who shed their skin and became immortal (*Pancavimsa Br.*, XXV, 15, 4). They became gods, *devas*, even supreme gods. Among the Adityas were Mitra; Varuna; Aryaman, protector of Aryans; and Bhaga, who ensures the distribution of wealth.

Aditi was *rajaputra* 'she whose sons are kings'; *uugraputra*, 'she whose sons are strong' (*Rig Veda*, VIII, 56, 11); *suputra*, 'she whose sons are good' (*Rig Veda*, III, 4, 11); and even *suraputra*, 'she whose sons are great heroes' (*Atharva Veda*, XI, 1, 1). She was the mother par excellence, and pregnant women carried with them the amulet 'which Aditi wore when she wanted a son' (*Atharva Veda*, I, 89, 10). She was therefore the guardian of childbirth.

A goddess apart

Aditi's name means 'the unbound', the free, and she was a primordial goddess.

The origin

'In the first age of the gods, Being was born of Non-Being. Then the Regions were born, brought forth from the one in labour. The World was born of the one who was in labour. The Regions were born of the world. Daksa was born of Aditi, and Aditi of Daksa. For Aditi was born, O Daksa, she who is your daughter. After her the gods were born, the blessed, the related immortals.' (*Rig Veda*, X, 72, 3–5)

'Aditi is the heavens, Aditi is the atmosphere. Aditi is the mother, father, and son. Aditi is every god and the five races. Aditi is that which has been born. Aditi is that which is to be born' (*Rig Veda*, I, 89, 10). Her attributes were sufficiently indeterminate to leave room for a kind of pantheism. While her sons, the supreme gods, had a function in divine society or the universe, Aditi was *everything* at the same time; she was the total, the beginning and the end, and, at the same time, she was the opposites. She was undifferentiated and also represented length, breadth and freedom.

As far as sacrifices were concerned, she was not treated as the other gods; she was outwith the divine world. Her honour was such that she received the first and last offerings or she received nothing. Her charge was to allocate to each divine couple what was destined for them.

Her work

Aditi was the goddess responsible for opening out. She freed everything which was restricted and made all traces of sin, impurity, suffering and illness disappear. She also gave good health (*Rig Veda*, X, 100).

Adopted by the Buddhist tradition, she became part of its legends. Thus she brought support to Buddha and drowned the armies of Mara, the tempter, who wanted to distract Buddha from his meditation and thus prevent him from achieving enlightment.

Her cult

Thailand, Birmani, Laos and Cambodia have represented her as a young woman winding her hair with both hands. From her hair a river flows which is the source of all riches. In these countries she was known as Dharani or Brah Dharni.

Adonis

God of Phoenician origin

The precocious seducer

His voilent, ephemeral and barren passion made unfaithful wives faint.

Originally from Phoenicia, he was first called Thammuz and then Gauas. However, it was as Adonis, meaning 'lord', that he became famous, particularly in Byblus, Alexandria, Cyprus and Greece.

Theias, the king of Syria, had a daughter named Myrrha or Smyrna. Aphrodite made Myrrha wish to commit incest with her father. She succeeded in tricking Theias and joining with him. When he realized what had happened, Theias was enraged and wanted to put Myrrha to death. To protect her, the gods turned Myrrha into a myrrh tree and ten months later a child, Adonis, came out of the bark of the tree.

The loves of Adonis

Adonis was very handsome, and Aphrodite gathered him up and concealed him in a chest which she entrusted to Persephone, the goddess of Hell. Persephone refused to

---

The passion of Aphrodite

'Seduced as she was by the young man, she was no longer to be seen in Heaven [. . .]. She went everywhere with him. In the past she was wont to savour the joy of sweet repose in the shade, but now she wandered around and crossed mountains. She kept her distance from the fearsome wild boars. You too, Adonis, she made you fear them: she wanted you to benefit from her counsel: "Be brave," she told him, "against those who would shun you; audacity is not proof against the audacious. Be careful, my young lover, of being foolhardy and risking my happiness."' (Ovid, *Metamorphosis*, X, 530–545)

---

give Adonis back, however, as she, like Aphrodite, had fallen in love with the young man. Zeus mediated in the quarrel between the two goddesses, and it was decided that Adonis should spend one third of the year with one, one third with the other and the remaining third with whomsoever he wished. Adonis, however, chose to spend two thirds of the year with Aphrodite (*Apollodorus*, III, 14, 3).

One can see in this myth a personification of the productive forces of nature and seasonal cycles. This has been the interpretation since antiquity.

The death of Adonis

Adonis was mortally wounded by a wild boar in a battle provoked by Artemis. This tragic end took him from Aphrodite's love and still inspires compassion. It was said that at Aphaca in Byblus, at the source of the river of Adonis, the Nahr Ibrahim, the waters flowed red once a year in memory of the blood spilled by the god.

The Adonia

Every year this event gave rise to great festivals which had two distinct moods. The first was funereal with wailing and sacrifices for the death of Adonis, and the second was triumphant with assemblies and joyous processions for his return.

In Alexandria the order of the ceremonies was reversed to reflect the order of events in the story. The festival began with songs and dancing, a banquet and entertainment which evoked the union of the two lovers and finished with a funeral procession. Theocrites tells of festivals celebrated in this way by Arsinoah, wife of Ptolemy Philadelphia, the king of Egypt (283–246 BC) (*Theocrites*, XV, 111–132).

In Athens the ceremonies were not connected with the cycle of the seasons and their relation to life and death. These were reserved for Demeter. The public festival was funereal with all the funeral rites: unction, the preparation and display of the dead, offerings and communal meals. Effigies of Adonis in wax or terracota took the place of the corpse. These effigies were held in high regard by the women who paraded them through the town while wailing and breaking into sorrowful songs.

Thereafter the celebrations became more private. Their object was sexual pleasure enjoyed outwith marriage, in secluded places. Joy was expressed through the more ephemeral trappings of seduction, such as flowers and perfumes.

The gardens of Adonis

The gardens of Adonis were earthenware pots, bottoms of cups, or light baskets which were planted with quick-growing plants such as fennel, wheat or lettuce. The vegetables grew in several days, and their development was speeded up by watering them with hot water and leaving them in full sunlight. Cultivated like this, they withered very quickly and thus symbolized the ephemeral existence of Adonis. In Greece, the expression 'the gardens of Adonis' was used to describe anything which was precocious and transitory.

Legend

According to the *Funeral Song of Honour of Adonis*, by Bion of Phlossa (I, 72), Aphrodite shed many tears, and each tear turned into a rose while each drop of Adonis's blood became an anemone.

The poet, obviously mindful of the need for accuracy, added that the goddess shed as many tears as Adonis lost drops of blood.

> **The country of Adonis**
> 'Aphaca is in a place halfway between Heliopolis and Byblus where a temple to the Aphacitide, Aphrodite, was founded. Close by, there is a kind of pond which resembles a man-made reservoir. Above the temple and the surrounding area, on a precise date, a fire burns in the air, like a flaming torch or globe, and people gather there and this flame still appears in our day and age.' (Zozime, *A New History*, I, 58).

Adonis is young, tall and handsome. The goddess uses all her powers of seduction and sensuality to attract and keep him.

Bartholomeus Spranger (1546–1611): 'Venus and Adonis', c. 1592. Oil on canvas.

Aeneas

Greek hero

Piety

To found the city which would dominate the world, Aeneas undertook a thousand adventures and faced a thousand dangers.

Aphrodite disguised herself as Otrea, the daughter of the Phyrigian king, so that she could sleep with Anchises. When she revealed her identity to Anchises and told him that she was going to bear him a son, Aeneas, she asked him to keep it a secret because Zeus, in his anger, would strike the child down. One day when he was drunk, Anchises boasted of his liaison, and the King of Olympus sent down a thunderbolt which made him lame (*Homeric Hymn to Aphrodite*).

Alcathous, Anchises's brother-in-law, made sure that Aeneas received an education. Aeneas proved to be the bravest of the Trojans after Hector.

The protection of the gods

His piety made the gods offer Aeneas particular protection. Zeus saved him when Achilles took Lynerssos; Aphrodite fought beside him against Diomedes; and, when he was wounded, Apollo carried him away in a cloud. Shortly afterwards, he returned to the battlefield, killed a great number of Greeks and replaced Hector in command. In his fight against Achilles Poseidon intervened.

When Troy fell, Aeneas took refuge in the mountains. He carried Anchises on his shoulders, his son, Ascanius in his arms and the penates (household gods) of the city in his hands. He gathered all the survivors on Mount Ida and founded a new city.

Destiny, however, called him far away. He went westward, passing through Thrace, Macedonia, Crete and Delos and meeting Andromache and Helenus in Buthrotum. He reached southern Italy, sailed round Sicily and was shipwrecked by storms on the coast of Carthage. There he was received by Queen Dido, who fell in love with him.

The gods ordered Aeneas to carry on his journey. He came to Cumae and encountered the Sibyl, who told him of perils ahead and led him down to Hell to visit his ancestors. There he saw the dead who had failed in their destiny, and he also saw the abode of the Blessed. Anchises, his dead father, told him the secrets of the universe. (Virgil, *Aeneid*, VI, 418 ff.)

The origin of Rome

Aeneas sailed close to the coast of Italy and reached the mouth of the Tiber. King Evander made an alliance with him. He then fought against Turnus, king of the Rutuli. Ascanius, his son, founded Alba Longa, and Romulus, one of his descendants, laid the first stone of the city of Rome. Aeneas himself disappeared during a storm. As the son of Aphrodite, Aeneas gave Rome its divine origin. The Romans, 'the most religious people in the world' (Cicero, *De Natura deorum*, II, 3, 8), said that they were the beneficiaries of the goddess's favours. The important families claimed descendance from Ascanius, whom Julius Caesar called Iulus.

The Sibyls were women who were thought to have the gift of predicting the future. Two were particularly well known, the one at Cumae and the one at Erythrea.

25

Agni

Indian god

The sacrificial fire

God of fire in the Vedic age, he was the mediator, through sacrifice, between men and gods.

Known to the Romans as *Ignis*, as *Ognito* to the Slavs, *Ugnis* to the Lithuanians and *Atar* to the Iranians, he was *vaicvanara*, 'he who belongs to all men'.

Agni was fire in all its forms: in the sky where it appeared in all its splendour as the Sun; in woods where it suddenly appeared; in homes where it warmed the atmosphere. He also appeared in the heat of anger and that of digestion. Agni was all fire.

His character

Agni was brilliant and dazzling, illuminating whatever came near him. He was said to have had 'flaming hair' and 'golden jaws'. He was very old, his origins lost in the depths of time, and at the same time, he was young, possessing the vigour and strength of youth. He was described as 'the god who never ages', *tanunapat*, as being 'brought forth from himself', for fire comes out of fire. He was also immortal, invincible

---

The indispensable

'I invoke Agni, in his role of official of this cult, god of sacrifice, officiant, oblator who confers treasures beyond measure. Agni is worthy to be invoked by the ancient prophets, just as by the present ones: may he escort the gods here!'
(*Hymns to Agni; Rig Veda*, I, 1)

The rsi

The rsi were the sages who passed the Veda on to men.

---

and a ruler.

He was a *rsi*, endowed with particular intelligence and perceptiveness. He was knowledgable, inspired, wise and prudent. He stirred the minds of men and led them towards Good.

He was frequently linked with water. The priest often invoked all the Agnis who were in the waters (*Aitareya-brahmana*, VIII, 6). The vegetation which grew in water was Agni's dwelling-place (*Rig Veda*, X, 91, 6), and he himself appeared when the lotus flower, an aquatic plant, was rubbed. He was called 'bull of the waters' because he made them fertile. He was also a child born of the river which engenders all beings. The Sun itself was born in the water (*Rig Veda*, II, 35, 6).

Mataricvan, the Hindu Prometheus, fetched fire from the sky and was also the first man to make a sacrifice. 'Mataricvan', however, was often considered to be the hidden name of fire.

Agni was a guide and protector of men. With his piercing eye he saw demons, chased them and then burned them. He protected against illness. He was 'master of the house' (*grihaspati*) and the eternally burning fire lit by the ancestors.

Sacrifice

Agni bit everything he met, ferociously. He had two faces: one calm, the other terrible. He gave life and death. His power made him the necessary intermediary between the earthly and the celestial, the god before whom 'the offerings are gathered'. He was the 'mouth of the gods' who ate their share of the sacrifice.

The offering reserved for him was the goat, symbolizing strength and virility, and it was one of his children whom the gods wanted to lead their armies against the *asura*, their enemies. (*Mahabharata*, III, 223 ff.)

Ahura Mazda

Indo-Iranian god

The wise lord

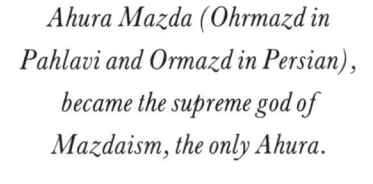

Ahura Mazda (Ohrmazd in Pahlavi and Ormazd in Persian), became the supreme god of Mazdaism, the only Ahura.

He had the form of the sun and nine wives. He inhabited the region of light, and his clothing was the sky. He held a royal court: at his right-hand sat Good Thought, *Vohu Manah*; Excellent Order, *Asha*; and Desirable Power, *Kshathra*. On his left sat Holy Devotion, *Armaiti*; Health, *Haurvatat*; and Immortality, *Ameretat*. In front of him sat obedience.

God and the gods

Ahura Mazda was a god amongst other gods, such as Mithra, Anahita, Vayu, Verethraghna and Varuna. After Zarathustra came, he was the only one left, above everyone and the one to whom everyone else was subject.

Ahura Mazda appeared in many forms. He made plants grow and allowed fire to give its heat, water to quench thirst, animals to reproduce, armies to be victorious, and so on. It was thought in those days that a god was behind each of these events. Zarathustra affirmed that it was always Ahura Mazda who was making things happen. Those believed to be gods were beings created by him, who acted only according to his orders and were his responsibility. They were the beneficent spirits or the *yazatas*, 'worthy of adoration'.

Ahura Mazda was eternal. He created the other living beings 'in the beginning' and created the world by his thought. (*Yasna*, XXXI, 7, 11)

The order of the world

The Lord established perfect order (*arta*), and all creatures had the right to a prosperous life on earth and, after their death, to a paradise filled with light. However, in order to receive these benefits, they had to be just (*artavan*) and remain faithful to the good religion, taking the side of the Godly, *Spena Manyu*, in his battle against Evil, *Angra Mainyu*.

Good, a beneficent spirit, and Evil, a destructive spirit, were twins: one had chosen good and life while the other had chosen evil and death (*Yasna*, XXX). The choice was made by Evil, and Ahura Mazda was not responsible for it. On the other hand, there was a profound unity between the Lord and Spenta Manyu (*Yasna*, XLIII, 3). Ahura Mazda left them both free to choose, just as he left all men free to choose.

Ahura Mazda in the stylized form of an eagle with its wings spread. He wears a crown and makes a sign of blessing.
Persepolis. East door of the Tripylon. Bas relief (detail), Achemenide period, c. 522–465 BC.

Amaterasu

Japanese goddess

The emperor's ancestor

Goddess of the sun and light, of growth and fertility, she is considered to be the divine origin of the imperial dynasty.

In the 8th century, the Japanese thought that the present was only justified by the past and the earthly by the heavenly. The emperor's authority, therefore, had to have a very ancient and divine origin.

The origin of Amaterasu

The *Kojiki* ('Notes on Ancient Matters'), the most ancient Japanese book, recounts how, in the beginning, there were five divine couples. The last of these were brother and sister, Izanagi and Izanami. Izanagi was the god who made the solid earth and was father of Amaterasu, the goddess of the sun; Tsuki-yomi, the god of the moon; and Susa-no-o, the sea-god. Amaterasu accepted the heavens as her charge, and Tsuki-yomi accepted the king-

---

How the Kami tried to make Amaterasu come out of the cave

'They uprooted a plant from Mount-Celestial-Perfume, whose leaves were always very luxuriant, and attached to its upper branches curved 'tama', strung onto long threads. From the middle branches they suspended a large mirror, and on the lower branches they hung cloth streamers of white and green. Majesty-Futodama took these objects as sacred offerings and Majesty-Celestial-Koyane chanted, while Kami-Masculine-Strong-Handed hid himself near the door of the cave.' (*Kojiki*, IV)

---

dom of night; but Susa-no-o, grieving for his dead mother, refused his kingdom and said he wanted to join his mother in hell.

The children of the jewels

Izanagi, weary of his pleas, chased Susa-no-o from the sky. But, before he left, Susa-no-o wanted to visit his sister, Amaterasu. He made such a noise, shaking the mountains and making the earth quake, that she was frightened and armed herself as if for war. The brother and sister confronted each other on either side of the Tranquil River. Amaterasu broke her brother's sword, and from it three goddesses were born. Susa-no-o sucked the five strings of jewels his sister had given him and male gods appeared. The children that came from the sabre were those of Susa-no-o, and the children from the jewels were Amaterasu's. Susa-no-o was then seized by a kind of madness, and he smashed the dykes and blocked the drainage in the paddy-fields. Finally, he threw a flayed horse through the roof of his sister's home, while she sat weaving clothes for the gods.

The resurrection

The goddess was terrified and shut herself away in a cave, blocking the entrance with a rock. Since she was goddess of the sun, this plunged the world into darkness. The other gods were very worried and searched for some feat of magic which would bring back the light. They placed a sacred tree at the entrance to the cave and attached mirrors, jewels and material to it. The goddess, Amano Uzume, started to dance. Holding some bamboo leaves, she climbed up on an upturned, empty tub and began to move to the music. As she writhed about to the strong rhythm, she was siezed by divine ecstasy and undid her clothing, letting it fall slowly, until she was completely bare.

At the sight of her nakedness, the gods burst out laughing. Amaterasu, surprised by the laughter, inched open the door of the cave and saw her face in the mirror set before her. Even more intrigued, she came out of the cave and one of the gods closed it behind her. Light returned to the world.

Thereafter the dance of Amano Uzume served as a model in certain popular rites. It was performed at the death of an individual, its aim being to call the person back to life. The dance was also a symbol of fertility.

The descendants of Amaterasu

Oshihomimi was a 'child of the jewels' and became the first sovereign of Japan. His father's domain was below the earth for

Situated near the village of Uji-Yamada, one hundred kilometres east of Kyoto, is the **Temple of Ise***. It is completely rebuilt every twenty years according to an absolutely identical plan. Its style is typically archaic, characterized by the use of unpainted* hinoki *(Japanese cyprus) and by crossing the two long beams placed diagonally on the gables of the building.*

Sanctuary of Ise (Honshu): the Great Shrine made of wood (last rebuilt in 1973).

three reasons: first, he was the god of the sea; second, he wanted to join his mother in the underworld; and finally, it was his fate to be exiled from the earth. Susa-no-o was a mediator. Amaterasu, who would be invoked by the emperors of Japan as a guardian force, came from the celestial domain above.

Her cult

At Ise, on the island of Honshu, are the Grand Shrines dedicated to Amaterasu, to which the imperial household of Japan has come to pay homage for countless centuries. The *Nai-Ku* (Inner shrine) and *Ge-Ku* (Outer shrine) are the most important Shinto shrines in Japan. A million pilgrims go each year to the New Year festival held there. In the Nai-Ku are the melted remains of the eight-pointed mirror, one of the three symbols of imperial authority, believed to have come directly from Amaterasu.

Custom requires that the shrines be rebuilt (in wood) every twenty years, and this has happened sixty times already (most recently in 1973). The architecture is pure, ancient Japanese, the simple lines patterned after prehistoric structures, a style used before the introduction of Chinese-style temple architecture.

Amazons

Warrior-women of Greek myth

Anti-men

The Amazons are described (Iliad VI) as antianeirai, that is 'those who go to war like men'. The idea of the Amazonian matriarchy was disturbing to ancient Greek society.

In the Amazon state the women were magistrates, directed public life and made up the army. They were *kreoboroi* 'devourers of flesh' (Aeschylus, *Suppliant*) and *androktones* 'killers of males' (Herodotus IV). Men were only tolerated for work of a servile nature. Once a year the Amazons met with men from neighbouring societies and chose partners from among them — preferably the most handsome. Their couplings took place in the darkness of the forest, so that the partners would not be able to recognise each other (Strabo XI). It could be said that the Amazons stole semen from the men. Later, when the children were born, the women killed the males or blinded or crippled them so that they were no more than a supply of male seed (*Diodorus of Sicily*, II). As for the females, one breast was removed so that they would not be restricted in the practice of archery and spear throwing.

Warriors

It was said that they were descendants of the god of war, Ares, and the nymph, Harmony. They worshipped Artemis and were fearsome warriors. It was considered a great feat of arms for a young warrior to face them in battle.

With Myrine as their leader, the Amazons crushed the Atlantians and occupied Gorgon and the greater part of Libya. They passed through Egypt where Horus, the son of Isis, ruled, and crossed Phrygia (*Diodorus of Sicily*, III, 54 ff.). With Penthesileia, they flew to the aid of Priam during the Trojan War. Achilles wounded Penthesileia in her right breast but found her so beautiful that he fell in love with her (*Iliad*, III, 189).

They fought against Heracles and invaded Attica following the abduction of the Amazon Antiope. They established camp on the Areiopagus, the hill of Ares, and the decisive battle took place at the foot of the Acropolis. The Amazons came very close to winning but were finally forced to swear an armistice (Plutarch, *The Life of Theseus*, 26–28).

The matriarchy

It is of little importance whether or not these people really existed and accomplished these great feats. Whatever the reason, it represented the guilt felt by a society which was too masculine, the fear of an irreparable separation of the sexes and/or the submission of men to women. It also called into question the male order.

> **Etymology**
> There is a scholarly etymology for the name 'Amazon'. It could come from the privative α and from $\mu\alpha\sigma o\zeta$, meaning 'breast' or the women who have lost a breast. Hippocrates is clear that, if they performed this operation on themselves, it was 'to move all their strength into the shoulder and arm' and in this way make them more capable of fighting.
> (Hippocrates, *Airs, Waters and Places*, XVII)

Amitabha

The divine Buddha

The saviour

Amitabha (Infinite Light) or Amitayus (Infinite Life) was worshipped as O-mi-to-Fo in China and Amida in Japan.

He was one of the five 'meditation buddhas', or *Dhyani buddhas*, sent by Adi buddha, the original buddha.

A bodhisattva

With the mission of Amitabha there was a kind of reversal of the original doctrine of the buddha. The ideal was no longer so much nirvana, the fruit of a personal discipline, but that of becoming a bodhisattva. No longer did the bodhisattvas tremble before the cycle of birth and death. They acquired merit only 'for the good of others': 'We wish to become a shelter for the world, a refuge for the world, the place where the world can rest, the final comfort of the world, the islands of the world, the guides of the world, the means of salvation of the world.' (*Ashtasakasrika*, XV, 293)

The pure earth

Although Amitabha was only a monk called Dharmakara, he wished to become buddha and to gather together on 'the pure earth' all those who would pray to him with faith. Thus they would enjoy perfect happiness until they entered nirvana.

This 'paradise of the west', *Sukhavati*, was paved with gold, flooded with light, and surrounded by seven walls of precious stones and palm trees. Bells rang out melodiously all the time and lotuses grew abundantly in ponds full of crystal clear water. From the heart of these lotuses, the inhabitants of this paradise were reborn. They all had a human, masculine form but were incorporeal. Here they attained their final rebirth, thanks to the merits which Amitabha had obtained for them and to their devotion (*bhakti*). Their joy was to listen to the teaching of their master.

The wish of Amitabha

Amitabha made the wish 'That his name would be known in all the existing regions; that whosoever would call on him would immediately fall within his jurisdiction; that, by a ray emanating from his heart, he could illuminate any being he wanted to, at any distance; that any person who was dying, however much of a sinner he was, and, repenting, wanted to be reborn in his kingdom, would be reborn there straight after death, so that he could be instructed, improved, and put on the road to his salvation'.
(L. Wieger, *Histoire des croyances religieuses et des opinions philosophiques en Chine* (History of religious beliefs and philosophical opinions in China), Paris, 1922)

Bodhisattva

A long personal asceticism led the bodhisattva to make no distinction between himself and others. He possessed nothing of his own, not even the benefits of the long road travelled. He would not even reach nirvana as long as he was concerned with himself and the eradication of the self could only be achieved by eradicating other 'selves'.

Among the bodhisattvas we also know of Maitreya, the next buddha; Avalokitesvara, who protected against all danger; Manjusri, the lord of the world; Vairochana, who spread light; and Siddharta Goutama, before his 'awakening'.

Amma

Dogon god

Distant and ethereal

A supreme god, he lived in the celestial regions and was at the origin of all creation.

At the beginning of time, Amma created the Earth and immediately joined with it. But the Earth's clitoris opposed the male penis. Amma destroyed it, circumcising his wife, and they had a child, Ogo, and then twins, the Nommo. Ogo had no partner and was barren, so he introduced disorder into the world by committing incest with his mother. The first menstrual blood came from this union, as well as Yeban and Andumbulu, the spirits of the undergrowth.

The infinitely small

There is another version of creation in which the world is said to have come from the word of Amma, who created the infinitely small—the size of a grain of millet, the smallest of cereals. This infinitely small swelled until it formed the primordial egg. The egg contained two placentas, each containing the seeds of twins.

The revolt of Ogo

Ogo prematurely came out of one half of the egg. He brought with him a part of the placenta, hoping to bring his sister, Yasigi, with him. He rushed forward into empty space. He made the Earth from the placenta and searched it to find the embryo of his sister. Amma, however, had entrusted Yasigi to the Nommo. This penetration by Ogo of the placenta from which he had been born was the first act of incest, and the Earth, which had been desecrated in this way, became impure and parched.

The sacrifice of the Nommo

Amma sacrificed one of the Nommo, *semu*, in order to make the Earth fertile. He spilled his blood and hurled bits of his body to the ground, where they changed into four trees. Then Amma brought the Nommo back to life in the form of a human couple, and thus man was created without the participation of the impure Earth. Amma sent the second placenta to earth and in it were found the ancestors of men as well as all the animals, vegetables, and minerals.

The division of the world

Ogo approached Heaven, but Amma transformed a remaining part of the placenta into a burning sun. And so Ogo tried to contact the risen Nommo and succeeded in taking some of his semen. But one of the other Nommo intervened and bit off the end of Ogo's penis, took back the stolen semen and tore out his tongue. The loss of speech turned Ogo into a pale fox, called *Yurugu*. In circumcising men, what was done to Ogo to separate him from the hidden spiritual principle is repealed.

Thus the world was divided into two domains: Yuguru's, containing disorder, impurity, sterility, drought, night and death; and Nommo's, consisting of order, purity, fertility, humidity, day and life.

Creation

'Amma created the stars by throwing pellets of earth into space. He created the sun and moon by modelling two white earthenware bowls, one encircled with red copper, the other with white copper. Black people were born under the sun and white people under the moon.
(Quoted in L. V. Thomas, *Les Religions de L'Afrique noire* (Religions of Black Africa), Paris, 1969)

Amun-Re

Egyptian god

The 'hidden god'

Of modest origins, the god Amun was likened to Re, the sun-god.

Did the fortune of the gods depend on that of their worshippers, or, indeed, did that of the worshippers depend on the fortune of the gods?

The god of Thebes

Amun was the local god of Thebes and was considered to be the god of the air or of fertility. He was given the form of a man, dressed in a loincloth and wearing a head-dress topped by two feathers. Sometimes, he also had the head of a ram. His wife, Mut, the goddess of Heaven, had the form of a vulture; and Khons, his son, had that of a child bearing a crescent moon on his head.

His name meant 'hidden god', as if he expressed the unknown and mysterious aspects of the divinity. He was a god with no history, and precisely because of this he borrowed that of others. When Amenemhat the 1st founded the 12th dynasty and Thebes became the capital of Egypt, Amun was made their protector and leader of the nation and was even made into a primordial and eternal god — the 'king of gods' (*nesou netjerou*). It was thought that the

---

The creator

'Men, God's flock, have been well provided for. The sun-god has made the sky and the earth for their benefit . . . He made the air to invigorate their nostrils, for they are images of him, issue of his flesh. He shines in the sky, he gives them vegetation, and animals, birds and fish for food . . .' (*Instructions for Merikare*, c. 2000 BC)

---

leader who had succeeded in reuniting Egypt under his authority could only have done so thanks to the god who was creator and organiser of the world.

Re

Amun was identified with the god Re, who possessed a secret name which was a symbol of supremacy. The latter was thought to be the incarnation of the sun, revered from the most ancient times. Two traditions exist which explain his origin.

The first says that he came out of Nun and that the pyramids represented the primordial hill on which he appeared. At Heliopolis, the *Benben* stone was an object of worship because it was said to be there that the god brought about creation by mastur-bating or spitting. Man was born from his tears.

The other version was that he was the son of Geb (the earth) and Nut (the sky), and that every morning he was born from his mother's belly and every evening he plunged into the domain of the dead (*Am-Douat*).

Re's creature was the phoenix, which is reborn from its ashes and is immortal. He was the god of the resurrection of the chosen ones. He was always one of the great gods in the official pantheon and was never dethroned. Sometimes, though, he was confused with other gods.

Amun-Re

Thus Amun became Amun-Re and the pharaohs developed his cult. It was made more attractive by his sanctuary at Karnak, and his riches became fabulous. His priests held such enormous power that they attained royal status at the end of the 20th Dynasty, but when Egypt changed its capital, his star began to fade and provin-cial gods once again found favour. Osiris, who was more popular, became his direct rival.

The 'divine women worshippers'

The people who worked in the service of Amun-Re were numerous. Under Ramses III there were 81,322 people because the management of his extensive properties demanded it. He was the only god known in Egypt to have had 'divine women worshippers' who were considered to be his earthly spouses. They were celibate and assured their continuation by means of adoption. Their role, since it was surrounded by royal prerogatives, was usually reserved for a princess, and little by little she came to take the place of the high-priest of Amun.

The wonderful festival

During the tenth month of the year, the god Amun of Karnak crossed the Nile in a boat in order to visit the necropolis and the 'gods of the West'. The boat at Amun's disposal was sumptuous. Called *Ouserhat*, its size was imposing and it was made of Libyan wood and covered in gold and precious stones. The procession, in which the pharaoh took part, stopped at all the royal temples on the route.

Other than this exceptional ceremony, the daily rites bore a strong resemblance to the attentions given to a royal person, including dressing, unction, offerings of food, libations and the burning of incense.

Spreading the cult

The worship of the ram-god spread beyond Egypt. It can be found in Merowe, in the Sudan and in Greece under the name of Ammon. The Siwah oracle, consulted by Alexander the Great, appears to be a subsidiary of the oracle at Thebes, the Egyptian capital.

> **The primordial**
> 'Pay homage to Amun-Re, king of the gods, the primordial, he who came into existence first, the only god, the well-loved, he who lifted up the sky, who made heaven and earth and the waters . . .' 'Come to me, Amun the valiant, he who saves the shipwrecked: let me reach dry land.' (*Inscription on a bas relief found in 1912 within the Deir el-Medineh temple*)

Anahita

Persian goddess

The immaculate

Goddess of the dawn and fertility, she was compared to the Indian Sarasvati and the Babylonian Ishtar.

Anahita is without a doubt the only true Iranian goddess. She was called Ardva Sura Anahita, which means the high, the powerful, the immaculate.

The portrait of her given to us in the *Avesta* is of a young girl with swelling breasts: 'She wears her belt high to give her bust fullness and charm.' She is adorned in finery, crowned with stars and wears otter-skin, brocade and jewels. On her feet are sandals of gold (*Yasna*). She was goddess of all the waters of the rivers and of all purifying and fertilizing liquids: rivers, lakes, and the sea, but also sperm, vaginal secretions and milk.

With the reform of Zarathustra, she became a spirit of prosperity, collaborating in the work of creation, fighting for justice and initiating men into religious rites.

> **The Holy One**
> 'Anahita is the holy one who increases energy, flocks, wealth and health, and who enhances the earth.' (*Yasna*, V)

Ancestors

Spirits of the forefathers

The mediators

Although considered to be inhabitants of another world, ancestors retained links with the earthly world.

In all parts of the world, ancestors have been held in high regard as founders of society, initiators of civilisation and guarantors of a certain kind of life.

In most countries they were considered to act after their death, often by perpetuating the influence they exercised during their earthly life, sometimes by taking on a greater dimension and becoming the representatives of men to the divinity, and vice versa. They had completed the full cycle of their life and because of this were thought to know more and to have more experience. They were free from the everyday occurrences of the earthly world and guardians who should be revered. The first in the genealogical order, who could only have been created by the divinity directly, was particularly revered.

What did they become?

Since they no longer had any bodies, the ancestors became spirits who could not be seen or heard but who communicated with the living in a specific way. Whether they were angels or demons, they were among those intermediary beings who were neither men nor gods, but who had something of the nature of both.

But could the spirit of a man survive without a body which located it in time and space? Without a doubt, no. Consequently, it was easy to imagine the ancestor reincarnated in the form of a living person who exhibited something of his character, his

physical appearance or his deeds, or who simply continued his existence.

Sometimes the ancestor's presence could be indicated by a stone or a tree. For example, in East Asia they speak of the 'seat of spirits', and all social and cultural life is organized around it. Or indeed, in central Australia the ancestor was transformed into a stone, a tree, or an animal so that there was more to these objects than was apparent. The world was inhabited by the ancestors.

Where were they?

By some link with the living, the ancestors were on earth. They were found in the mountains, in the far west, in caves or in places where they had lived during their life. These places were always somewhat disturbing, indeed dangerous: like the mountains where the *qentilis*, the ancestors of the Queshuas of the Andes, retired and which became their tombs. A person who approached them saw his skin wrinkle and become covered in callouses, and then he died.

They were also in another world, underground or heavenly, a world imagined as the inverse or double of our world. It was

---

Invocation to death

'You have appeared in glory like Re: see, he has come to see you, rejoicing in your beauty. His solar disc is your solar disc; his rays are your rays; his crowns are your crowns; his greatness is your greatness; his appearances are your appearances; his beauty is your beauty . . . He does not die and you do not die; he has no need to be victorious over his enemies and you have no need to be victorious over your enemies; no harm can ever come to him and no harm can ever come to you.' (*Book of the Egyptian Dead*, Ch. 181)

also imagined that this afterlife consisted of several stages. One of these was provisional, a kind of purgatory, and the other final. The latter corresponds, for example, with the deification of ancestors in Japan (after seven, thirty-three or fifty years, the ancestors become gods), or with their establishment in an intermediary state. In any case, they were closer to the living in the time immediately after their death. Thus the Sotho of South Africa invoked the *Badimo*, the new gods or ancestors: 'New gods, pray for us to the old god.'

What did they do?

Either they were all harmful, or all good; or, according to other traditions, some were harmful while others were good. Generally speaking, because of this great importance was attached to the cause of death of the

person concerned. A violent death could only mean that the resultant spirit was evil.

Most often, the ancestors were jealous of the living. A visit from them was to be feared, in case they took someone back with them into death. This is a likely origin for the fear of ghosts.

In general, their actions served to preserve civilisation and the prosperity of the living. Their concern was to complete what they started during their earthly life.

The worship of the ancestors

The memory of the ancestors was often perpetuated by an inscription on a tablet, as in China and Japan, or in a wooden or bamboo sculpture, as in Melanesia and Vanuatu. The Tungus in Siberia did the same, calling their statuettes *Dzuli* or *Muxdi*.

In Siberia effigies were always put in places of worship, just as in the Far East they were left in monasteries or temples. The Greeks took great care of their tombs, and the Romans had altars to the benevolent spirits of the dead who were nothing more than their ancestors.

It was common to feed the ancestors, as one would the living, by giving them offerings. The Greeks placed their gifts on the tombs in bowls with holes in the bottom, so that they could reach the dead. These offerings often took the form of sacrifices.

Zombies

In Haiti and Latin American there were brotherhoods of particularly evil sorcerers who met in secret places. They held great feasts there to celebrate their crimes and performed rites designed to take away the souls of their enemies so they could have complete mastery over them. It was said that 'they had consumed them'. Those enemies became, through their magic rites, what was known as Zombies, the living dead. They were total automatons, under the orders of those who 'had consumed' them. They vommitted, without hesitation or scruple, crimes and atrocities which had been dictated to them, and thus they enabled those who *were* really responsible to escape punishment.

Contrary to the ancestors or angels, who were spirits without bodies, Zombies were bodies without spirits, who provoked evil and destruction. They were ready-made heroes for a certain kind of literature which has made them famous.

The prayer of the traveller before leaving

'Our ancestors! Since my body has left and gone to the forest, it is insubstantial here. But you still hear what I say [. . .] If I do not reach my ancestors my body will not be made permanent. That is why I sprinkle on water to keep my skin cool. If I stay safe and arrive at the house of my father, I will give a fattened animal to my ancestors.'

(Quoted by L. V. Thomas, *Les Religions de l'Afrique noire* (Religions of Black Africa), Paris, 1969.)

Angels

Heavenly creatures

The messengers of God

Spiritual beings and intermediaries between God and men, they carried the word of God to men.

The Old Testament called them *beney 'elohim* 'sons of God' (*Job*, 1, 6), 'holy' (*Psalm* 89, 6), 'sons of the Most High' (*Psalm* 82, 6), 'strong' (*Psalm* 78, 25), 'mighty ones' (*Psalm* 103, 20) and 'Watchers' (*Daniel* 4, 13). They were pure spirits who accompanied men throughout their lives.

The celestial hierarchy

The celestial court consisted of 'nine choirs of angels' divided into three ranks: the seraphim, cherubim and thrones; the dominions, powers and virtues; and the principalities, archangels and angels. The function of the first class was to praise and worship God, and they constituted the highest order in the hierarchy. The function of the last was to assist the course of the stars, nations and people. (Denys l'Aréopagite, *Les Hiérarchies célestes*) (The celestial hierarchies)

Angels or lesser gods

Long ago, it was common to believe that a superior god would send a lesser god on missions to men, to pass on messages, give order or bring help. It would have seemed ridiculous not to recognize the numerous powers at work in life. 'The angels,' said S. H. Newman, 'are the real cause of movement, light, life and the elementary principles which are offered to our senses in different combinations, and thus suggest the idea of cause and effect and what we call the laws of nature'. (*Apologia pro vita sua*, 1864, p. 152)

Messengers

Faith in a single God did not make this belief disappear. Since the creator was too great or too far away to attend to minor matters directly, these lesser gods acted as messengers. They were called *angeloi*, angels whose job was to reveal divine secrets to men concerning Heaven and Earth (*Ethiopian Enoch*, LX. 11). Paul's *Apocalypse*, an apocryphal work found in the apostle's house in the 4th century, gives them the responsibility of guiding men's souls towards Heaven.

That said, one can assume that the god who was encountered near the Lahai Roi wells and promised Hagar, in the name of Yahweh, many descendants, was only an angel (*Genesis* 16, 7–15). For there was only one God: 'I am the Lord, there is no other; there is no god beside me.' (*Isaiah* 45, 5)

Raphael, Michael, Gabriel and others

Elsewhere, the assertion of Raphael ('God cured') regarding his functions is clear: 'I am Raphael, one of the seven angels always ready to enter the presence of the glory of the Lord.' (*Tobit* 12, 15).

We can be just as precise as regards

> **Sanctus**
>
> 'In the year of King Uzziah's death I saw the Lord seated on a throne, high and exalted, and the skirt of his robe filled the temple. About him were attendant seraphim, and each had six wings; one pair covered his face and one pair his feet, and one pair was spread in flight. They were calling ceaselessly to one another, "Holy, holy, holy is the Lord of Hosts: the whole earth is full of his glory."'
> (*Isaiah* 6, 1–3)

Michael ('He who is like God'), 'the great captain, who stands guard over your fellow-countrymen' (*Daniel* 12, 1).

He is also the protector of Israel, and the *Ethiopian Enoch* (XX, 5) places him before the throne of God. He is the leader of the celestial armies (*The Assumption of Moses*, X, 2) and the prince of light (*Rules of the Qumran Community*, XVII, 6).

But the one who, by virtue of his mission, appears most often is Gabriel ('Man of God'). It is he who came to enlighten the people's understanding (*Daniel* 9, 23). He told Daniel of the coming of the Messianic age (*Denial* 8, 19), Zechariah of the coming of John the Baptist (*Luke* 1, 19), and Mary of the birth of Jesus (*Luke* 1, 24 ff.).

To these three great angels, the *Book of Enoch* and the *Book of Esdras* add Uriel, who is in charge of lamps and also administers justice, as well as the lesser angels Raguel, Sarakiel, Jeremiel and so on.

There are many angels. 'Thousands upon thousands served him and myriads upon myriads attended his presence.' (*Daniel* 7, 10)

Gabriel, Azrael and the others

The Koran talks of angels just as it talks of demons and jinn: 'Praise be to God, creator of Heaven and Earth, whose messengers are angels with two, three or four wings' (*Koran*, XXXV, 1). Gabriel, the angel of tidings, has an important place in it. The Koran also recognizes Azrael, the angel of death, and Munkar and Nakir, the angels of the questioning at the tomb.

Guardian angels

Guardian angels are responsible for protecting and guiding men. God 'has charged his angels to guard you wherever you go, to lift you on their hands for fear you should strike your foot against a stone' (*Psalm* 91, 11). Each of us has an angel by us who intercedes for us to God (*Job* 5, 1). In Paul's *Apocalypse* we find a very developed doctrine of the guardian angel.

The mystery of human realities

Origen was worried about preaching to Christian gatherings because, he said, since each Christian was accompanied by his angel, the sermon was aimed as much at the angels as at the men, and angels are particularly sensitive to mistakes. Did this mean that the men would be more than men?

The angel is a celestial image, a model example, what psychoanalysts would doubtless call a 'super ego'. There is an angel for each nation and for each civilisation . . ., and these angels do not die; they are always there before the throne of God. It is as if they are the sign of and the foundation for a celestial immortality in the affairs of men, the real link between God and the Earth.

The worship of angels

The worship of angels has developed greatly between the time of the Old Testament and our own time. Saint John Chrysostom, Saint Augustine, Saint Thomas Aquinas and, a little closer to us, the popes Pius XII and John XXIII have contributed to this.

According to Dante

This hierarchy of divinities consists of the Dominions first, and next the virtues, and the third are called the powers.

In the next to last of the last dancing trio whirl principalities, and then Archangels; the festive Angels fill the last with play.

And all the angelic ranks gaze upward, as downward they prevail upon the rest, so while each draws the next, all draw toward God. (Dante, *The Divine Comedy*, xxviii, trans. Mark Musa, London, 1984)

Pope John XXIII

After the recital of the Angelus on 12 December 1962, this pope declared, 'Our desire is to expand the worship of guardian angels, the heavenly companions given to us by God.'

Angra Mainyu

The Persian demon

The destructive spirit

Also known as Ahriman, he was the creator of darkness and of evil things.

There is no cold without heat, damp without dryness, black without white. The two complementary opposites were representations of the omnipotence of Ahura Mazda, The Wise Lord. One was personified in Spenta Mainyu who chose the Arta—the right direction, the true Reality of things, the truth—and was identified with Ahura Mazda himself. The other was personified in Angra Mainyu, who chose the *Druja* and trickery and became the destroyer.

Angra Mainyu was the foul spirit; he belonged to death, filth and rottenness, inspiring disgust. As a sign of contempt, many texts wrote his name back to front with vile descriptions. They even went so far as to say that he did not exist and never would. The forces he took—those of the lizard, the serpent and the fly—were only lent to him for a time and were to disappear. Evil was the opposite of existence.

> **The disappearance of Angra Mainyu**
> Anga Mainyu, who started off as the equal of Ahura Mazda, the Wise Lord, ended up by gradually disappearing. A Mazdean catechism of 1910 does not mention his name.

Anna Perenna

Roman goddess

Queen of the joyous feast

Worshipped in a sacred wood situated north of Rome, she was represented as an old woman.

It is not known whether she was the old woman who, when the plebeians withdrew to the Holy Mount in the 5th century BC, fed them with 'rustic cakes' (Ovid, *Fasti*, III, 661–674), or if she was the sister of Queen Dido of Carthage (Ovid, *Fasti*, III, 557–656). The second legend, however, seems more worthy of a goddess.

Anna, who was fleeing from an invader, reached the hills of Latium where Aeneas ruled. Aeneas welcomed her, but Lavinia, Aeneas's wife, was jealous. Forewarned, Anna fled and met the god of the Numicius, the nearby river, and became a nymph. She then got her name *Perenna*, meaning eternity.

When Anna was old, she was approached by Mars and asked to be an intermediary between himself and Minerva. However, since Anna knew that her mission was impossible, she substituted herself for the chaste goddess and, much to the surprise of Mars, made fun of him in a most improper way. It was said that this was the origin of the obscene songs which were to be heard during her feast.

Antigone

Greek heroine

The guardian of the family

Against orders from the state, Antigone defended the sacred duties to the family and the dead.

Antigone was the fruit of the incestuous union between Oedipus and Jocasta. Distraught by the unhappiness of her blind father who was reduced to begging far away from Thebes, she helped him, guiding his footsteps and easing his sufferings. She stayed with him until his death in Colonus in Attica, whereupon she returned to her homeland and resumed a more normal life, accompanied by her sister, Ismene.

A war of fratricide

War soon broke out. Jocasta's brother, Creon, a dictator who had imposed his rule by trickery, was defending his throne against the Argives. The Thebans were split: Eteocles, Antigone's brother, was on Creon's side, while Polyneices, another of her brothers, sided with his adversaries. Fighting took place at the gates of the city: cruel, relentless and merciless hand-to-hand combat. The two brothers found themselves face to face and, enraged by the

---

The unwritten laws

'I do not believe that your edicts have so much power that they can allow mortals to break divine laws. These laws are unwritten but inviolable. This is not of today, nor yesterday, but they have been in force since the beginning, and no one witnessed their birth. To disobey them by a cowardly respect for the authority of a man — is this not to incur the severity of the gods?' (Sophocles, *Antigone*, 460 – 464)

---

struggle, killed each other. Gradually, Creon got the upper hand and routed the Argives. Victory was his; all that remained was to bury the dead.

The king decided to have magnificent funerals for those who had died for his cause: they had fought the good fight and shed their blood for victory. Thus, Eteocles received funeral honours. But Creon also decreed that it would be punishable by death to bury the warriors from the opposing side, as they were traitors who had endangered the power of the sovereign and were thus unworthy of any kind of burial. Polyneices therefore would not be buried.

The inflexible

Antigone, however, did not agree with this and announced that she would disregard the royal order because it was contrary to divine laws. She thought that it was better to obey the gods than men. Ismene tried to convince her to submit to the powerful Creon for her own good, but Antigone remained steadfast. She declared to Creon, 'I was born to share love, not hate', to which he replied, 'Go, then, and share your love with the dead.' (Sophocles, *Antigone*, 522–523)

She then went and scattered earth over the body of Polyneices, thus fulfilling the rite of burial.

The inexorable

Creon, who was furious at having been defied by a woman, would not yield to the pleas of his son Haemon, Antigone's betrothed. He had her buried alive in the family tomb, and she hanged herself in her prison.

The story has a terrible ending: Haemon killed himself over the corpse of Antigone and Eurydice, Creon's wife, committed suicide when she learned of the death of her son. (Sophocles, *Antigone*)

Anu

Sumerian god

The just but distant king

An, Anum or Anu rarely intervened in human affairs but delegated his power to Enlil instead.

At the beginning of the world when everything was covered in water, the first divine couple, Apsu and Tiamat, appeared. After them, other couples appeared, like Lakhmu and Lakhamu, Anshar and Kishar. Then Anu was born, the god of Heaven who, in his turn, begat Ea. With Ea and Enlil, Anu formed the trinity of the great gods. Anu, nonetheless, is first in time and space (*Enuma Elish*, 1).

In the court of the gods, Anu is the *sarru* king. The gods took refuge with him when the flood came. He found Adapa guilty of having broken the wings of the wind and heard the complaints of Ishtar about the insults of Gilgamesh (*Gilgamesh*, VI).

The cosmos was divided between the three great gods into spheres of influence: 'They threw dice and divided it.' The sky fell to Anu and crowns and sceptres were set before him. Earthly royalty was descended from him (*Etana*, I), and as the god of Uruk, he gave back the city to Rim-Sin of the Larsa dynasty. On Anu's orders Rim-Sin hollowed out the Euphrates and, by his strength, conquered the neighbouring cities.

Worship of Anu was not restricted to Uruk. There were also temples at Deir, Assur and Adad.

Anubis

Egyptian god

The embalmer

Anubis was the guide of souls, to the world beyond.

As a jackal-god, he was often represented with a human body and the head of a jackal or dog. Anubis was the god of the desert and the necropolis and watched over the tombs. He introduced the dead to the other world and helped them before Osiris, the judge-god.

He was the embalmer—'The bandages are his,'—and was said to be the son of Osiris and Nephthys. He helped Isis put together the pieces of the corpse of Osiris, killed by Seth. He embalmed the body, and the magician-goddess succeeded in resurrecting Osiris.

His cult spread far beyond Egypt, into the Graeco-Roman world. There was a statue of him in the serapeum at Delos.

Embalming

As for Anubis, it is he who repels the swelling of his own body, and who is himself covered in bandwagon.' (*Jumilhac Papyrus*, vii, 5–6)

Aphrodite/Venus

Greek and Roman goddess

The ideal of feminine charm

The poets celebrated the perfect shape of her face, the sparkle of her eyes, her smiling mouth and the beauty of her breasts.

A proud and cruel goddess, she haunted animal nature and reigned over the hearts and senses of men. Her worship was assimilated by the Romans with that of Venus, a goddess of ancient Italy.

Her origin

According to Homer, she was the daughter of Zeus and Dione (*Iliad*, V, 312). According to Hesiod, she was born from the foam impregnated by the sexual organs of Uranus, which Cronos had severed and thrown into the sea. 'The woman born of the waves' was thus one of the first goddesses (*Theogony*, 188 ff.). As soon as she came out of the water she was transported by the Zephyrs, first to Cythera and then to the shores of Cyprus. There she was dressed, covered in jewels, perfumed and taken to the immortals.

From these two different origins, Plato identified two Aphrodites. One, the daughter of Uranus, also called Urania, was the noble goddess of pure love. The other, the daughter of Dione, also called Pandemos, was the goddess of 'common' love. (*The Banquet*, VIII, 180)

Her loves

She married Hephaestus, the lame god (*Odyssey*, VIII, 266–366), but outrageously deceived him with Ares, the god of war. The two lovers were discovered by Phoebus, who rushed to inform Hephaestus. Hephaestus set a trap for them in the form of a net with invisible mesh and invited all the gods from Olympus to witness his misfortune. Surprised like this, Aphrodite fled in shame to Cyprus, and Ares to Thrace. From their union were born Eros (Love), Anteros (Love in return), Deimos and Phobos (Terror and Fear).

The frivolous Aphrodite however, did not have only one lover. Her passion for Adonis was well-known (*Apollodorus*, III, 14, 3). She also loved the shepherd, Anchises, whom she met on Mount Ida. Aeneas was their son (*Iliad*, II, 819). She had relationships with Hermes and with Dionysus, by whom she had Priapus. Her favourites were Phaethon (*Theogony*, 988), Cinyras (*Iliad*, XI, 20), Butes and Paris.

Jealousy

She was jealous and made Eos (Dawn) conceive an impossible love for Orion, because she had seduced Ares. Her weapons were varied and cruel, and she punished all those who would not succumb to her. She led the daughters of Cinyras into prostitution and inflicted a foul smell on the Lemnians who had neglected to worship her. These women, abandoned by their husbands, killed all the men on the island and founded a society of women.

Her power was immense. She made Pasiphae fall in love with the bull of Minos. Her victims included Helen, Medea, Ariadne, Phaedra and Hippodameia, to name but a few.

The beauty competition

Who was the most beautiful of the three goddesses: Hera, Athena, or Aphrodite? This was the question posed by Eris (Discord), and the prize for whoever won the contest was a golden apple (the apple of strife). The contest itself was organized by

Zeus and took place on Mount Ida, and there was only one judge, Paris. The three goddesses each knew how to make the best of certain advantages which did not necessarily have any bearing on the subject of the contest. Thus Hera offered Paris kingship of the universe, Athena offered him invincibility in war, and Aphrodite offered him the most beautiful mortal, Helen. In this way, Aphrodite won the prize and also became the cause of the Trojan War. (Stasinos of Cyprus, *Cyprian Songs; Iliad*, XIV, 29 ff.)

Eros and Aphrodite

One was the god, the other the goddess, of love. Their functions, however, were not the same. Eros was often considered as a primordial god and was the power of instinct.

When Aphrodite appeared, he adapted himself to her and joined forces with her. Aphrodite marked the moment when the sexes became distinct. Along with Aphrodite were born the chatter of young girls, smiles, deception, charm and seduction.

Artemis and Aphrodite

Marriage was one of the boundaries which separated the domains of Artemis and Aphrodite. The former was the chaste goddess who preferred hunting to seducing men. Her kingdom was that of the young girl. However, for the young girl it was only a place through which she must pass; she could not stay there, and leaving it would cost her her toys and dolls. The rhetorician Libanus said, 'Girls go from Artemis to Aphrodite.'.

Aphrodite's kingdom was elsewhere. It was the place of desire. No one could escape. Remember Atalanta who tried to flee from 'Aphrodite's gifts' and keep her virginity? She had dedicated her life to the hunt, even turning her relationships with men into a manhunt, a game of chess. But when she was unable to keep her virginity any longer, Atalanta was trapped by Aphrodite's wiles and turned into a lion.

Sometimes Aphrodite consumed women with violent and ungovernable passions. Think of the story of Diomedes, king of Thrace, who sent his mares to devour passersby. Those horrible animals were

*Charm, beauty, seduction and sensuality were all qualities of **Aphrodite**. Here we can see the even features of her face, the penetrating gaze, and the flowing drapery which both reveals and hides her perfect body.*
Terracota figurine from Myrina or Pergammon; end of the 11th cent. BC.

The Venia

The Romans were particularly religious. Their religion consisted essentially of making agreements with the gods. However, they also knew that they could not force their 'partners' in the same way. From this comes the prime importance of the Venia, the grace, the free benevolence which they expected more specifically from Venus, hence her name. Venus was the goddess that they particularly 'venerated'.

like young girls filled with lust who entwine their lovers and drag them to their deaths. (*Scholies to Aristophanes, Lysistrata*, 1029).

Young women discard the characteristics of Artemis but they are afflicted with Aphrodite's madness all their lives. Nevertheless, even Aphrodite's nature was sometimes tempered with moderation. After all she rejected her deformed son, Pripaus, even though he was the son of Zeus himself, because Priapus had such an enormous phallus Aphrodite thought she would be made a laughing stock. Priapus was abandoned in a wood and left to become a rustic deity.

The cult

The oldest Sanctuaries to Aphrodite are in Cyprus and Cythera, two Phoenician settlements. But it seems likely that the original cult began in Asia where a lunar deity has always been worshipped as a symbol of fruitfulness and fecundity in animals. This deity was known as Atargatis by the Philistines, Ishtar by the Assyrians, Astarte by the Semites. The cult spread over most of Asia Minor as far as Mount Eryx in Sicily, to Carthage and to Latium.

She was a real 'Lady of Succour' who calmed the wind and sea, and in Paphos she was consulted by sailors before they set sail.

But, above all, she was the goddess of love and her temples, particularly those on Mount Eryx and in Corinth, were inhabited by women who offered themselves to passing strangers. At first, this function was reserved for young girls who, in this way, gave their virginity to the goddess, but gradually the practice became restricted to the slaves attached to the temple—the genuine professionals of love.

The Roman Venus

In Rome, well before any Greek influence, there was a divinity of nature, goddess of all that blossoms, and goddess of fecundity whose name was Flora. She had two temples in Rome and festivals called the *Floralia* were dedicated to her. Venus was a similar goddess, but it was her similarity to Aphrodite that made her of major importance. In the beginning, she was the goddess of fields and gardens; later, she became the

goddess of female beauty. Temples were built to her and festivals arranged. On 23 April were the *Vinatia priora* and on 1 April, the *Veneralia*.

In time, the cult of Venus developed. Scylla, the dictator (138–78 BC), worshipped her as *Venus Felix*, and named himself, in Greek, Epaphrodite. Under the name of *Venus Pompeiana* she was the patron of Pompei. Caesar built her a monument in the Forum Julium, calling her thereafter *Venus Genitrix*.

Soon Aphrodite was to be not only the mother of Aeneas and his race but also the protectress of the Roman people. Among the patrician families there were many who prided themselves on being descendants of Aphrodite and Aeneas. Augustus, who presided over a whole movement of patriotic and religious rebirth, took great care to unite Venus Genitrix with Rome. Later (AD 135) Hadrian completed another temple to Venus in Rome. Like Aphrodite in Greece, Venus had many forms, such as Venus Victrix, Venus Calva, Venus Salacia, Venus Equestris, and others.

Dione was a first generation goddess, daughter of Uranus and Gaea.

The Zephyrs were the gods who represent the west winds.

Phaethon was the son of the Sun.

Cinyras, who was king of Cyprus and a prophet, lived until he was 160 years old, thanks to the favour of Aphrodite.

Butes, the Argonaut, was saved from the Sirens by the goddess.

Orion was a giant and Poseidon's son.

Paris, the son of Hecuba and Priam, king of Troy, kidnapped Helen and was thus the cause of the Trojan War.

Apis

Egyptian god

The sacred bull

Menes, the first Egyptian Pharaoh, was said to have started the cult of Apis about 3000 BC

A god of strength and fecundity, Apis was represented as a bull for whom divine honours were reserved.

His cult

During the great public festivals, a bull was chosen for its strength, appearance and, above all, for the number of patches on its body. It was supposed to be black with a white patch on its forehead and a white crescent on its neck and sides. The bull represented the reincarnation of Apis. It was solemnly led to the *sekos* (Herodotus, *History of the Persian Wars* II, 153), the temple of the living Apis, which was a court where the bull was cared for, fed, and had an entourage like a king.

When the animal died, a procession was arranged to transport the body to the *ouabet* which was a room specially reserved for embalming. The faithful went into mourning and began a complete fast for four days, and then a less strict fast for a further seventy days. A funeral vigil also took place from the first evening after the bull died.

Once the mummification had been completed, a new procession took the body from the ouabet to the 'pavilion of purification'. Here the faithful presented their offerings, and there was a funeral cortège consisting of the army and the priests of Ptah (it appears that Apis did not have his own priests), the mourners and a crowd which made its way towards the *serapeum*, the tomb of Apis.

The serapeum

The serapeum was a passage twelve metres beneath the ground, and on each side of it were the vaults of Apis. The furnishings were the same as they would have been for a human mummy: a sarcophagus, amulets and jewels. Sarcophagi were originally made from wood but were later cut from granite.

All those who had participated in the funeral ceremonies had, in return, the right to erect a stele inside the serapeum. These were usually small, and were generally made from limestone. They bore witness to the mourners' devotion to the god.

*One of the faithful, his hands outstretched in a gesture of adoration, kneels before the god **Apis**.*
A stele of painted limestone from the serapeum at Memphis, Egyptian. 20th dynasty, c. 1200 BC (New Empire).

A holy calculation
'Five squared is the number of the letters in the Egyptian alphabet and it is also the number of years that the bull Apis lives' (*Isis and Osiris*, 56). It is curious to note that the period of twenty-five years, or the Apis period, corresponds to the period at the end of which the phases of the moon return on the same day.

Apollo

Greek and Roman god

The god with the silver bow

Young, handsome and dazzling, seer, poet and musician, Apollo had all the qualities of a great god.

The Romans often call him Phoebus, the bright one, and he was often identified with the Sun. Apollo's sparkling and brilliant nature also had a terrifying side. He was said to be 'the most powerful of the gods'.

Delos

Zeus had an affair with Leto and she became pregnant. Hera, who was jealous, pursued Leto the length and breadth of the earth to prevent her from bringing her children into the world. Asteria, a small, floating, barren island, was the only place that would welcome her. There Leto was finally able to give birth, first to Artemis and then to Apollo. Because the god of light first saw day on its soil, the island was immediately covered in gold and became prosperous (*Homeric Hymn to Apollo*, 135). It was set in the middle of the sea of Greece and became known as Delos, the shining one. The sacred swans flew round the island seven times because it was the seventh day of the month, and finally they bore the child away beyond the home of the North Wind, to the Hyperboreans (Callimachus, *Hymn to Delos*, 141–145).

Delphi

After he had stayed with the Hyperboreans for a year, Apollo went to Delphi. There he found a dragon, Python, who guarded the oracle of Themis and also raided the country, killing men and animals, polluting springs and ravaging the earth. Apollo destroyed him with his arrows and thus delivered the country. He then founded the Pythian Games, consecrated the shrine and made the tripod one of his symbols. Henceforth, Pythia, priestess of Apollo, pronounced her oracles sitting on a tripod (*Homeric Hymn to Apollo*, 127 ff.).

Youth

Handsome, young, tall, outstanding in word and deed, he had 'the appearance of a robust, strong man' (*Homeric Hymn to Apollo*, 449–450). God of ever-renewed youth, but not immature, he was full of energy and sometimes even violence. He was the model for, and protector of, the *kouroi* (young

---

The Corybantes were mysterious spirits.

Diomedes was Ulysses' faithful companion during the Trojan War.

Leto was the daughter of Coeus, the Titan.

Themis, goddess of the law, was the daughter of Gaea and Uranus.

Daphne was a nymph, daughter of the river-god Peneius. Eros made Apollo fall in love with Daphne because he had made fun of the way Eros used his bow, his favourite weapon.

Admetus obtained Apollo's promise that he would not die on the day fixed by destiny if someone else would offer himself in his place. On that day his wife, Alcestis, died in his stead.

people). His long curls were black with silver tints, hair which had never been cut. Young men made him an offering of the hair they had cut for the first time, in a traditional rite which marked their entrance into manhood.

This portrait of Apollo can only be that of a seducer, and Apollo's charm attracted a multitude of followers. The most graceful images of him were made. He was the archetype of virile beauty and, at the same time, of masculine qualities. Apollo was as successful in making feminine conquests with goddesses as with mortals, but despite his beauty and glory, he was often unhappy in love.

The loves of Apollo

He loved the nymph Daphne, a love inspired by Eros who was annoyed by his jests. She, however, did not reciprocate his desires and fled to the mountains, where she was transformed into a laurel tree, the tree dedicated to Apollo.

He also loved the nymph Cyrene and had a son by her, Aristaeus. With her, he fulfilled all the matrimonial rites (Pindar, *Pythian Odes*, IX, 104 f.), but this did not prevent him from roving. By the muse, Thalia, he had Corybantes; with Urania, the musicians Linus and Orpheus; by Coronis he had Asclepius, but he killed her because she married Ischys (Pindar, *Pythian Odes*, III, 41–2). The same thing happened with Marpessa who preferred Idas, a mortal, to him, since she feared that she would be abandoned in her old age by the ever-young Apollo. We also know of his love for Phthia, by whom he fathered Doros, Laocodos and Polypoetes, and of Rhoeo by whom he had Anius.

He did not love only women; he loved Hyacinthus, too. The jealous Boreas and Zephyrus, however, who also loved the hero, caused the discus which Apollo had thrown to strike Hyacinthus on the head, killing him.

Insane arrogance

Apollo never mixed with humans other than out of capriciousness or when he was obliged to. He was very proud before Diomedes: 'Go back, do not seek to pit yourself against the gods, for they are not of the same race; immortal gods and men merely passing through on the earth.' He was 'insanely arrogant', says the *Homeric Hymn*, and would not lower himself to look at 'that pathetic race which grows and withers like the leaves on the trees'.

However, he did help the Argonauts, in whom he saw something of his own pride, and he was able to sight the Achaeans from far off in order to protect Troy, whose side he had taken. His arrogance made him scoff at Zeus himself.

The tests of Apollo

Twice, Zeus reacted by testing him and ordering him to be a slave, for a time, to certain mortals.

The first time, along with Hera, Poseidon and Athena, Apollo tried to tie up Zeus. For this he was condemned to serve the King of Troy, Laomedon, who where he built the walls of the city and kept flocks on Mount Ida. Since the king refused to pay him, he sent a plague which devastated the country. (Pindar, *Olympian Odes*, VIII, 40–1).

The second time, Zeus had killed Asclepius with a thunderbolt, and Apollo killed the Cyclops in rage. As a punishment he was sent by the Olympian king to Admetus, king of Therae, for whom he worked as a herdsman. He was well received and so brought prosperity to the land. (Callimachus, *Hymn to Apollo*, 47)

His exploits

Music was one of Apollo's talents. One day, his flock was stolen from him by Hermes; but when he found the sheep on Mount Cyllene, he let the thief keep them in return for the lyre he had invented. On another occasion he was challenged by the satyr, Marsyas, who claimed he could play more melodious music on his flute than Apollo on his lyre. Marsyas was defeated and Apollo had him flayed alive and nailed to a pine, which is why the bark of this tree is said to be red like the blood of the victim. Marsyas obviously did not know that the music of Apollo charmed 'the gods, the wild beasts, and even the stones' (Euripedes, *Alceste*, 579).

He was leader of the choir of Muses and inspired soothsayers and poets alike. Indeed, his oracles were expressed in verse.

The terrifying god

Apollo's weapons were just as fearsome as those of his sister, Artemis. He took part in the massacre of the children of Niobe; decimated the Greek army before Troy (*Iliad*, I, 43 ff.); and killed the Cyclops, the serpent Python who came from his dark lair, and Tityus, the giant who came out of the earth. The death of Achilles is attributed to him and, because of the hate he bore towards Achilles, he pursued his son, Neoptolemus, killing him at Delphi where he was consulting the oracle.

Apollo was 'the Lord Archer who has the appearance of a star which burns brightly in daylight; countless sparks fly out from his person and their brilliance reaches Heaven' (*Homeric Hymn to Apollo*, 440–447).

Even Apollo's friends were afraid of him. He appeared to the Argonauts, whom he supported, but he was so dazzling that they dared not raise their eyes. They were dumbstruck and trembled, and when they did want to look upon him, he had already gone (Apollonius of Rhodes, *The Argonautica*, II, 680). When he arrived at Delphi, 'the Crisean women and their daughters with beautiful waists screamed in fright at the sight of Phoebus because he inspired great terror in them' (*Homeric Hymn to Apollo*, 446–447).

The god who knows everything

Just as he was good at killing, Apollo also knew how to cure and get rid of evil and illness (*apotropaios*), and to fight the monsters who spread unhappiness. He was a doctor, rather like his son, Asclepius. He knew the purification rites (*katharsios*) and was invoked against plague. His effigy was set in dangerous places, and it was to him that people turned when they were in serious situations.

Because Apollo's gaze reached every-

His curls, 'pour out perfumed oil which they distill: but the drops are not at all greasy'. (Callimachus, **Hymn to Apollo**, *36–40*). **Apollo** *is a handsome man; well-balanced, strong, arrogant, a musician and a poet.*

Cytherean Apollo: Detail of a bronze statue from Pompeii. It is an antique copy of a Greek original.

where, for him there was no distance, and nothing escaped him — words, thoughts or actions (Pindar, *Pythian Odes*, III, 25). He was omniscient, knowing the cause of evil and the cure. He also knew 'how many grains of sand there are, and the dimensions of the earth.' (Herodotus, *Histoires*, I, 47).

'It is for Apollo to dictate the most important, the most beautiful, the first laws' (Plato, *The Republic*, IV, 427).

The oracle

Apollo spoke at Delphi. Pythia said 'I' and spoke Apollo's own words. She was the only one who knew what the master of the world thought and the judgments he made in his mind. 'Know thyself' was the inscription on the pediment of the temple. The oracle could read the answers written in the hearts of those who questioned it, but 'never pronounced an oracle on a man, woman or city that was not an order from Zeus' (Aeschylus, *The Eumenides*, 616–619).

The whole of Greece came to this place, which was different from others. There they could receive advice on their private lives, directives for political life and orders for their rituals and religious life. But Apollo made his power felt there, and it was a place of violence. The 'Delphic cutlass' was the instrument of the famous murders carried out because of Apollo's promptings. Aesop, the writer of fables (6th century BC), lost his life there.

The festivals

The festivals in his honour, the Thargelia, had two phases. Firstly, two poor wretches,

physically and morally destitute, were chosen. One represented women and the other men. They were paraded through the town, beaten with sticks, stoned and sent to be burned or chased into the mountains. They took with them the sins of all, and this formed the rite of purification. Next they sang the *paean*, the song of Apollo, and offered the god the first fruits of the earth in the form of bread, fruit and cakes.

Animals and plants

Certain animals have a particular connection with Apollo: the wolf offered to him in sacrifice, the deer, the swan, the kite, the vulture and the crow, whose flight signifies omens.

The laurel tree was, above all, Apollo's tree, and Pythia chewed a leaf when she delivered her oracles.

The cult of Apollo

Apollo was very important in antiquity. It was he who promised salvation and eternal life in the Orphic religion and started Pythagorism. He also reigned on the island of the Blessed, a paradise.

In Rome, the first temple dedicated to him was built in the Flaminian meadows. It was erected following a serious epidemic and was known as Apollo Medicus (*Livy*, IV; XL).

The first Roman Emperor, Augustus, took Apollo as his protector, claimed to be descended from him and attributed his victory at Actium to him. In commemoration of this battle Augustus built the Palatine temple of Apollo.

The Paean

'Be silent, listen to the Song of Apollo. Even the waves are quiet when the bard plays the cithera and bow of Lycorean Apollo. Thetis, sad mother, no longer bemoans the fate of Achilles when she hears the clamour of *lé Paian, lé Paian*, and the stone which cries lays aside its cares for a time, the damp rock on the phyrgian shores; marble which was a woman whose mouth maoned. *Ié, lé*, may your cry ring out.' (Callimachus, *Hymn to Apollo*, 17–24)

The haughty god

In the course of the Trojan War, Apollo declared to Ares, 'O, you who shakes the earth, you would not say that I was sane if I went into battle against you for miserable humans who, like the leaves, grow and burn with vigour as they eat the fruits of the land, and then perish in weakness. Let us, therefore, cease this battle and let them continue the struggle themselves.' (*The Iliad*, XXI, 462–466)

Ares/Mars

Greek and Roman god

Murderous violence

Identified with the Roman god Mars, he was escorted by the gory Enyo, Eris (Discord), Deimos (Terror), and Phobos (Fear).

Ares was the son of Hera, who bore him without the assistance of male seed (*Iliad*, XV, 166), and one of the twelve great gods. He was a supreme fighter who cared little for the interests he defended, changing sides without scruple. He loved fighting for fighting's sake and delighted in bloody massacres. He was the god most hated by the Olympians.

A brute of immense stature, he wore bronze armour (*Iliad*, V, 704), a gleaming helmet with a long plume (*ibid.* XXII, 132), and carried a spear (*ibid.* XV, 605) and a leather shield (*ibid.* V, 289). Endowed with enormous strength, he cast aside all obstacles: warriors, chariots and even walls (*Homeric Hymn*, VII, 1). He surprised his enemies with his incredible speed and terrified them by shouting '*alale, alala!*', his war cry.

His wild energy

He was the god of war, not the god of victory, and his thoughtless ardour resulted in many setbacks. He was the opposite of Athena, the goddess of restraint and forethought, and she sometimes disarmed him

---

The Aloeides

These were the two sons Poseidon had by Iphimedeia, the wife of Aloeus. They were extraordinary giants who declared war on the gods after climbing up to the sky by piling mountain upon mountain.

---

to prevent him from interfering in battles which did not concern him (*Iliad*, XV, 110–42). She fought directly with him by arming Diomedes (*ibid.* V, 590 ff.) and once even succeeded in knocking him down by throwing a stone at him (*ibid.* XXI, 391 ff.).

Ares was well acquainted with defeat, having been attacked by the Aloeides, Otus and Ephialtes, sons of Poseidon, and he was chained up and kept for thirteen months in a bronze jar (*Iliad*, V, 385 ff.). Heracles, too, brought him down on several occasions and even went so far as to strip him of his weapons (Hesiod, *The Shield of Hercules*, 359 f.).

He fought until he was exhausted and was sometimes left for dead. He was then taken to Olympus, where Zeus himself looked after his wounds: 'a god must not die' (*Iliad*, V, 590 ff.).

Male power

Such excessive ardour did not leave people indifferent. Aphrodite herself was conquered by him and had to keep her illicit liaison with him a secret (*Iliad*, VIII, 266–366); according to certain traditions, Eros and Priapus were born of this liaison. Ares was as impetuous in his adventures with women as he was in war. He raped Astyocha and made her pregnant with Ascalaphus and Ialmenus (*Iliad*, II, 512).

Meleager

Just after the birth of Meleager, his mother was warned that the child's life was linked to a brand which burned in the hearth.. Althaea immediately extinguished it and Meleager grew up. As an adult, he fought the wild boar of Calydon, killed it and offered the pelt to Atalanta, whom he loved. Althaea, who was furious, threw the brand into the fire and Meleager died.

He also raped Pyrene, by whom he had Diomedes of Thrace, Cycnus, and Lycaon (*Apollodorus*, II, 5–8). Chryse bore him Phlegyas (*Pausanias*, IX, 36, 1); Astynome bore him Calydon; Althaea, Meleager (*Apollodorus*, I, 8, 2); Periboea, Tydeus (*Diodorus of Sicily*, IV, 35); Protogencia mothered Oxylus (*Apollodorus*, I, 7, 7); Harpina, Oenomaus (*Pausanias*, V, 22, 6), and so on.

His cult

Thrace was the country of Mars's origin, and the fierce and warlike people of that region dedicated a cult to him. From there it then developed in Thebes, Athens and Sparta. In this last city, two of the priests walked before the army and gave the signal for battle by means of flaming torches.

In Rome, the cult of Ares was assimilated with that of Mars, one of the most ancient and venerated gods on the peninsula. He was honoured by a brotherhood of respected priests, the Salians (*Salii Palatiini*), who looked after the twelve serrated shields said to have fallen from the sky and at certain festivals performed war dances. Mars was said to be the father of Romulus, the founder of Rome, and to have helped Rome become the greatest empire in the world.

Ares-Mars in *ceremonial costume: thichset and impassive, he wears a Corinthian helmet with a high plume, a breastplate, a chiton (a light tunic), and a chlamys (a short mantle attached at the shoulder).*

Marble statue from the Trajan Forum, AD 81–96.

Artemis/Diana

Greek and Roman goddess

The unshakeable virgin

Eternally young and active, Artemis was the equal of any man. Her only pleasure was hunting.

Daughter of Zeus and Leto, she was marked by the jealousy of Hera, the legitimate wife of the Olympian master. Since she was the first to be born, she assisted at the birth of Apollo, and the bond between brother and sister was much stronger because of this.

She was tall and imposing (*Homeric Hymn to Pythian Apollo*, 271), a queen with a beautiful face (Callimachus, *Hymn to Artemis*, 204) and golden curls (Euripedes, *Hippolyta*, 80 ff.). She was proud of her shape and took great care of it, and because of this she made sure that she kept her virginity.

Artemis of the golden arrows

Coming from Delos, Artemis would have hunted for the first time in Attica (*Pausanias*, I, 19, 6). She was armed with a bow and arrows made by Hephaestus and the Cyclops. The god Pan gave her dogs, 'swifter than the wind' and capable of knocking down even lions (Callimachus, *Hymn to Artemis*, 90–95). She lived in the mountains and woods where she hunted stags, hinds, roe deer and occasionally even lions and panthers (*Pausanius*, V, 19, 5; *Iliad*, XXI, 485).

Tityus was a gaint, a son of Zeus. Jealous Hera sent him to fight with Leda.

Acteon was the grandson of Apollo and the nymph, Cyrene.

The bad-tempered girl

She was a warrior, joining with Apollo in the murder of the serpent Python, in the punishment of the giant Tityus, and in the massacre of the children of Niobe, who had insulted her mother. Anyone who offended her paid a severe penalty. She was 'the invisible and unviolated virgin' (Sophocles, *Electra*, 1239) and turned mercilessly against anyone who attempted to force her against her will. Otus, the Giant, was killed by one of her ruses (*Odyssey*, XI, 305 ff.); Orion was stung by a scorpion sent by her (*Apollodorus*, I, 4, 3); Acteon happened to see her bathing naked in the river Partenius and was turned into a stag (Hesiod, *Theogony*, 977); and Buphagus was pierced by her arrows on Mount Pholoë (*Pausanias*, VIII, 27, 17).

She defended modesty, stood up against fierce violence and excesses, and punished illicit love. She also avenged the rapes of the nymphs Opis and Chromia (*Pausanias*, VIII, 47, 6), and Tartarus, the tyrant, was put to death because he took advantage of his power to take the virginity of the young women of his city before they were married (*Antonius Liberalis*, XIII).

Artemis took her anger out on those virgins who gave into love. She turned Callisto into a bear because she had let herself be seduced by Zeus (Hesiod, *Fragments*, XCIX). She also demanded that Comaetho, her priestess, and Melanippus, Comaetho's lover, be sacrificed (*Pausanias*, VII, 19, 20).

She had a particular care for young women, those who had not yet acquired a taste for the talents of frivolous Aphrodite. These were the priestesses who celebrated her, dancing in front of her temple and meeting together in the woods. Artemis was not against their marrying, but when that happened, they came and laid in front of her altar all the paraphernalia of their virginity — locks of hair, toys and dolls —

and they left her domain. The goddess had no time for trifles. On the other hand, when it was a question of something serious, she was there. She became the protectress of women in labour and newborn children (Callimachus, *Hymn to Artemis*, 20–25).

Diana the huntress

Her worship was brought to Rome under the name Diana. She was a very demanding goddess, since one could only become the keeper of her temple on the shores of Lake Nemi by killing the priest who already held the office (Ovid, *Fasti*, III, 275). It is said that Artemis hid Hippolytus, the son of Theseus, in this shrine, after his death and resurrection.

It was the influence of the Greek Artemis that made Diana a huntress. She reigned in the forests, and on the Ides of August, the feast day dedicated to her, she rewarded the hounds and allowed the wild beasts a respite (Stace, *Les Silves*, III, 1, 55).

Her cult

There were several temples to Diana in Rome. One of them, the one in the vicus Patricius, had a distinctive characteristic: men were not allowed there because one of them had tried to violate a woman in the sanctuary itself, and the man had been torn apart by the hounds of Diana. The most important of her temples was built by Servius Tullius (578–534 BC) on the Aventine. It was a meeting place for followers of Diana, and the festivals which took place there were especially for women and slaves.

The assimilation of Diana with Artemis was completed when Augustus gave her a place beside her brother, Apollo. She became *Diana Victrix*, Diana the victorious, and was celebrated in the secular song by Horace. The song was written for the greatest festival in the Empire, given in her honour by Augustus. In it Diana symbolizes the moon and Apollo, the sun, two planets which influence procreation, birth, and death.

But above all, brother and sister were considered to be the protectors of the imperial city and guarantors of the peace imposed by the Empire on the world.

Artemis *was a lunar goddess; her wings symbolized the course of the stars at night.*

Gold plaque from Rhodes, 7th cent. BC.

Artemis, transformed into a hind, made the **Aloeides**, Otus and Ephialtes, run after her, and this caused them to kill each other.

Apollo, when he wanted to found his shrine at the foot of Parnassus, found a serpent named Python which he had to kill.

Apollo's sister
'Give me, my dear father, eternal virginity [. . .] Give me a bow and arrows . . . give me the office of bringing light and let me wear a fringed tunic reaching to my knees so I can hunt wild beasts'. (Prayer of Artemis to Zeus. Callimachus, *Hymn to Artemis*, 7 – 10)

Arthur

Celtic hero

Sovereign of the western medieval world

Valour, chivalry, conquests and the service to the Church are what made the court of King Arthur (or Artus) so renowned.

Son of Uther Pendragon, the king of Britain, and Igerne, the wife of the duke of Cornwall, Arthur symbolized the union of the two peoples 'who could hear each other talk from one shore (of the Channel) to the other' (Geoffrey of Monmouth, *Historia regnum Britanniae*, 1137).

King-knight

Arthur was brought up by Merlin the magician and crowned at the age of 15. Armed with Excalibur, his magical sword, he rid his country of monsters and giants, drove out the invaders, conquered the continent, reached Rome and in some stories even as far as Palestine, from where he brought back the Cross of Christ.

But he was also a deceived king. Queen Guinevere accepted the chivalrous love of Lancelot of the Lake, and Arthur's nephew Mordred took advantage of the king's absence to steal the crown from him. He sought to revenge himself on them both and was mortally wounded, in 542, as he fought against the usurper. It was the end of

his kingdom. 'The great king exchanged his existence for another' (Thomas Malory, *La Mort d'Arthur*, 1470).

Morgan le Fay and the fairies took him on a barge to the island of Avalon, and from there he will one day return to deliver his people.

The Knights of the Round Table

Arthur's court was known as Camelot; valour and chivalry were the key words there. He founded the Order of the Knights of the Round Table so that there would be no problems of precedence among the knights. The Round Table made all the knights equal, and each went his own way in search of adventure. Above all, the knights respected the Code of Chivalry, honour, the brotherhood of arms and the protection of the weak and the Church. When they returned, they gathered together at the castle of the Joyous Gard, and there they told of their exploits. At his great feasts, the king would not sit down to eat until some adventure had been retold in his house.

The quest for the Grail

The knights of the Round Table were obsessed by the quest for the Grail. The Grail was a mysterious chalice, thought to be the one in which Pilate washed his hands, or perhaps the one in which Joseph of Arimathea gathered some drops of the blood of Christ. This quest could only be undertaken by a pure knight. Galahad, the son of Lancelot, was the only one found worthy of the task. He was regarded as the true knight, the desired one, the promised one, the one descended from the highest lineage of King Solomon and Joseph of Arimathea, the one who would succeed in the quest for the Holy Grail and thus end the age of adventure.

Camelot

The location of Arthur's court varies with local tradition. Such tradition places it at Carleon castle in Wales, at Tintagel in Cornwall, in Cumberland or the lowlands of Scotland, or even in Brittany.

Asclepius/Aesculapius

Greek and Roman god

The one who loved mortals the most

Asclepius possessed the magic power (metis) to cure and revitalize.

Asclepius was the son of Apollo. His mother, Coronis, was the daughter of Phlegyas, king of Thessaly. Coronis was killed by Artemis because she had been unfaithful to her divine lover with a mortal, Ischys, son of Elatus. But just at the moment when her body was burning on the funeral pyre, Apollo tore the child, who was still alive, from his mother's breast and entrusted him to Cheiron the Centaur. Under the guidance of this master, Asclepius acquired the knowledge of incantations, love potions, drugs and surgery (Pindar, *Pythian Odes*, III). Athena gave him a magic potion from the blood of the Gorgon. When taken from the left side of the monster, the potion was a violent poison; but when taken from the right side, it was a miracle remedy which could bring corpses back to life (Apollodorus, *The Library*, III, 10, 3).

Miracle-worker

Asclepius used his knowledge to serve mortals, and his powers were so great that the ill were cured and the dead brought back to life. Among those who benefited from this were Lycurgus, the orator; Glaucus, the son of Minos; and Hippolytus, the son of Theseus. However, this upset the order of the world as it was not known if men were going to become immortal or if the privilege of the gods would be taken away. Zeus, the master of the universe, could not accept such disorders; he became enraged and killed Asclepius for upsetting the natural order. In spite of this, Asclepius did not disappear, nor did he enter Hades. Instead, he became a god himself. We can see him in the sky in the form of a constellation, the serpent-eater.

He was a kingly god, the god of the earth, the son of Phoebus (the Sun). His symbol was a snake wound round a staff, a symbol which was with him in most of the representations. He was portrayed as an old bearded man, thoughtful and benevolent.

Epidaurus, centre of healing

Epidaurus was the centre of his cult and people came there to be cured.

The rules that had to be observed were very stringent. To obtain the blessings of the god one had to have great purity. Fasting, abstinence, and refraining from sexual relations were all obligatory. The dormitories where the faithful slept on the bare ground were visited by non-poisonous snakes. The god came to them in dreams while they slept. In this way he accomplished the miracle of his cure and specified the treatment to be given.

Hippocrates

Under the patronage of Asclepius, schools of medicine were established and spread to many towns. The island of Kos is the cradle of one of the most famous of the Asclepeides or descendants of Asclepius: Hippocrates, the great doctor of antiquity.

Hippolytus, son of Theseus, had rejected the advances of Phaedra, his father's new wife. Afraid of being unmasked, she accused her step-son of trying to rape her. Theseus, to avenge her, called up a great sea monster to kill Hippolytus.

Glaucus was the son of Minos and Pasiphae. While he was still a child, he chased a mouse, fell into a jar of honey and drowned.

Aten

Egyptian god

The Sun's radiant disc

As the supreme god, universally accessible, Aten eclipsed all the other gods for twenty years.

Aten was unique. He showed himself to all mankind in the form of the solar disc, he gave life, he was the creator of all things and all things depended on him. He was close to the people and spoke their language.

He had no connection with the other, numerous gods who had powerful priests, complicated and mysterious rituals, a secret language and temples which were closed in on themselves.

Aten's temples were open to the sky so that the devotees could see and worship the solar god without any hindrance. Amenhotep IV (1372–1354 BC) became Akhenaten ('He who is pleasing to Aten'),

developed the cult of Aten and imposed it to the exclusion of all others. He chose a capital for the god (now called Tell-el-Amarna), built his temples and made himself his messenger and prophet.

This religion with only one god lasted throughout his reign. With the pharaoh's death, however, Thebes once again became the capital and Amun's clergy regained their power.

Prayer to Aten

'You appear, splendid one, on the horizon of the sky, O living Aten, creator of life. You fill the whole land with your perfection . . . When you disperse the darkness by throwing out your rays, the inhabitants wash, dress and lift their arms to worship you; the whole country sets to work, livestock is happy with its grazing; tress and plants grow green, and birds fly from their nests.' *(Hymn to Aten)*

*Akhenaten gives a buckle to his daughter, Meretaten, under the symbol of **Aten**, the sun-god. The oblong headpieces are noticeable, characteristic of the style imposed by the pharaoh.*

Relief from an altar from Tell-el-Amarna. XVIIIth Dynasty, c. 1379–62 BC).

Athena/Minerva

Greek and Roman goddess

Intelligence and skill

Radiant in her bronze armour, Athene, like the city whose protectress she was, combined the love of art with that of wisdom.

When Metis, 'the goddess who knows more than any god or mortal man', was pregnant by Zeus, he was warned that, if the child was a girl, a boy would be born after her and would depose his father. Zeus, therefore, swallowed the mother, and when it was time for the child to be born, he asked Hephaestus to crack open his skull. Athena came out of his brain in full armour, shouting out a war cry which rang out in the Heavens and on earth. She was born 'equal to her father in strength and careful wisdom' (Hesiod, *Theogony*, 896).

Virgin and warrior

Athena was called 'Parthenos', the virgin. However, she was not a virgin goddess like the others. Having no fear of men, she lived amongst them as one of them. Indeed, she always took their side and confronted the most powerful. 'In all things,' she said, 'my heart leans towards men, except in marriage' (Aeschylus, *The Eumenides*, 736). She defended Agamemnon against Clytemnestra in the case against Orestes, who had killed his mother to avenge his

---

Agamemnon was the king of kings. At the time of the Trojan War, he sacrificed his daughter, Iphigeneia, in order to obtain favourable winds, and for this reason was killed by his wife, Clytemnestra. Orestes, their son, murdered his mother to avenge his father.

---

father. (Aeschylus, *The Eumenides*, 736–738). Her protégés—Odysseus, Heracles, Diomedes, Achilles, and Menelaus—were, without exception, all men.

Her protection was by no means ineffectual. Athena followed Odysseus in all his wanderings and took the form of a mortal in order to help him. She suggested to Nausicaa that she should go and wash her linen when Odysseus was due to reach the island of the Phaecians, and she was the instigator of the order given to Calypso to release the hero. She defended Heracles and assisted him in his trials (*Pausanias*, III, 18, 11). She restrained Achilles' anger (*Iliad*, I, 194), but always moderate herself, denied Tydeus immortality because of his brutishness.

She was a warrior (*areia*), powerful (*stenias*), and a champion (*promachos*). She took an active part in the war against the giants; Enceladus and Pallas became her victims and she made a shield from the skin of the latter. At Troy she fought on the side of the Achaeans, because Paris had not given her the first prize in the beauty contest. Ares was her sworn enemy (*Iliad*, XXI, 390 ff.), as she hated the god for his reckless abandon, his murderous folly and his love of blood. Athena did not fight

---

Menelaus, Agamemnon's brother, was the husband of Helen, kidnapped by Paris in the event which provoked the Trojan War.

Calypso, the nymph, held Odysseus back for ten years, for she had fallen in love with him.

Tydeus committed a murder and then ate the brain of his victim. Athene was outraged by this.

---

in that way: she used strategy, ambush, cunning and even, on occasion, magic. Protected by the aegis, her shield on which the terrifying head of the Gorgon was represented, she paralyzed her adversaries and made her companions invincible. War to her was not an end in itself; it was undertaken as a necessity and its savagery had to be tamed.

The city

When the gods divided the earth among themselves, each of them claimed a group of worshippers. Athena was in competition with Poseidon for the possession of Attica. The god of the sea arrived first and caused a spring to gush out on the Acropolis. The goddess, on the other hand, made an olive tree grow out of the sacred rock. Zeus settled the difference, and Poseidon was declared to have been beaten (*Apollodorus*, III, 14, 1). Thus the era of civilization began for the city of Athens.

Erichthonius was the adopted son of Athena. Hephaestus, abandoned by Aphrodite, tried to force Athena to make love with him. She resisted, however, and managed to free herself. The sperm from the smith-god had spurted against her thigh, so Athena collected it and planted it in the earth. Erichthonius was born from this, the son of Hephaestus and Mother Earth (*Apollodorus*, III, 14, 6). The child was to be a protégé of Athena and became the king of Athens, founding the cult of Athena there and forever linking the name of the goddess with his people.

As in war, Athena was against any excesses in everyday life. She taught men to conquer their savage streak, to tame nature and become masters of the elements. She was the initiator of all skills and taught Pandora how to spin and weave (Hesiod, *Works and Days*, 64), and the Phaecian women too (*Odyssey*, VII, 110). She was invoked by blacksmiths; she trained horses and invented the chariot. She was also the one who obtained for Bellerophon the bridle which he needed to subdue Pegasus (Pindar, *Olympian Odes*, XIII, 63–87). She presided over carpentry and, with Danaus, built the first ship (*Apollodorus*, III, 1, 4). It was Athena herself who went up on to Mount Pelion to cut down the trees to build

Marble statue of Athena of Varvakeion.
A Roman copy of Phidias's statue (5th cent. BC)

the Argonauts' boat (Apollonius of Rhodes, *The Argonautica*, II, 1187–1189), for she wanted to teach men what *metis* was: 'that is to say, intelligence and not strength makes a good woodcutter' (*Iliad*, XV, 412).

Minerva

Assimilated to the cult of Athena, Minerva was an Etruscan goddess, introduced to Rome under the name of *Minerva Capta*, 'captive Minerva'. Craftsmen celebrated her in a festival on 19 March.

Baal

Phoenician god

The fighter

Baal, after a well-fought battle, won his palace, his realm and his powers as god of fertility and fecundity.

Baal was a young man or a 'bull-calf with sharp horns' and an energetic fighter. He won his title of king of the gods by attacking El and was known as the 'prince-lord of the earth'.

Anat, his sister and perhaps his lover, was inseparable from him. She was a bloodthirsty goddess, always ready to kill. As Baal, the god of storms, sent 'invigorating rain, so Anat sprinkled the dew and brought forth springs from the nourishing earth. The blood which she loved so much was a catalyst for fertility. Both were responsible for the universal prosperity of people and animals.

The battles of Baal

Baal had to fight for his sovereignty as Yam, the god of the sea, was his enemy. They started by hurling abuse and insults freely at each other and then came to blows. Kothar, or Koshar-wa-Hasis ('deft and skilful'), the god of arts and crafts, made Baal two clubs. He conquered Yam with the second one, and this victory over the god of the sea gave sailors the courage to set their boats on the water.

Baal needed a palace, just like other gods. Since it was necessary to obtain the permission of El for this, he asked Kothar to make gifts which he would offer to Athirat, the wife of the god, and so make her benevolent towards him. In this way he persuaded her to intervene on his behalf. The palace was to cover almost 10,000 acres and would be built by Kothar himself. From the very first day of the inauguration, Anat exercised her murderous talents.

God of fertility

In a final battle, he confronted Môt, the god of war and barrenness. A seven-year cycle, either of fertility or of drought, depended on the outcome of this struggle. Thus, Baal's success meant abundant harvests and fecundity for both humans and animals.

El took on the responsibility of maintaining the balance between the two rivals, and each year Baal voluntarily accepted death. He fell from his celestial palace, descended to earth and rose again to heaven, carried by the solar goddess, Shapash, and by Anat, goddess of springs. Thus the death and resurrection of crops are linked with Baal (A Caquot, M. Sznycer, and A. Herdner, *Textes ougaritiques*, t.I: *Mythes et Légendes*, Paris, 1974).

There were altars to Baal throughout almost all of the ancient Near East, as far as Egypt and Jerusalem, where the faithful 'filled the temple (of Baal) from one end to the other' (2 *Kings*, 10, 21).

Anat, the sister and wife of Baal

Anat arrives at her dwelling place and makes her way to her palace. But she is not satisfied with the massacre in the valley, with the battle between the two fortresses. She moves some chairs to accommodate the courageous troops, moves some tables to accommodate the warriors, the foot soldiers, the knights. When they are crowded together she massacres them. Then Anat contemplates the battle scene and rejoices. (A. Caquot, M. Sznycer and A. Herdner, *Texts ougaritiques*, Paris 1974)

Balder

Norse god

The wisest and most beautiful

The 'fairest of the Aesir', slain by pure wickedness, it was said he would preside over the golden age to come.

Balder belongs to the group of Aesir gods who were aristocratic, the gods of sovereignty and power. The son of Odin and Frigg, he was the opposite of the others: they were harsh and violent, while he was gentle and kind, pleasant and willing to help. 'He is so beautiful to look at and so radiant that he gives out light, he is the wisest of the Aesir, the most skilful in speech and the most merciful' (*Gylfaginning*, II). He lived with Nanna, his wife, in Breidhablik (Great Brilliance) within Asgard, the world of the gods.

His mother, Frigg, made him invulnerable by asking all the plants—the material for weapons—to swear that they would not injure him. His immunity was put to the test by playful gods who knew that they could not harm him. However, one of them, Loki, who was wicked and jealous, found one plant—the mistletoe—which had not been asked to swear the oath on account of its youth. He put some into the hands of Höchr, the blind god who was hanging back, and said to him, 'do as the others, enjoy yourself, I will guide your hand.' As soon as it was said, it was done. The mistletoe hit

Balder and, as it was now a weapon too, it pierced him through and he fell. (*Gylfaginning*, XXXIII–XXXV)

The Aesir organized a great funeral for Balder. He was set on a boat which they pushed out to sea after setting fire to it. Balder did not die in combat, so he had to go to the home of Hel, the terrible. The Aesir wanted to get him back from there and asked the goddess of hell to free him. They asked and then begged her, and eventually she was moved to pity and agreed to give back Balder. She made one condition, that every creature, without exception, must weep for him.

The whole world wept for him, except a hideous little old woman, Thökk (who was in fact Loki in disguise). Thus, Balder had to remain in hell until the end of Ragna rök. Then he will come out to preside over the 'return of the sons of the dead gods to the fold of the Aesir'.

Ragna rök is the last battle. It will bring about the end of the world.

The Aesir and the Vanir

The Norse countries had two families of gods, the Aesir and the Vanir. The latter, doubtless the gods of the indigenous population, were patrons of the fertility of plants and the fecundity of beasts and men. They were close to the people, and the most important ones were Njord, Frey, Freyja. The Aesir were probably the gods of invaders or gods of war, and were aristocratic rulers. They were called Tyr, Odin, Thor, Heimdall, Balder and Loki. Legend tells us of a war between the Aesir and the Vanir, a war with many stages after which there was a reconciliation (*Ynglinga Saga*, I). It has since become difficult to decipher which family, or even, sometimes, to distinguish between them.

Balder's dream

'I still want to know who will be Balder's murderer and who will rob the son of Odin of his life [. . .] Höd will be Balder's murderer and will rob the son of Odin of his life. I have been forced to speak; now I will be silent.' (from *Baldrasdraumar*, 8–9)

Brahma

Indian god

The lord of all life

Considered as the creator, he was above and beyond all devotion and worship.

Brahma was born of himself or was even called the 'unborn'. He emerged from the original egg of the world (*Mahabharata*, I, 1, 32) or from the waters (*ibid*. XII, 166, 12). He was assimilated to Prajapati, Dhatar, Vicvakarman, Brihaspati, Hiranyagarbha and Purusha. He reigned in splendour in a heaven which was his own, a paradise to which everyone aspired. With Vishnu, the preserver, and Shiva, the destroyer, he formed what was called the Hindu *Trimurti*.

Brahma and Sarasvati

Brahma had decided to create. To do this, he divided himself in two to make a couple. Thus Sarasvati, or Savitri, came into existence. She was feminine energy, necessary to the fecundity of Brahma, but she was also like his daughter. Creation, then, could only happen through incest.

Brahma immediately fell in love with Sarasvati. She, in order to show her respect for her father, circled him constantly. Brahma, who wanted to look at Sarasvati all the time, saw himself grow another head on his right, another behind, and a third on his left. Brahma now had four heads, all full of the desire inspired in him by Sarasvati (*Matsya-purana*, III, 30–41). He was also

given four arms to show his power. He is often represented as being mounted on a goose.

Brahma was the creator, and his son, Marici, helped him in his task. Kashyapa, Marici's son, was the father of the gods, men and other beings. Brahma travelled a lot and often intervened. When the gods were having difficulties, they came to him for advice. He was like the 'grandfather' (*Pitamaha*), and he gave each his office. In this capacity he made Indra king of the gods (*Mahabharata*, I, 212, 25).

Brahma organized the world which, for him, was like one day in a lifetime. He knew what the future had in store and revealed the Vedas to humanity. He also laid down the rules of *karma*, the standard of reward for one's actions, and he never changed his position. He was impartial, instituted laws and punishments, created death and was responsible for the destruction of the world.

He was not a god of grace and free gifts, and no one expected any favours from him. Consequently there were few prayers to him and few temples were dedicated to him. He also represented untouchable fate, an inflexible iron law which was applicable in all circumstances. He was a distant and proud god.

He was the personification of the *brahman*, the sublime and mysterious being which permeated all things, men and gods. This being was the absolute in their hearts: it preceded them, transcended them and was at the same time inherent in them. Brahma, therefore, evoked the impersonal and neutral reality which encompassed everything.

Visvakarman was the divine creative power of the world.

Dhatar was the organizer of the world.

Hiranyagarbha was the primordial egg at the root of all creation.

Brihaspati was the chaplain of the gods.

Buddha

Founder of Buddhism

The wise man of India

His long search showed him the way to escape from illusions and pain.

Legend has it that Siddharta Gautama was born around 560 BC near Kapilavastu, at the foot of the Himalayas. He came from a noble family and spent his childhood in luxury and pleasure. He was very intelligent, a good archer, and endowed with extraordinary strength, and so he knew only the joys of existence. His father took care that he did not leave the palace, from which all sorrow, suffering and trouble had been banished. He married the beautiful Yashodara, who bore him a son, Rahula.

The search for truth

One day, disobeying the orders of his father, he went out of the palace. He saw an old man, and thus he came to know of old age and poverty; he saw a sick person, and learned of suffering; he saw a corpse and discovered death. He lost all joy in living and decided to save humanity from its evils. The sight of the calm and serene face of an ascetic finally consoled him, and Buddha left his father's palace.

First of all, he listened to the teaching of a brahmin master, Arada Kalama, who taught him to distinguish the different constituent elements of things. He became learned in this doctrine and knew all its subtleties and formalism, but he felt it to be insufficient and so left Arada Kalama.

He became the disciple of Udraka and managed the most difficult yoga exercises that he was taught, practising all the techniques to gain an exceptional mastery of them. However, this path did not seem to him to be the right one either, and he left there too.

Then Buddha became a monk and was called Çakyamuni (monk of the Çakya family). He laid aside all his possessions and began to observe the most rigorous asceticism. Eventually he reached the stage where he ate only one grain of millet a day and became almost a skeleton. However, he began to understand the futility of such mortifications.

He had tried everything—the life of pleasure, philosophy, yoga, and asceticism—and nothing had satisfied him. He sat down under a fig tree and began to meditate. Concentrating for a long time on the sorrowful nature of existence changed him profoundly, and he saw again his countless previous lives.

And so Buddha came to the last tests. He was tempted by the demon, Mara, monsters threw stones at him; and pretty girls offered themselves to him. The stones turned into flowers, and the girls left him indifferent. Little by little, he discovered the law of the infernal cycle of birth and

---

Buddhism

It can be said that Buddhism is a religion without God. At least, we can acknowledge that it does not pose the question of God's existence, and is more like a school of wisdom than a system of worship. However, that is not to say that it has no relationship with the 'unknowable'.

The illusion

'Just as in the vast ethereal sphere, stars, darkness, light, mirage, dew, foam, lightning and clouds emerge, become visible and then vanish, so do the outlines of a dream, and so you should consider all things as being endowed with an individual form.'
(*Vajracchedikd*, 32)

rebirth and grasped the four 'great truths', attaining awakening and enlightenment. Thus he became Buddha.

He acquired disciples at Benares and explained to them the four great truths about pain, the origin of pain, stopping pain and the road which leads to the cessation of pain. From then on, there were more and more conversions and his community expanded. He died at the age of 24 after a long meditation.

The Buddhas

The Buddhas were beings who had attained enlightenment. Gautama was to be the seventh, with Vipashyin, Shikhin, Vishvabhu, Krakucchanda, Konakamuni and Kashyapa coming before him and Maitreya after him. But there were many others—indeed, a vast number of them.

Buddhas have three bodies which should not be confused. Firstly, there is a material body (nirmanakaya), by which they are made manifest in the world. These are the historic Buddhas. Secondly, there is what is called the 'glorious body' (sambhogakaya), thus named because it manifested the wealth of virtue accumulated by the Buddha in his previous lives. It is in this form that they revealed themselves to those who were just awakening. Finally, there is the body of law (dharmakaya) and this was the most important one. It represented their true spiritual reality, their profound essence, their common ground, which was integrated with universal reality.

The glorious body of the Buddha could be recognised by the thirty-two 'marks of the superman' and by the twenty-four subsidiary marks. The most important of these were the urna, a curl of snow-white wool which hung between their eye-brows, and the ushnisha, a turban or cap often represented as a protuberance on top of the head.

The body of the Buddha is always enveloped in light. A halo around the head indicates holiness, a symbol used by Christian art from the 4th century onwards.

Buddhahood is a state which can be attained by all beings. Perhaps there is only one Buddha, a pan-Buddha, a kind of 'body of the essence', present everywhere: not only in physical elements, but in the most enlightened consciousnesses.

The posture of **Buddha**, *sitting. The soles of his feet turned upwards indicates concentration.*

Gupta stele, 5th–6th cent. A.D.

> **The samsara** is the principle whereby each death is followed by a new birth which, in turn, is followed by a new death. This infernal cycle is still called 'reincarnation'.

> **His birth**
> 'I am the highest in the world, I am the best in the world; this is my final birth; there will be no more new existences for me.'
> (Majjhimanikaya, III)

Castor and Pollux

Greek heroes

The young sons of Zeus

These twins were very close, sharing everything, even death and immortality.

Leda, the wife of Tyndareus, king of Sparta, was visited by Zeus in the form of a swan. She lay with him, and on the same night also had intercourse with her husband. Two pairs of twins were born of these couplings, Pollux and Helen being the children of Zeus and Castor and Clytemnestra the children of Tyndareus.

Castor was a good fighter and a fast runner. He was audacious and quickly came to blows, fighting fiercely to win victory. He is often depicted as being accompanied by his hounds with whom he hunted. As the son of a human he was mortal.

Pollux was a skilled boxer. He was very strong and knew how to fight intelligently and use clever tactics. He also tamed horses. Castor and Pollux were inseparable and complemented each other very well. They fought the same battles and defended all those close to them.

Theseus kidnapped their sister, Helen, and shut her up in the fortress of Aphidnae. Taking advantage of the absence of the Athenian who had gone to the underworld to ask for Persephone's hand, the Dioscuri, as Castor and Pollux were called, went to Attica. They freed Helen, drove the son of Theseus from the throne, installed Menestheus, the Pretender, and took back with them Aethra, the mother of their enemy.

They were powerful enough to be called on in times of difficulty. During their search for the Golden Fleece with the Argonauts, they saved the ship, *The Argos*, from a storm. Castor and Pollux also took part in the deliverance of Prometheus, the hunt for the boar of Calydon and the devastation of Iolcus.

Their home was in Sparta. They went there disguised as handsome foreigners and then disappeared, taking with them a young virgin who lived there. They were the patrons of youth and resided over army exercises and sporting activities.

At the battle of Lake Regillus they supported the Romans, and that evening they went into the city to announce the victory and to let their horses drink at the fountain of Juturna. Rome built them a temple in the Forum — an unusual honour for foreign gods.

Inseparable

They both fell in love, at the same time, with two sisters, Phoebe and Hilaeira. Their betrothed, Idas and Lynceus, went after them, and in the struggle, Castor and Lynceus were killed. Zeus then killed Idas with a thunderbolt and took Pollux up to Heaven. He was Zeus's son and therefore immortal, but he did not want to be separated from his brother. Moved by his pleas, Zeus agreed that they should share immortality, and they both spent every second day with the gods. They became the constellation *Gemini*.

The Battle of Lake Regillus took place between 496 and 449 BC. The Romans fought against the Latins who had revolted under the leadership of Tarquin the Great, the deposed king.

Jason asked the Dioscuri for their help to destroy Iolcus, where he had been driven out after the death of Pelias.

Centaurs

Mythical Greek monsters

Uncivilised boors

Half man, half horse, centaurs were aggressive and unintelligent beasts.

Zeus turned a cloud into the likeness of his wife, Hera, and sent it to Ixion to see if he would dare seduce it. From this sacrilegious union the centaurs were born, monsters whose torso was that of a man and whose lower half was that of a horse. Thus a very strange creature was created.

They were monstrous, both in shape and character. They were riotous, violent and savage and 'lived away from the towns and cities. They ate only living flesh, respected nothing, hunted with nothing but stones and branches, rebelled against each other over trifles and flew into terrible fits of rage.

Only two of them, who were of different origins, were kindly: Cheiron, who was born of the love between Philyra and Cronus; and Pholus, born of Silenus and a nymph. They were welcoming, wise and the friends of man.

Cheiron and Pholus

Cheiron was the tutor of Apollo, Achilles, Jason, Asclepius and many others. Because of his sense of harmony with nature, he accumulated much knowledge of hunting, war, drugs, ointments, medicine and even music. He helped Peleus by giving him back his sword when he had been handed over to the centaurs by Acastus, who was jealous.

Pholus warmly welcomed Heracles, setting cooked meat before him while he kept the raw meat for himself. When Heracles asked for some wine, he replied that he had none, other than a jar which was owned jointly by all the centaurs. He decided to open it, but the smell of the wine provoked the centaurs to come and attack the cave.

Heracles repelled Ancius and Agrius and went after the others, who had gone to Cheiron. He wounded Elatus and, accidentally, Cheiron. Despite every care the wound remained open, so that the wounded centaur, born immortal, preferred death. Prometheus therefore exchanged his death for Cheiron's immortality.

However, this was not the only fight the centaurs were involved in. One day they were invited to the wedding of Peirithoüs, the leader of the Lapiths. During the feast the centaurs got drunk very quickly as they were unused to wine, and one of them, Eurytus, assaulted the bride. A general free-for-all ensued, and a great massacre in which the Lapiths finally gained the upper hand.

They were not indifferent to women. They could not resist their natural urges and so were well acquainted with rape and kidnapping. Eurytion tried to kidnap Mnesimache, to whom Heracles was betrothed. Nessus tried to rape Deianeira, and Hylaeus joined with Rhaecus to ravish Atalanta, a worshipper of Artemis.

Ixion was the son of Ares. He killed his wife as soon as they were married. This crime was not pardoned, except by Zeus, who took pity on him. However, he did great harm when he tried to seduce Hera.

Deianeira was the wife of Heracles, who killed Nessus when he tried to rape her. Nonetheless, as the centaur was dying, he gave the young woman a drug which he said was a love potion. Later, when Heracles turned his attentions elsewhere, Deianeira sent him a tunic soaked in the potion. As soon as the tunic touched Heracles' skin, the hero experienced great pain. The 'love' potion was, in fact, a poisonous potion causing death.

Cernunnos

Celtic god

Master of wild beasts

The horned god, Cernunnos, was a god of plenty.

His nature was essentially that of a country-man. He is represented as being old, with the ears and antlers of a stag, and he wears a torque, a kind of Celtic necklace. He was often accompanied by a serpent with the head of a ram. On a gilded silver bowl found in Gundestrup, in Denmark, he is represented sitting cross-legged, surrounded by a great stag, two bulls, two lions, and two wolves. Nearby, a child sits astride a dolphin. In this way, Cernunnos appears as the master of wild, earthly and aquatic animals.

Obviously, he manifested strength, power and durability (symbolized by the antlers), and on an altar, kept in the museum of Reims, he is shown with a basket of food, cakes and coins beside him.

Certain Roman steles from Dacia (Romania), identify him with Jupiter, the master of heaven.

> **Cernunnos** has left traces in the French countryside. Cernune, Cernone, and Kernone (7th cent.) have become Sanon, a tributary of the Moselle. Towns are also named after him, such as Cernay in the Haut-Rhin and Cernay-la-Ville in the Yvelines.

Chac

Mayan god

Rain-god

Chac was also called Ah Hoya (he who urinates), Ah Tzenul (he who gives food to others), or Hopop Caan (he who lights up the sky).

Chac was characterized by two wide eyes, a long turned-up nose and two curved fangs, and his hair was made up of a tangle of knots. He came from the four points of the universe: in the East he was red; in the North, white; in the West, black; and in the South, yellow. He made thunder with stone axes and threw down the rain by emptying gourds full of water.

Chac was beneficent and a friend of man. He taught them how to grow vegetables and was the protector of their cornfields. They appealed to him for rain by means of particular ceremonies. The men would settle outside the village and adhere to strict observance of fasting and sexual abstinence.

Chac is an important god in the Mayan pantheon. He is comparable to the Aztec god Tlaloc.

> **Chac** is likened to the Aztec god Tlaloc. The animal associated with him is the frog, because it signals the coming of rain by its croaking. In portrayals of this animal, it is shown spitting out water.

Cú Chulainn

Irish hero

The supreme warrior

When the rage of battle reached him, Cú Chulainn became a ruthless fighter.

Cú Chulainn was the son of Dechitme, King Conchobar's sister. He was also said to be the son of the god Lug, who was always close to him in battle and sometimes even took his place.

He was brought up by his aunt, Findchoem, but four other people helped in his education: Sencha, the pacifist, who arbitrated in conflicts; Blai, the hospitable, who stood by and defended the honour of the men of Ireland, even in their pillaging; Fergus, the brave, who protected them against evil; and Amargin, the aged poet, who was esteemed by all for his eloquence and wisdom.

The warrior

At the age of seven, Cú Chulainn heard the druid, Cathbad, say that the young man's life would be short from the day he took up arms, but that he would achieve eternal glory. He then rushed to the king and asked him for weapons.

Exempted from the curse of Macha which prevented the king and warriors of Ulster, Conchobar's kingdom, from taking part in battle, Cú Chulainn was able to halt the progress of the enemies who were united against his country. He killed the wild dog of Culann with his bare hands. He also challenged to combat the sons of Queen Maev, who had decimated the army of Ulster, and killed all three of them. He was the wily one who knew how to dodge blows, the champion who could be hit only by surprise, the swift one who could cross water as quickly as a swallow.

Mild mannered in daily life, Cú Chulainn became a madman in war, and he could do nothing to free himself from these fits of rage. He had to be plunged into three vats of cold water to help him recover from his battle frenzy.

The seducer

Cú Chulainn had many amorous adventures. He tried to seduce Emer, the daughter of Forgall; Uathach ('terrible'), the daughter of Scathach, the female warrior; and Aife ('beautiful'), Uathach's adversary in battle. He also had a great love affair with the goddess Fand.

In the end he was beaten by Queen Maev. He was caught in a trap and forced to eat dog's flesh, which was absolutely taboo for him. This transgression led to many others, and he was finally killed by Lugaid, the son of one of his victims.

Emer, the wife of Cú Chulainn

'When I walk, you can see intelligence and shrewdness in my face. When I go forward, victorious, you admire the beauty of each of my features [. . .] When you were looking for a wife for Cú Chulainn, you could not find what you needed anywhere: beauty, gentleness and shrewdness, sensitivity, generosity and chastity. A tender and intelligent wife. It is I whom all the Ulstermen desire. It is I who possess the heart of Cú Chulainn.' (*The Ulster Cycle*, B, 23)

Conchobar

Conchobar was the king of Ulster just as Arthur was the king of Britain. Like him, he had extraordinary adventures; like him he was the founder of a brotherhood of arms. Arthur founded the Order of the Round Table and Conchobar the Order of 'The Red Branch'. And finally, just as Arthur was aided by his nephew, Gawain, so Conchobar was aided by his nephew, Cú Chulainn.

Cybele

Phrygian goddess

The mother of the gods

Mistress of wild animals, Cybele was worshipped as a goddess of the earth.

Agditis, a hermaphrodite monster, was born from a stone which had been fertilized by Zeus. The gods decided to mutilate him and make the goddess Cybele from him.

Cybele lived in the forests and mountains with wild animals and the Corybantes, her priests.

Attis

Her love for the shepherd, Attis, made him mad, and he castrated himself for her. Cybele took Attis on her chariot, which was pulled by lions.

According to other traditions, Attis was the son of Nana, who became pregnant from eating the fruit of the almond tree. When Attis was celebrating his own wedding, Agditis (Cybele) got into the banquet room and all the guests were seized by madness. Attis fled, castrated himself under a pine tree and died. Zeus granted Adgitis's prayer and agreed that the body of Attis would be incorruptible, his hair would not stop growing, and he would continue to be able to move his little finger.

Pessinus, in Phrygia, was the main centre of the cult dedicated to Cybele. There she gave oracles and was honoured in the form of a black, sacred stone.

Her cult

Cybele's cult spread throughout Greece, and then to Rome, where she was officially received in 404 BC. Her priests, or *galli*, were eunuchs, dressed in women's clothing and decked out like prostitutes. They danced to the sound of cymbals and the dulcimer and went into a kind of trance. At first, the Roman authorities were very suspicious of these ceremonies and forbade any citizen to become part of her priesthood. Then, things changed, and the emperor established himself at the head of the priesthood, whereupon great festivals were instituted.

As spring approached, the Romans enacted the myth of Attis. There was a procession to a pine tree, at the bottom of which a young man castrated himself. There was a period of fasting and abstinence for eight days and then a festival of blood, during which each follower flagellated himself and certain priests (*galli*) castrated themselves. Next, there was a funeral vigil for Attis, accompanied by a very noisy show of mourning with much gesticulating. After this the participants celebrated his resurrection with a great outburst of jubilation. Finally, there were ceremonies incorporating the silver statue of Cybele and the sacred stone, and these were transported in a chariot drawn by cattle through the town. Finally the goddess herself was purified in the Almo.

From the 3rd century on, the cult of Cybele also made its mark in the increasing performance of another rite—the taurobolic baptism. This involved sacrificing a bull and sprinkling the faithful with its blood.

The initiate

'Happy is the man who is beloved of the gods. Happy is he who, instructed in the divine rites, sanctifies his life, whose soul makes its way to the mountains, for he will experience raptures by virtue of the holy purification. Happy is the man who, according to canons, gives himself over to the orgies of the Great Mother Cybele, where he will brandish the thyrsus and be crowned with ivy, for he is in the service of Dionysus.' (Euripedes, *The Suppliants*, 72)

Demeter/Ceres

Greek and Roman goddess

Spirit of the cultivated soil

Ceres had dominion over all plant life. She presided over the interplay between life and death, and she provided food.

Demeter was the daughter of Kronos and Rhea. She was the goddess of corn, and her cult particularly flourished in the regions where grain was grown: in Sicily, in the region of Eleusis, in Crete, in Thrace and in the Peloponnesus.

Persephone (Kore) was the child from the union of Zeus and Demeter. She was the goddess's only child and grew up happy, playing with Artemis and Athena, the other children of Zeus. Her uncle, Hades, fell desperately in love with her. One day, while she was picking a narcissus, he opened the earth wide, and, as she cried out in surprise, he appeared and dragged her down to the underworld with him.

The long search

Demeter, hearing her daughter's screams, rushed to her aid but could not find her. Heartbroken, she searched the length and breadth of the world without stopping to eat, or drink, or in any way care for her appearance. After ten days she finally discovered the identity of the abductor. She decided to leave Olympus and renounce her divine duties until such time as her daughter was returned to her.

Disguised as an old woman, she visited cities and watched men working. Finally she came to Eleusis and ended up among the chattering old women at the court of King Celeus. Iambe, one of the women, managed to make Demeter smile with her banter, and Demeter decided to break her fast. She prepared '*kykeon*', which was barley water flavoured with mint. She was then taken on as a nurse and brought up Celeus's son Demophoön, to whom she gave the task of spreading the knowledge of the cultivation of corn.

The goddess's exile had made the earth barren, and Zeus, who was responsible for order in the world, demanded that Hades give back Persephone. She, however, had already eaten a few seeds from a pomegranate, and this bound her forever to the underworld. A compromise was nonetheless reached: Persephone would rise up into the world above with the first growth of spring and return to her subterranean home when the seed was sown in autumn.

The Eleusian Mysteries

'I am Demeter, revered by all, the power most useful for gods and men.' So the goddess made herself known to the children of Eleusis. They raised a temple in her

---

Iambe was the daughter of Pan and the nymph, Echo. She made Demeter laugh by hitching up her clothes to show the goddess her backside.

Demophoön was the son of the king of Eleusis. It was said that one night Demeter pushed him into a fire in order to burn away his mortality. He had a brother, Triptolemus, to whom is sometimes attributed the mission of spreading the cultivation of crops.

To Demeter
'Greetings, goddess; keep this city in harmony and happiness; make the earth abundant, fatten our livestock, give us fruits, and ears of corn, and crops.' (Callimachus, *Hymn to Demeter,* 135 – 140)

---

honour and soon plans were made for the Eleusian Mysteries.

In September–October, the candidates for initiation purified themselves in the sea. The procession then followed the sacred path from Athens to Eleusis and arrived at the sanctuary by nightfall. 'I have fasted, I have drunk *kykeon*, I have completed my tasks and put the objects in the wicker basket and the rush basket' (Clement of Alexandria, *Prokeptic*, II, 21): these were the words spoken by the neophytes. This was followed by secret rites carried out in silence, and the first part of the initiation was complete.

The 'mysteries' are so called because their secrets have been very well guarded. Was the symbolic task the search for a rudimentary mill for grinding corn — seen as a step in the progress of civilization — or, indeed, the performance of sexual acts? It is still not known.

The second phase of initiation was a spiritual experience. Aristotle expressed it clearly: 'The initiates were not meant to learn anything, but rather, to experience certain emotions and moods.' (*Fragment 15*; ed. Rose)

Finally, as Demeter again took her place among the immortals, the initiates returned to Athens and to the life they had left for a short time. The Eleusian Mysteries were only an interlude in the life of the city, an interlude where men, women and slaves found themselves awarded the same status, devotees of a single cult, following the same path. It was a brief and controlled hiatus in the political life of the country.

The Romans gave Demeter the name of Ceres, an ancient divinity of the fertile earth.

Demeter, *portrayed as serious and dignified, dressed plainly in a long robe. She brings to men the cultivation of grain (wheat and barley) which, according to one legend, allowed them to stand upright.*

'Demeter giving an ear of corn to Triptolemus'. Detail from an Attic bowl, end of the 5th cent BC.

Demons

Evil celestial beings

Mischief-makers

Perverse and formidable spirits, demons forced men to do evil and also did harm to men themselves.

As the personification of all evil powers, demons took on the appearance of foreign gods. The demon is known in Israel as Beelzebub. In the story of creation, he is given the form of a serpent: an evasive, sly reptile whose venom was particularly feared.

Fallen angels

For Dionysus the Areopagite, demons were angels who had rebelled against God and fallen. Their leader was Satan. Before his fall he was known as Lucifer, meaning 'Bearer of Light'. He was very powerful, clever, beautiful (the beauty of the devil), arrogant, seductive, wily, a rebel against any law, treacherous and perverse. He was the 'prince of the world' and was below, while the gods were on high.

Demons were invisible and innumerable. Each person had a thousand to his right and ten thousand to his left. They preferred to live in isolated and unclean places like deserts and ruins, and they were to be greatly feared, especially at night. They attacked animals and men and were the cause of physical ailments and mental problems. They also provoked wild passions and rage and caused jealousy.

Demons were tempters. In the beginning, Satan, in the form of a serpent, won Eve over. 'He said to the woman, "Is it true that God has forbidden you to eat from any tree in the garden?" . . . The serpent said, "Of course you will not die. God knows that as soon as you eat it your eyes will be opened and you will be like God, knowing both good and evil." ' (*Genesis*, 3, 1–5)

There have been many incidents of possession throughout history. This is when a demon inhabits the body of a man, who is then stripped of his willpower and awareness and becomes nothing more than an instrument in the hands of the possessor. Exorcisms are religious rites whose aim is to remove the demonic influences.

Faust and the diabolic pact

For men it has been a very great temptation to use the power of demons. Merlin the Magician, Robert the Devil and Tannhaüser all made alliances with them, and through these contracts acquired marvellous powers.

Faust's ambition reached outrageous proportions. He was a magician, inventor, and scholar in every sphere, and he wanted to go beyond ordinary knowledge and become acquainted with the innermost nature of things.

In Faust, Satan found a weakness and exploited it. He sent his representative, Mephistopheles, to him in order to assist and direct him in his research and in his adventures, as well as to save him from traps and guarantee his power. There was only one condition attached to all this: that after Faust's death, his soul should remain the possession of Satan. A deal was made.

In the legend we hear all about the trials

The fall of the Angel

The Lord said to the Angels: I am going to create a mortal made from a clay of moulded mud. When I have made him well proportioned and breathed my Spirit into him, fall down before him. All the angels bowed down together before him, except Iblis who refused to bow down. God said: O Iblis why are not among those bowing down?'
(*Koran*, XV, 28 – 32)

and tribulations of Faust, his successes and failures and his encounters with Margaret and Helen. However, when the day of his death arrived, he had to fulfil his contract and give himself up to the Evil One. Did God perhaps come to his aid at that point?

Shayātīn

Shayātīn were Islamic demons. Iblis (Satan), their leader, refused to bow down before Adam when God had created him from clay. The shayātīn bred and spread very quickly, like fire which is the basis of their nature. They circulated in men's bodies as blood circulates in the veins, and they set their heads, which were like those of serpents, onto the hearts of men.

The effects of the shaytān (singular of shayātīn) were permanent. He won men over, deceived them, led them astray and made empty promises. His aim was to turn men away from God and take on the appearance of an animal such as a horse, a camel or indeed of a monster. Shayātīn were often confused with djinns.

Babylonian demons

Babylonian demons were the children of Heaven and Earth. Neither gods nor men could recognize them because they were surrounded by a halo which made them invisible. They shone like stars. They were dirty and stank. They also destroyed men's virility. They pervaded everything surreptitiously, like snakes, robbing men of their wives and separating sons from their fathers. They fed on blood and secreted a terrible poison.

The demon Alû fell on top of men and crushed them; Gallû killed men mercilessly. Namtar 'seized a man by the hair', the demon Lamast attacked babies at their mothers' breasts and Pazuzu made mountains tremble.

> **Portrait of the demon Lamastu**
> 'Her face is that of a lioness whose face is pale, her ears are the ears of an ass, her breasts are bared, her hair is in disarray, her hands are dirty, her fingers and nails are long, her feet are like those of Anzu, her venom is the venom of the serpent and the scorpion'. (Th. Dangin, in *Revue d'assyriologie*, no. 18, p. 170)

The Chinese kouei

The *kouei* were repulsive creatures. They were very large, with a black or green face

Demons were hideous, grimacing monsters. They were shown in the form of dancing cadavers, torturing men and leading them to Hell.

Tibetan painting on cloth (undated).

*The **demon Trinavarta** takes on the form of a tornado in order to kidnap the child Krishna. His mother covers her eyes to protect them from the dust.*

Gouache. Pahari school at the beginning of the 18th century. Illustration from the Bhagavata-Purana.

and long sharpened teeth. Their faces were covered with long hair. They wandered in corrupt places and through filth, transforming themselves into water demons and getting into men's lungs so that they could introduce harmful and even lethal substances.

Illness, accidents and catastrophes were all their doing, but they could be pacified by exorcisms and sacrifices. They were, however, rarely sympathetic to humans and were the incarnation of *p'o*, the evil spirits which surrounded corpses when they had been freed of their transcended souls. They were often identified with the spirits of the dead, especially those who had died by accident, suicide or murder.

Tch'e-yeou was a well-known demon. He had the body of a man, the feet of a bull, four eyes and six hands. His head was made of copper and his forehead of iron. He invented weaponry and enjoyed war. According to legend, he battled for a long time with Huang-ti, the yellow emperor, but was finally vanquished by him. He is portrayed as being absolutely terrifying.

The Raksava of India

In India, the *Raksava* represented every hostile force. They appeared either in horrible guises or in a very beguiling form. It was said that they entered abandoned corpses, ate the flesh and then made them obey their will, in order to spread evil all around them.

The Raksava's leader was Ravana, the enemy of Rama. He was at the head of a kingdom which was always in conflict with the gods and the work of the devout.

The Japanese tengu

Closely bound to the mountains, *tengu* appear suddenly, bewitching humans. They possessed magic powers, changed their appearance, stole and could make themselves invisible. Their actions were generally malicious, kidnapping children, sowing discord, making buildings crumble, disrupting religious ceremonies and even setting fire to temples. They were usually represented as birds with powerful claws.

Dionysus/Bacchus

Greek and Roman god

The lord of exuberance and drunkenness

God of wine and the vine, Dionysus (or Bacchus) unleashed frenzies, orgies and mystical ecstasy.

Dionysus was the son of Zeus and Semele, who was the daughter of Cadmus and Harmonia. 'He is a young man, his lovely blue hair streams down around him, and over his strong shoulders he wears a dark robe' (*Homeric Hymn to Dionysus*, 3–6). He is often represented as being in a chariot drawn by panthers and decorated with ivy and vines. His escort was composed of bacchantes, sileni, satyrs and gods who were more or less insane.

He was a marginal god and upset everything which got in his way. He did not respect laws or customs and overturned the city's hierarchy. He also allied himself with women and slaves and loved masks, disguises, wild screaming, licentious dances and wild places. Dionysus placed himself before and outwith the social order.

He was a drunken god who had no home and wandered about in caves. He preferred the luxurious vegetation of plants and men's debauchery and was said to be an 'eater of raw meat'. He made his followers coarse and vulgar and taught them to drink wine, with 'much cheering' (*polugêthês*). He was acquainted with excess and madness. Delirium, elation, flagellation and murders were all part of his world, but so too were mystical ecstasy and possession.

As a foreign god he was ill received. His cult was condemned and closed off in a ghetto; indeed, it was repressed. He had to win over and conquer an empire, and to this end he used all his talents and cunning, combining extravagant acts and mystery. Dionysus employed many methods which allowed him to push elation towards paroxysm and to weaken the barriers between the gods and men.

Thrice-born god

His mother asked the king of Olympus to reveal himself in all his glory to her, but she was unable to bear the flashes of lightning. She was struck down, and Zeus just had time to tear the child from her womb. He kept it inside his thigh until the pregnancy had reached full term and Dionysus emerged fully formed. Thus he was born of an intense joining of divinity and humanity.

At first, Dionysus was brought up by Athamas and his wife, Ino. Hermes advised them to dress him in women's clothes to divert Hera's jealousy away from this fruit of her husband's adulterous liaison. Hera, however, was not deceived, and she punished Ino and Althamas with madness. Zeus then transformed the child into a kid and entrusted him to the nymphs of Mount Nysa.

When he was still very small, Dionysus was led into a trap by the Titans. They enticed him with a whole range of toys: fir cones, spinning tops, golden fruit, and tufts and balls of wool. They took the child away, tore him to shreds, threw the pieces into a cauldron and boiled and then roasted them. Athena, however, saved the little one's heart, and Zeus gave the child's limbs to Apollo, who buried them on Parnassus. The goddess Rhea reassembled the scat-

Athamas was the king of Thebes. His wife, Ino, jealous of his children from his first marriage, bribed a messenger sent to Delphi to demand that they be sacrificed. The scheme was discovered, however, and it was Ino who was led to the altar. Dionysus rescued her by enveloping her in a cloud which allowed her to escape.

tered pieces and brought the god back to life. He was therefore a god who had been both dead and resurrected. (O. Kern, *Orphicorum fragmenta, 36, Berlin, 1922*)

The conquest of divinity

In her hatred, Hera continued to hound Dionysus. She drove him mad, and he wandered across Egypt, Syria and Asia to Phrygia. There he was received by Cybele, the goddess of nature, who made him join in her mystical frenzies and orgies. Through her, his madness itself became a force over which he gained mastery.

Still discredited, Dionysus travelled towards Thrace, where Lycurgus tried to enslave him. He managed to flee to Thetis but left the bacchantes, who were escorting him, in the hands of the king of Styrmon. Dionysus then grew furious: he drove his attacker mad, made his entire country barren and, in an oracle, demanded that the king be put to death (*Iliad*, VI, 135–136).

Dionysus boarded a Tyrrhenian pirate ship to get to Naxos. The pirates wanted to make him their slave, but he completely paralyzed the ship by turning their oars into serpents and making ivy and vines grow all over it. The pirates went mad, threw themselves overboard, repented, and were turned into dolphins friendly. (*Homeric Hymn to Dionysus*, 40).

Dionysus was to conquer India at the head of his army, which was composed of warriors, sileni, bacchantes and satyrs. His strength came as much from military power as from magic.

The god of wine

Dionysus discovered wine and the vine and presented some to Icarius. Unfortunately, Icarius started to drink in the company of the shepherds who were with him. They were overtaken by drunkenness and soon jokes turned into quarrels and quarrels into brawling. In the ensuing fray, Icarius was killed and Erigone, his daughter, hanged herself above her father's body. In revenge for these pointless deaths, Dionysus ensured that all the young women of Attica went mad.

In Boeotia he introduced the Bacchana-

lia, joyful festivals where everyone, but especially women, 'let their hair down', screamed wildly and were taken over by frenzy. King Pentheus was against these savage rites, but the bacchantes chased him. In her delirium the king's own mother, Agave, tore him to pieces with her bare hands (Euripedes, *Bacchanals*, 416).

Now Dionysus was recognized as a god. His empire was limitless and his power unquestionable. He took part in the war of the gods against the giants and killed Eurytus with his thyrsus. He went to hell to look for his mother, Semele. Hades was quite happy to let her go, on condition that he left something which was of particular importance to him. Dionysus left myrtle. Finally he married Ariadne, abandoned by Theseus on Naxos, and gave her a golden diadem crafted by Hephaestus.

Dionysus and Apollo

As Apollo was calm, so Dionysus was mad; as the former was dignified, proud and distant, so the latter was simple. He mixed with all outcasts and those on the fringes of society. As Apollo loved light and glory, so Dionysus haunted night and dark places.

Together they represented two opposing aspects of man and society. Without doubt, Dionysus was just as indispensable to the world as Apollo.

Icarius was host, on earth, to Dionysus; he spread the use of the vine throughout Greece.

The bacchantes were drunken and lustful women who conducted themselves like savages in Dionysus's procession.

Rhea was a Titan, the wife of Cronus.

Dragons

Legendary animals

Guardians

Ambivalent symbols of good or evil, dragons represented the mysterious forces which man had to confront.

The dragon was a fabulous being which usually breathed fire. It had the claws of a lion, the wings of an eagle and a powerful serpent's tail with which it caused a great deal of damage.

It is presented in different forms in Chinese art, Greek mythology, and medieval Christian legends. Sometimes it had a hundred heads, a back as sharp as an and skin covered in sharp scales. It always inspired terror and enhanced the standing of whoever vanquished it.

Above all, it was the guardian of treasure. It guarded the Golden Fleece and was put to sleep by Medea; she was in love with Jason, who had come to look for the fleece (Apollonius of Rhodes, *The Argonautica*). It watched over the garden of the Hesperides, where the famous golden apples which were guarantees of eternity were located (Hesiod, *Theogony*, 333 ff.). It was, in fact, the guardian of immortality.

Evil

As an incarnation of Satan, the dragon might be called Leviathan (*Psalms*, 74, 14). It was the beast Christ conquered (*Apocalypse*, XIII, 1 ff.), as did Saint Michael and Saint George. It represented hatred and evil, ignorance and darkness. There is evidence of dragon myths on the banks of the Rhône between Arles and Avignon, in Normandy near Villedieu-les-Roches, or on the island of Batz. It was a killer who terrorized the land. But in the end there was always a hero who came along and, after a hard battle, put an end to its slaughtering.

Good

In India, the dragon was a primordial principle, identified with Agni or Prajapati. He was ridden by immortals and secreted the first waters from which all creation emerged. His power was fantastic, and he was the symbol of the power of the emperor in China just as in the Celtic countries.

*Siegfried had to confront and kill an enormous and terrifying **dragon** so that he could get hold of the treasure of the Nibelungs and the cloak which would make him invisible.*
Painting by K. Dielits, 1880.

76

Durga

Indian goddess

The inaccessible

Shiva's wife, Durga, was the power of the god's work personified, the feminine part of himself.

According to various traditions, Durga was called Devi ('the Goddess'), Mahadevi ('the Great Goddess'), Kali ('the Black One'), Uma ('the Peaceful One'), or Parvati ('the Chaste Wife').

Durga was a formidable goddess, a force for leading astray as well as for salvation, and a warrior who enjoyed battle and bloodshed. She was both the creator and destroyer of the world.

She was the protector of the tribes who lived by hunting, and she fed on raw meat.

Her court consisted of *yogini*, wicked spirits and wizards; *vetala*, vampires; and *bhuta*, the spirits of those who had died a violent death.

She had two sons by Shiva: Skanda, whose purpose in life was to fight against the demon Taraka, and Ganesha, the leader of the heavenly armies.

When Mahisa, the leader of the demons, seized the world, all the energies of the great gods were incorporated into Durga. She took Shiva's trident, Vishnu's discus and Indra's thunderbolt and went in to a battle which lasted for nine nights. Durga killed the buffalo which had been taken over by Mahisa (*Devi-Mahatmya*).

The Koli and Cabara tribes offered her blood and intoxicating drinks. Others honoured her by sacrificing goats or performing ritual suicide.

> **The beneficent**
> '(Durga) is the mother of the gods, the power of desire, of action, and of knowledge. She introduced yoga . . . she is the daughter of Savitar (Savitri), and she grants favours; she is the future, destiny and the power of death at the end of the world; great Maya, the impetuous, who holds a bull on a leash, carries a pike and practices abstinence.'
> (*Saura Purana*, VIII, 14 – 22)

*The goddess **Durga**, mounted on her lion, listens to the claims of the demon. Ready for battle, she brandishes weapons in each of her eight hands.*

*Gouache from a series of **Dugra Charita** (undated).*

Enki

Sumerian god

Lord of the earth

The organizer of life on earth, Prince Enki was the one who ruled destiny.

Enki appeared on a boat at the bottom of the Persian Gulf and settled in the swamps which edge the Tigris and the Euphrates. He subjugated the area and built a temple of metal and rare stones, which was called 'the House of the Abyss'. The city of Eridu sprang up around it, and Enki was its god.

The life of the world

Enki was not the creator but he gave life and developed the world. He came from Dilmoun, the land from which copper comes. There, he slept beside his virgin wife. She called him and asked for the water necessary for life. Enki replied, 'In one revolution, the sun will bring you sweet water. For you, it will make water gush forth in your vast domain.'

Enki coupled with his wife, then with his daughter, and then with his grand daughter. He alone was the source of all life. Before this last union, Ningursag, the wife, suggested to her grand daughter that she ask the god for fruit; thus, this coupling was the origin of plants. However, Enki forgot to give plants their destiny and made do with eating them. This was an insane course of action, totally contrary to his

nature as creator, and it weakened him greatly. He was cured by the 'gaze of life' from his wife.

The civilizer

'God of great understanding', magician and master of practical knowledge, he spent his time making up for the weaknesses of the other gods. His every gesture and word contributed something to civilization. At his bidding all livestock and grain came out of the 'holy hill'.

During a banquet, Ninmah challenged Enki to find work for all the faulty men whom she had taken from the mould. Enki accepted the challenge and found a position for each of them. To the one who was weak and incapable of effort he gave the job of officer of the king; he made the blind man a poet, the sterile woman a prostitute, and so on (*Enki and Ninmah*).

The Me

Inanna was the goddess of Uruk, and she wanted to steal the *me* from Enki for her own city. *Me* were the elements of social life and civilization.

There were many *me*. Among them were divinity, royalty, pastorate, prostitution, sexual commerce, kissing, the family as a unit, obligatory work, argument, superiority, dishonour, uprightness, happiness, the ability to give advice, reflection and the sense of justice—in fact, everything that made Eridu superior.

In order to steal them, the goddess tried to get their keeper drunk (*Inanna and Enki*).

Creation

'When he bestowed destiny on every created thing in the year of plenty brought forth by the sky god, the Enki, Lord of the Abyss, the master, multiplied the peoples like grass.'
(*Hymn to Eridu*, I, 204)

Enki invented man and made a mould from him. This was standard practice in a land of potters, and Ninmah was responsible for using the mould.

Enki, lord of the earth. He holds Zu, the bird of storms; from his body flow waves in which little fish swim.

Impression of an Akkadian cylinder, known as the 'Cylinder of Adda', c. 2250 BC (detail).

However, like fire, the *me* could be split up without losing their strength, and Enki was not angry with the thief. He was an intelligent god, thoughtful and very sensible.

The wily one

Enki even intervened on Inanna's behalf and discovered a machine capable of capturing the terrible Ereshkigal, who held her prisoner (*The Descent of Inanna into Hell*). He defended humanity when Enlil wanted to reduce it by famine, epidemic or flood. He helped Atrahasis in the construction of his arch (*Atrahasis*). He found a champion to fight the giant, Anzu, who was disrupting the world, and showed him various ruses to

use during the battle (*Anzu*).

In spite of appearances, Enki succeeded in all his undertakings, resorting to subtle and somewhat deceitful ploys. Thus, Nergal, who was sent to hell to face the goddess Ereshkigal, became her husband and so 'colonized' the infernal abode, and Adapa, on the god's treacherous advice, refused immortality but kept his position with Enki.

Ea

For the Akkadians, Ea, who was very clever, wise, able, and omniscient, was the equivalent of Enki for the Sumerians. He put his father, Apsu, to sleep and stripped him of his clothes, took off his diadem, robbed him of his radiance and wore all these himself (*Enuma Elish*, I, 64–68). Ea was the father of Marduk, the wisest of all, who received from Anu, the supreme god, a twofold divinity.

The 'holy hill', doul-kong, is still called the 'mountain of heaven and hell' and is the place where the gods lived, unworshipped, before the creation of man.

Enlil

Sumerian god

The lord who keeps his word

The true keeper of sovereign power, Enlil was a formidable god whose decisions were binding.

Enlil was the king of the gods, the universal sovereign. Through his power he maintained order in the world. He slept on his mountain, assured of his power, and wished to be left undisturbed. His rages were frightening, and his decisions were often cruel: he imposed his authority regardless of the people involved. He was a weak dictator who found himself naked and helpless when he lost his crown.

Enlil and the Igigi

Enlil was the leader of the Anunnaki, the great gods who were dominant but idle and lived off the work of the Igigi. The Igigi were proletarian gods who worked like human beings. Exhausted by their tasks, they rebelled and decided to depose Enlil (*Atrahasis*, tablet I, 44). They burned their tools, and one of them actually declared war on Enlil. The sovereign then woke up and assembled the gods, demanding that the instigator of the revolt be put to death. Ea, who was more conciliatory, proposed that a living being—man—be created to take over a part of the labours necessary for the maintenance of the world and thus free the Igigi from this task. The great gods agreed to this, for the final decision was theirs.

Enlil and mankind

Soon the prosperity and din of mankind, whose number was steadily increasing irritated Enlil. He wanted to reduce their number and so sent illnesses, epidemics, suffering and death. Ea, however, who could not directly oppose the universal sovereign, suggested remedies, sent drugs and medicines and ensured the advance of humanity. This all meant failure for Enlil. He was so stubborn in his wish to destroy those who had disturbed him that he invented famine. Once again, though, Ea managed to save mankind. Enlil was furious and decided to have done with them once and for all. He sent a flood and made the gods swear that they would not disclose the extent of the anticipated catastrophe. Ea did not break his word by telling any man directly. Rather, he gave Atrahasis a premonitory dream in which he learned how to build an ark and thus save all the elements of the world.

Enlil and Anzu

Enlil asked the giant Anzu to inform each person of his or her particular responsibility. As he went about this task, Anzu slowly gained his master's trust and became so close to him that he was allowed to be present when he bathed. But, in order to take his bath, Enlil laid down the insignia of his power: the diadem and his divine clothing. Without his diadem, the god was unarmed. Anzu stole it from him, and the world ended up in chaos. Ninurta had to intervene so that Enlil could regain his position and the insignia of power.

> **God of nature**
> 'Enlil, who makes the seed of the land sprout from the earth, dreamed up the idea of separating Heaven from Earth and dreamed up the idea of separating Earth from Heaven'.
> (Hymn to Eridu)

> **Atrahasis**, he who is 'more than wise', was the sole survivor in the Sumerian myth of the flood.

Epona

Gallic goddess

The guardian of horses

The importance of the cult of Epona was due to the worship of the horse in ancient Europe.

Epona can be seen in countless portrayals from Gaul to North Africa, by way of England and Italy. She is shown on horseback, either alone or accompanied by a little girl. She was the patron of civil and military horsemen, travellers and, in an extension of this, those who were on their way to the Great Beyond.

It seems that she was sometimes seen as a goddess of fertility because near her statues, horns of plenty and baskets of fruit have been found. She was also identified with Rhiannon.

The Erinnyes

Greek goddesses

Primitive forces

Inhabitants of hell, the Erinnyes were responsible for punishing bloody crimes.

There were three Erinnyes: Alecto, Tisiphone, and Megara. They were winged spirits who had long hair entwined with snakes, and they carried whips and torches. They hounded their victims, delighted in torturing them, and drove them mad.

The Erinnyes were born from the drops of blood which fell from Uranus's severed penis, and they did not recognize the authority of the gods of Olympus. They were also called the Eumenides ('Good Ones') in order to divert their wrath. The Romans assimilated them to their Furies.

They were blind and carried out their punishments indefinitely. Thus they made Clytemnestra kill her husband, Agamemnon, who had sacrificed his daughter, Iphigenia. Then they made Clytemnestra's own son kill her to avenge his father. Finally, they hounded the son for the murder of his mother. Similarly, they were at the root of the curse on Oedipus and his descendants.

The Erinnyes were implacable and demanded punishment for every murder. For them murder was a stain: the man who had committed it had to be banished from his city, become a wanderer and be seized by madness. Then he had to be purified.

Resolute, the goddesses made sure that everyone knew his place in life and forbade the soothsayers to reveal too much of the future; men should not have too much power. They condemned *hubris* (insolence and arrogance). In Tartarus they tortured the dead.

> **Terrible Erinnye**
> 'Pitiless-hearted Erinnye who walks in mist in the depths of Erebus'. (*Iliad*, IX, 571)

Eros/Cupid

Greek and Roman god

Amorous desire

He was responsible for keeping the world together and for the continuation of the species.

Eros became Cupid for the Romans and Phanes, Metis, Protogenus or Ericepaius for the Gnostics.

Origin and empire

Cupid was a primordial god, a contemporary of Chaos, in existence long before Cronus and Zeus. He came out of the egg which formed the earth and sky when it broke in two. He was responsible for the embraces of Gaea (the Earth) and Uranus (the Heavens), and from their union were born Oceanus, Tethys, Coeus, and Cronus. The embraces of Gaea and Uranus, however, were too tight, and none of the children could rise towards the light until Cronus castrated his father.

Cupid was associated with Aphrodite, who moderated his power. Where she was grace, tenderness, gentleness and sweet pleasure, Eros was desire, the power of instinct and the violence of sex. Thus he yielded to her, as was appropriate for such a woman. Because of this it was thought that

---

God of the origins

'In the infinite bosom of Erebus, Night with black wings first produced an egg without a seed. From it, in the course of the seasons, Eros was born—the desired, whose back sparkled with golden wings, Eros like swift whirlwinds. It is he who joined one night with winged Emptiness in Tartarus, hatched our race and made it appear first in the light.'

(*Aristophanes*, Birds, 693 ff).

Cupid was Aphrodite's son (*Pindar*), the son of Aphrodite and Hephaestus (*Ibycus*), the son of Aphrodite and Ares (*Simonides*) or the son of Aphrodite and Hermes (*Cicero*). The important point being made was that desire is provoked by charm and seduction.

Cupid's action did not always seem to be beneficial. He made people lose their reason, paralyzed their willpower, and even inspired Zeus's capricious sexual desires. He hatched intrigues and then resolved them. He also enjoyed the company of Dionysus, the foreign god responsible for orgies, confusion and wars. Some thought he was a demon, perhaps because of his lack of scruples in his unending quest for the beautiful and the good, which excluded him from the company of gods who were themselves beautiful and good. The story which seems to back up this opinion had its supporters.

They said that Porus (Expedience) was drunk and fell asleep in the garden of Zeus. Thereupon Penia (Poverty) passed by and 'thinking that, for her, nothing is ever expedient, contemplated having a child by Expedience himself' (*Plato*). She stretched out beside him and became pregnant with Eros. Like Penia, the child was always in search of something, and like Poros, he always found some means of achieving his aims.

Eros and Psyche

However, the goal aimed for was not just any goal, and those who saw in him only unbridled passion, lust and depravity were mistaken. Eros was in love with the soul (Psyche) as Apuleius tells us in a well-known tale (*The Golden Ass*, Book IV, 28 to Book VI, 24). Psyche had two sisters. The three of them were very beautiful, but Psyche was the most beautiful—so beautiful that she frightened the young people and could not find a husband. The oracle was consulted, and it said that the girl should be finely dressed and exposed on a rock, where a monster would come and marry her. Psyche went along with this plan and was carried off to a magnificent palace of gold and marble, where she was treated like a princess. But there was no monster. When evening came she went to bed. Soon she felt the presence of something close to her, but this presence did not feel like the hideous monster she had feared. However, she was not allowed to look at him as he had expressly asked her not to. Psyche was happy until the day when the temptation became too great for her. The light from a lamp she had hidden revealed that her companion was a handsome young man, Eros in person. He immediately disappeared and Psyche, now abandoned, underwent a thousand torments. Eros, however, could not forget her. One day, when she had fallen asleep, he took her up to Olympus and asked Zeus to let him marry her.

Cult and powers

Because Eros (Love) is experienced through life more than through worship, there were not really any important cults of Eros in Greece. There were statues of him in gymnasiums, however, where beautiful young men exercised. He was like one of them but more handsome, the most loved and the most loving.

In the 4th century BC Praxitelus portrayed him as a chubby-cheeked child, plump and happy with life. In the representation, he keeps himself apart, hiding away in the shadows, and it seems as if he is there for no one.

Eros has wings to show how quickly he acts. Here he is a young man, colluding with the charm and beauty of Aphrodite, who helps him in his plans.

'Eros and Aphrodite'. Detail from an Attic vase, 5th cent. BC.

Faunus

Roman god

The sympathetic one

A rustic deity, Faunus was both honoured for the favours he bestowed and feared for the turmoil he represented.

Faunus was the son of Circe and Jupiter and one of the most ancient kings of Italy, where the cult dedicated to him always remained active.

Wild and rather savage, this god of agriculture was responsible for the fertility of plants and the extraordinary energy of living nature. He was at the root of the wealth and prosperity of Rome and lived on the Palatine Hill.

He gave his oracles at night, when the person who had come to consult him slept on a goatskin and received his revelations in the course of terrifying dreams. Faunus was the protector of the Italic peoples. It was he who announced that Aeneas would come and prepared for his arrival. Aeneas's descendants were to make the city great (Virgil, *Aeneid*, VII, 96–101).

The Lupercalia were the great festivals dedicated to Faunus. During them young people ran through the streets and used leather straps to beat any women they met. This flagellation was thought to be beneficial to the victims (Ovid, *Fasti*, II, 445 ff.). Faunus was sometimes linked to the Arcadian god, Pan, and he was often seen as being lustful.

Fauna, his sister and wife who was a fortune-teller, gave Hercules a son, King Latinus. She was the guardian of women and was often identified with *Bona Dea*. This was the good goddess, an expert in all household arts and so modest that she never came out of her chamber and saw no man but her husband. Her shrine was on the Aventine Hill.

Faunus reproduced himself in fauns, satyrs who were half man, half goat.

Fauns were rural spirits who, like the Greek satyrs, rejoiced in nature and the company of nymphs. Thus Faunus's personality was spread and increased.

Faunus the god of animals and shepherds in a Dionysian procession. He is accompanied by Pan and one of the bacchante.

Detail of an ancient bas-relief.

Finn mac Cumhal

Irish hero

Warrior and magician

Finn means 'fair, beautiful, blonde and of good breeding'.

Finn mac Cumhal (the son of Cumhal) was the father of Ossian. A fearsome warrior, Finn avenged his father who was killed in battle and reorganized the troops of the *Fiana*.

The Fiana were an elite troop 'composed of handsome young men'. Their qualities were phenomenal strength, intelligence, cunning, faithfulness, a hatred of money, indifference when fated with death and respect for women and for their vanquished enemies. They had to give whatever was asked of them, even if it was a precious possession. They were lords.

Finn mac Cumhal's stronghold was at Almu in the south of Ireland, but he loved wild and uncultivated regions. There he hunted deer and wolves, fished for salmon and lived off his catch.

A poet and seer, Finn knew the twelve books of poetry and possessed the gift of receiving visions when he bit his thumb.

> **Lendebair, the wife of Finn mac Cumhal**
> 'My husband is Cumhal [. . .] whose proud and noble passage of arms in battle surpasses all others. He is handsome when he comes back after a victory carrying the heads of his enemies. (*Ulster Cycle*, B, 23)

Freyja

Norse goddess

The great magician

Mistress of magic, Freyja gave fertility, fecundity, victory and peace.

She was also known as Vanadis, Vanabrudh (betrothed of the Vanir), Gefn, or Gefion. She was the daughter of Njord and the sister of Freyr. On her chariot drawn by cats 'she is so beautiful that all ornaments are named after her' (*Gylfaginning*, 34). She was the wife of Od (holy fury), a god who periodically disappeared for so long that he was believed to be dead, and Freyja shed tears of red gold for him.

Freyja was mistress of *seidr*, a magical science. Its main aims were to know the future and the fates of men, and to cause the seasons to be fertile and creatures to be fecund. She is linked to the cult of the dead, keepers of wisdom and guardians of the living. 'Wherever she goes in battle she receives half of those who fall, and Odin receives the other half.' (*Gylfaginning*, 23). She took on the form of a falcon to travel between one world and the other.

Freyja was also the goddess of love and sensual pleasure, and her personality had a licentious and lascivious aspect which could be found in her cult.

Freyr/Frey

Norse god

The most handsome of the gods

Divinity of fertility and fecundity, Freyr presided over love, wealth and orgies.

Freyr was the son of Njord and the brother of Freyja. 'Clear and shining', he personified the essence of beauty itself. He lived in Alfheimr and owned a marvellous ship, *Skidhbladnir*, 'which could be folded up like a handkerchief and put in your pocket'.

No one was ever able to hate him: this was a privilege he received when he was born. He was the god of peace and thought only of freeing the hands of those who were bound and bestowing gifts. Also, he never made anyone cry.

One day Freyr sat down on Hlidskjalf, Odin's holy seat. From there he could see, in the world of the giants, a beautiful girl called Gerda. He was overcome with desire for her and became very sad. He asked Skirnir, his servant, to go and ask her to marry him and gave him his horse and sword. Gerda, however, would not be bought, either by presents or by threats. Magic alone could make her yield, and she told the messenger, 'Barri is the name of the place where we both know a peaceful grove: it was there, nine nights later, that Gerda granted the pleasures of love to the son of Njord.' (*Skirnisför*, 39)

Married to Gerda (the Earth), Freyr created abundance and dispensed wealth.

He also brought sun and rain, just enough of each to make the crops grow. He succeeded Njord, settled in Uppsala, erected a large temple and allocated all his income, lands and his personal estate. 'He was all the more venerated because, under his reign, people were better off, in terms of peace and good season' (*Ynglinga Saga*, X). When he died he was carried, in secret, to the burial mound, and nothing was said to anyone. Tributes were still given to him and they were emptied into the mound, 'gold through one window, silver by another, and copper coins by a third. Thus the good seasons and the peace continued.' (*Ynglinga Saga*, X)

Freyr was one of the great Viking gods. He was god of the sexual act and represented by a horse's phallus when the whole family made incantations to him (*Völsa Thattr*). It was, however, mostly women who worshipped him and who took part in processions.

*Amulet representing **Freyr**, phallic god of fertility. This image is of the same type as the numerous phallic representations shown in inscriptions on rock.*

Bronze, 11th cent. From Lunda, Rällinge (Södermanland), Sweden.

Ganesha

Indian god

Leader of the heavenly troops

Master of intelligence, Ganesha was the patron of artists and writers.

Ganesha, or Ganapati or Ganpati, was the son of Shiva and Parvati and the brother of Skanda. He was young and well developed and had the head of an elephant. He sat on soft cushions, holding a bowl of rice, to which he was very partial. He travelled on a rat. Since he was clever, Brahma gave him the task of copying the *Mahabharata* (*Mahabharata*, I, I, 74).

His origin was very curious. Parvati was often surprised in her bath by her husband. She was unhappy about this and, wanting a 'keeper of the door', she created Ganesha from the dirt which was left after her ablutions. She then set her son, who was already a young man, on guard. Shiva wanted to force his way past, but Ganesha prevented him. So, Shiva created a pretty woman, Mayra (a magical illusion), who distracted the sentry and allowed Shiva to cut off his head. Parvati was furious and demanded that her child's life be given back to him. Shiva, engaged in this task, could not find the severed head; consequently, he replaced it with that of an elephant who happened to be passing by.

Ganesha and his brother, Skanda, were always in competition. Ganesha was cunning and Skanda strong. When they wanted to get married, Shiva decided that the first to do it would be whoever could go round the earth the fastest. Skanda rushed off without waiting, but Ganesha first took

leave of his parents by going round them seven times. This was a Vedic rite which corresponded to going round the world seven times. Because he had followed the proper ritual, he received two wives: Buddhi (Intelligence) and Siddhi (Success).

He was also Vighnesvara, the master of obstacles. His mission was to ensure the smooth running of earthly affairs. He produced wealth. He was, however, ambivalent: two of his hands pacified while the other two bore weapons. He put obstacles in the way of those who neglected him and spared others. He was invoked at the beginning of all undertakings.

Ganesha was very popular and had temples throughout India. He was vegetarian and was offered red flowers, little bunches of 21 sprigs of herbs and, most importantly, little cakes in the shape of figs.

The god 'with the elephant's head', surrounded by a musician and a servant who fans the air with her fly-swatter.

*Miniature from the **Bhagavata-purana**. 18th cent.*

Genii

Mythical spirits

The hidden essence of things

Scattered everywhere, genii mixed with men, joined with objects and presided over events.

The world of the genii was like a parellel world, less beneficent than that of angels but less wicked than that of demons. Genii were like the doubles of objects, beings and events. They were their essence or spiritual aspect, expressing the deep inclinations that make them act despite themselves.

Genii were supposed to have a separate existence. They gave support for the doctrine of animism of primitive societies and the expression of the mystery of the elements of existence. They were ambiguous and often bizarre beings, and their reactions were so unpredictable that it was better to appeaase than to antagonize them.

The iskoki

There were numerous races of genii throughout the world, and their presence was explained in many ways. The Hausa of Africa, for example, thought that God (the father of the house) created Adamu, the first man, and Adama, the first woman. These two brought 70 pairs of twins into the world. One day, God, called Ubangiji there, announced his arrival. Adamu and Adama were ashamed of having given birth to so many children and hid half of them in the trees, in caves, in deserts, and so on. God, of course, saw everything. As he was not going to allow himself to be duped, he decided that he would punish the first men for their lack of trust. The children

who were hidden would thereafter remain invisible. They would live like the others and reproduce like the others, but they would harm their visible brothers—who, in turn, would have to feed them with offerings of animals. The invisible men were known as *iskoki*, meaning genii.

The Romans

Apart from the genii attached to people and things (streams, trees, paths, the sea and so on), there were others who presided over events such as war, hunting and victory. The Romans had a genius of the matrimonial bed, who dispensed the fertility of the home, and one of the table who ensured good food.

The coming of the Empire did not prevent the increase of genii. The great gods themselves had their own, and sacrifices were made to the genius of Mars or that of Jupiter to enable the devotee to transcend the god's character and concentrate only on his deep being or spiritual aspects.

The Grand Siècle

By the 17th century, the genius was no longer a being endowed with a certain independence. Rather, it was a talent or exceptional creative power. To explain why it was unattainable and unpredictable, genius was described as 'a gift of the gods'.

The guardian

'Genius, guardian of the temple, protect your temple.' 'May god the protector of the temple remain in the temple, and may Udug the good and the beneficent Lama enter the temple.'
(Cunieform texts from Babylonian tablets in the British Museum)

Giants

Mythical beings

Strength

'Big, strong and stupid' — these were often the characteristics of giants.

Gluttons in Burgundy, guzzlers or Gorgons in Brie, there were giants in every region. They left their footprints on the landscape, played with boulders as disci, and changed the course of rivers. Some were well known, like the wicked ogress who kidnapped little girls who did not do their work, or the giant who protected travellers.

The Bible says that the giants were the product of an unnatural union between fallen angels and daughters of men. They were closely connected with the earth, usually living underground, and they taught man harmony with nature, which they dominated. They also taught men the rudiments of the knowledge they had from being able to see from high up, as well as other secrets which were probably forbidden to humans.

For the Irish, giants were fallen former gods. This gave them a rather ambivalent character, for they had almost divine strength contained in human bodies and they knew neither good nor evil. Consequently, they were dangerous and disconcerted everyone in the path.

The giants of ancient Greece

They were sons of the earth, born from the blood which flowed from Uranus's wound when he was castrated by Cronos. They fought against Zeus for the sovereignty of the world. They represented youth, strength and virility. Zeus wanted to exterminate them, but to do this, he needed something smaller than himself — a man. One of the characteristics of giants was that they could be killed only by a god and a man together. Heracles, therefore, who had not yet been deified, came to Zeus's aid.

Earth wanted to save her children and undertook to find the herb of immortality. But Zeus was quicker: he plunged the world into darkness and made the miraculous herb disappear. The giants were therefore vanquished, and there was nothing left to prevent the force they represented from being placed in the service of the law. (Pindar, *Nemean Odes*, VII, 90)

The Norse giants

In Norse mythology too, giants were unruly. They lived in Jotunheim and wanted to seize sovereignty of the world, symbolized by Thor's hammer. The giant Thrym succeeded and prepared to take possession of the universe.

However, after many appeals, he agreed to give back the instrument of power, but asked for compensation in the form of the goddess Freyja, who had a great reputation for lasciviousness. Loki then thought of a ruse to trick the giant. He disguised Thor as Freyja and himself as a servant, and they both went to the banquet given by Thrym. Just at the moment when Thrym handed over the hammer, Loki massacred his host's entire family.
(*Thrymskvida*, 1–32)

The enemies of the gods

'Hlorridi's heart leapt for joy in his bosom when he recognized the hard-hearted hammer. First Thrym was killed, then the giant's family. He killed the giant's old sister, who had been expecting wedding presents; she received punches instead of silver and hammer blows instead of lots of rings. Thus Odin's son recovered his hammer'.
(*Thrymskvida*, 31–32)

Gilgamesh

Sumerian hero

The quest for immortality

Tyrannical king and then intrepid adventurer, Gilgamesh illustrated the human condition in a very dramatic way.

Gilgamesh, the son of the goddess Ninsun and a mortal, was the king of Uruk. He was a great builder and made his city an impregnable fortress, surrounded by a wall and edged with more than 900 towers.

Enkidu

Gilgamesh was a tyrant. All the women waited on him at his pleasure and all the men were his servants. His subjects, crushed by this oppression, begged the gods to free them from their torturer and decided to create a giant to fight and kill him. This giant's name was Enkidu.

Enkidu was the opposite of Gilgamesh. He was half savage, more like a beast than a man, with a completely hairy body. He lived in caves and wild places among the wild beasts and had no knowledge of civilisation. Endowed with enormous strength, he destroyed everything in his way and picked a quarrel with anyone he came across.

Gilgamesh first saw him in a dream and then learned of his existence from a hunter who had seen him drinking at a spring. He sent a courtesan to seduce Enkidu. She coupled with him for seven days and seven nights and succeeded in making him a man rather than a beast. Enkidu followed her to the city where, gradually, he learned to be civilized. He then met the king, but it was a harsh confrontation since each of them wanted to win and thus confirm his supremacy. Gilgamesh, who was more cunning, had the upper hand, but he took a liking for his adversary.

The death of Enkidu

They went together to fight Humbaba, a phenomenally powerful monster who spat fire and could kill by his breath alone. They found him in a forest of incredible cedars of which he was the guardian. After many mishaps, they managed to kill him.

On Gilgamesh's return, the goddess, Ishtar, bewitched by his exploits, made advances to him. He refused her with great insolence, calling her 'a shoe which hurts the foot'. Ishtar was furious and created a heavenly bull capable of destroying Gilgamesh and his whole city. Enkidu managed to grab the animal by its tail and Gilgamesh plunged his sword between its withers and its horns.

Enkidu, intoxicated by the victory, scoffed

An exceptional being
'Two thirds of him are divine and one third is human. The gods themselves perfected his body; his mother Ninsun, moreover, endowed him with beauty. Within the walls of Uruk he displayed strength as great as that of a buffalo with its head held high, and his weapon blows are without rival.' (*Gilgamesh*, II, 3 – 15)

Acceptance of being a mere man
'When the gods made men they gave them death and kept life for themselves. Gilgamesh,, you should fill your belly and rejoice night and day. Make every day a festival and take your pleasure day and night . . . and embrace the child who takes your hand so that the woman with you is delighted. This is man's only purpose'. (*Epic of Gilgamesh*)

at the goddess and insulted her unrestrainedly. She took revenge on Enkidu by making him ill, and he died after suffering 12 days of agony.

Gilgamesh was inconsolable, and for seven days and seven nights he wept for his friend, hoping thus to bring him back to life. After the burial, Gilgamesh wandered in the desert, terrorized by the prospect of death. Then an idea came into his mind: he should gain immortality. He knew that Uta-Napishtim, the sole survivor of the flood sent by the gods, was still alive, and he decided to find him. Thus began his adventures.

The tests

The door of the sun was opened to him by its guardians, men-scorpions, of whom it was said, 'the sight of them is enough to kill you' (*Epic of Gilgamesh*, IX, 11, 7), because they recognized the divine part of him. For 12 hours he made his way through the underground darkness. Along the way he met the nymph Siduri who tried to divert

him from his plan. He then crossed the waters of death and finally reached the bank where Uta-Napishtim lived.

Uta-Napishtim asked him not to sleep for six days and seven nights in order to accustom himself to immortality. Gilgamesh, however, fell asleep and did not wake up until after the seventh night. He was then anxious and said, 'What am I to do, Uta-Napishtim, where am I to go? A demon took possession of my body, death lives in the room in which I slept, and wherever I go, death is there!' (*Epic of Gilgamesh*, X, 6–9)

Eventually, Uta-Napishtim revealed to him where he would find the plant called 'the-old-man-becomes-young-again'. Gilgamesh went to look for it at the bottom of the sea and then set off for home, intending to share the plant with his subjects. On the way he stopped to bathe in a stream, and a serpent, which had been attracted by the scent of the magic plant, ate it. Gilgamesh was thus stripped of immortality. He went back to Uruk to accept his fate and resume his former life.

Gorgons

Mythical Greek monsters

Terror

The Gorgons used their repulsive appearance as a terrible weapon.

The three Gorgons were the daughters of Phorcys and Ceto, who were gods of the first divine generation. Their hair was made of angry serpents, they had tusks like a boar's, their hands were made of bronze and they had golden wings. Their eyes were so terrifying that anyone who looked at them was turned to stone. The gods themselves were seized with horror before them. Poseidon was the only god who dared to couple with Medusa, one of the Gorgons.

Euryale represented sexual excess, Stheno, social perversion, and Medusa,

vanity. Of the three, only Medusa was vulnerable because she was mortal.

They were believed to live in the far west, near the kingdom of the dead.

Medusa

Perseus went to kill Medusa. Thanks to the winged sandals Hermes had given him, he was able to fly. This meant that he would not be affected by the gaze of the monster. He used his shield like a mirror, waited for his victim to fall into a deep sleep, and cut off her head. Pegasus and Chrysaor, the children of Poseidon, emerged from the wound.

Athene later affixed Medusa's head, which had retained its power, to her shield. The blood which had been spilled was used as a magic potion by Asclepius.

Hadad

Assyrian god

The thunderous one

Hadad, Haddu or Adad was the god of storms. He was the destroyer, but he also made plants grow.

Hadad was the son of Anu. As the god of storms his symbol was thunder. He was often compared to a wild bull, and in terms of astrology he was sometimes identified with the crow constellation.

He was invoked in curses when he was begged to send torrential rain to the lands of wicked men or to one's enemies. However, he also brought agricultural fertility.

His cult spread throughout the Middle-East, where he was identified with Baal the Syrian and Teshub the Hurrite.

The last resort

'. . . they built a temple . . . they no longer worshipped their own gods . . . but hurried to Adad's door.' (*Atrahasis*)

Hades/Pluto

Greek and Roman god

Lord of hell

The merciless god of hell, Hades never gave up those who had entered his kingdom.

Hades was the son of Cronos, and therefore the brother of Zeus and Poseidon. When the world was divided between the three brothers, the underworld and hell fell to Hades while Zeus took the heavens and Poseidon, the sea.

The Cyclops gave Hades a helmet which made him invisible. He was formidable in battle and took part in the fight against the Titans. Hades ruled the dead, assisted by demons over whom he had authority. He forbade his subjects to leave his domain and became enraged when anyone tried to steal his prey from him. Among mortals, he was the most hated of the gods, and the gods themselves had an abhorrence of him. (*Iliad*, XX, 61)

He fell in love with Kore, but Zeus forbade him to marry her, the Olympian king was disgusted by the idea of this sweet young girl shut up forever in the underworld. Hades therefore kidnapped her. By the time Zeus had ordered him to give her back to Demeter, her mother, it was too late: Hades had already made her eat a seed of the pomegranate, which bound her forever to hell. Kore became as cruel as her husband.

Although forbidden by Hades to enter hell, Heracles wounded Hades with an arrow and won victory (*Iliad*, 395 ff.).

People were afraid to say Hades's name. He was also known as Pluto, 'the rich one', perhaps because, as Sophocles says, 'dark Hades is enriched by our trembling and our tears.' (*Oedipus Rex*, 30)

Hanuman

Indian god

Conqueror of the planets

Hanuman was deft, shrewd and physically agile.

Hanuman, also known as Anuma or Maruti, was the son of Anjani, a monkey, and Vayu, the god of the winds. He was leader of the army of monkeys, a superman endowed with extraordinary strength. He also showed exemplary devotion. He was close to nature and fought without arms, using only rocks and uprooted trees. He was a vegetarian, faithful to his friends and had no relationships with women.

As soon as he was born, Hanuman was starving; seeing the sun, he thought it was a ripe fruit. With one leap he rushed towards it, crashing into all the planets on his way. Indra was furious and threw his club at the baby, whereupon Hanuman fell unconscious on top of a high mountain. When Vayu saw his son dead, he went on strike. The world, deprived of wind, could hardly breathe and was in danger of suffocating. The gods, seized with panic, rushed to the child and brought him back to life. Indra left him his club and Brahma promised him invincibility.

Hanuman was the ally of Rama, whose beautiful and virtuous wife, Sita, had been kidnapped by the demon Ravana and shut up in his palace at Lanka. With one enormous leap Hanuman reached Lanka, found Sita and promised that she would be freed shortly. He did not free her himself as he wanted to leave that glory to Rama, but he did light a big fire to herald the disaster to come. He then went back to tell Rama about his mission. War broke out, and Lanka was invaded and completely destroyed. Ravana was killed and Sita was freed and returned to her own kingdom (*Ramayana*).

It is understandable that, with exploits such as these, Hanuman was the god of athletes and gymnasts. As protector, he destroyed the death rays emitted by the planets.

The strength of the monkey-god

'I would have enough strength, certainly, to go round this colossus which seems to lick the sky, Mount Meru, without resting a thousand times. If the vigour of my arms could toss the sea about, I would have enough strength to submerge the world, with its mountains, rivers and lakes. With the vigour of my thighs and loins I could lift up the sea, Varuna's residence and all her monsters with her.'
(*Ramayana*, XIII)

Hanuman, the king of the monkeys, and his army discover Sita locked up in the palace of the demon Ravana.

*Gouache on Rajasthan paper, from a series of **Ramayana**, end of the 18th century.*

Harpies
Greek genii/spirits

Kidnappers

The harpies were swifter than the wind and as frightening as a thunderstorm.

The harpies were the daughters of Thaumes and Electra. There were three of them: Aello, who was also known as Nicothoé or 'swift-footed'; Ocypete, 'swift of flight'; and Celaeno, the dark one. They were either women with wings or birds with the heads of women, and their claws were sharp and cruel.

They were the 'hounds of Zeus' and seized children and souls. Thus, one day, during the absence of Aphrodite who was

The torment of vice
The harpies symbolized the torment of vice and wicked obsessions. Only the sons of Boreas, the wind (breath of the spirit), managed to drive them away.

raising them, they abducted the daughters of Pandareus and gave them as slaves to the Erinnyes (*Odyssey*, XX, 77). On tombs they were depicted carrying out their crimes.

The harpies were very skilful at torturing their victims. King Phineus suffered from their curses. They fouled or stole from him all food that was put before him. He could stand it no longer and asked the Argonauts to free him from these furies; and so the Boreades, Zetes and Calais agreed to chase them away.

It was said that the harpies could only be killed by their own hand, and that the Boreades would die if they did not overcome them. The first of the harpies fell in a river. However, Iris, the rainbow and messenger of Zeus, intervened. In exchange for saving the harpies' lives, she promised that they would no longer trouble King Phineus (Apollonius of Rhodes, *The Argonautica*).

By their union with the god Zephyr, the harpies gave birth to the two horses of Achilles, Xanthus and Balius, and the Dioscuri's two horses, Phlogeus and Harpagus.

The harpies with their wings spread flee before the Boreades, who want to kill them.

Detail from a proto-attic jug. Terra cotta, Aegina, c. 610 BC.

Hathor

Egyptian goddess

The Lady of Dendera

Known as a wild lioness outside Egypt, Hathor became the queen of peace and love in the country which adopted her.

Hathor, represented as a woman bearing the sun between two cow's horns, was the ideal mother. She represented the intoxication of pleasure, love and fertility. The Greeks identified her with Aphrodite.

During the reign of Re, Hathor lived in Nubia where she was a blood thirsty lioness. Re felt the need to have her near him, so he sent Shu and Thoth to look for her. They managed to persuade her to come to Egypt, the land of joy and wine. Once she was there she lost her wildness and became the epitome of grace and charm. She was the wife of Horus, whom she visited once a year during the festival of 'the Good Meeting'. During the festival, her statue was taken in a procession to the temple of Horus at Edfu. The rest of the year she stayed at Dendera.

Heimdallr

Norse god

Guardian of the gods

Heimdallr, the most radiant of the Aesir, was the first born at the dawn of time, and it was said that he would be the last to disappear.

Heimdallr was born of nine mothers. He lived in Himinbjorg (the Mount of Heaven). He could see everything and never closed his eyes. He listened to everything and could even hear the grass growing in the fields and the wool growing on the sheep's back. Because of these qualities he was the guardian of the gods' abode and was on watch at the foot of the rainbow which led men to the gods.

Heimdallr was responsible for the society of men. Under the name of Rig he came to earth incognito. There he was welcomed by a first couple, Great-grandfather and Great-grandmother. He spent three nights with them in the conjugal bed and produced a son called 'Slave'. Then he went to another couple, Grandfather-Grandmother, and there he produced 'Free Peasant'. Finally, with Father–Mother, he produced 'Noble'. This time he did not abandon the child but looked after his education, and the child eventually became king. He was at the origin of social class (*Rigsthula*).

At the moment of the end of the world, or *ragna rök*, it was said that Heimdallr would rise and blow into Gjallarhorn, his trumpet, to call all the gods to hold a council (*Gylfaginning*, 50).

Helen

Greek heroine

The woman loved by men

She was the most beautiful of women. She captivated all men and, as a result, was the cause of the Trojan War.

Helen was the daughter of Zeus and Nemesis. Nemesis fled from the Olympian king's advances, travelling throughout the world and hiding in various forms until, at last, she transformed herself into a goose. Zeus, however, who would not allow himself to be declared beaten, took the form of a swan and thus succeeded in coupling with her. This union took place at Rhamnus in Attica. Nemesis then laid an egg, which was taken to Leda by a shepherd. From this egg — it is sometimes said that there were two eggs — came Helen, Clytemnestra, Castor and Pollux. Another tradition has it that Helen is the daughter of Leda (see *Castor and Pollux*).

The girl of a hundred suitors

Helen was brought up by Tyndareus, her human father. As she grew up, he thought about her marriage. Every prince of Greece came forward and wanted her hand, and her father was very uneasy. Would they not tear each other to pieces for the love of this beautiful woman? So he listened to the advice of Ulysses and made all the suitors swear an oath that they would agree to respect the choice Helen made. Also, should the need arise, they would help the one she had chosen.

Helen chose Menelaus and everyone acquiesced. The most beautiful woman in the world was married. She gave her husband a daughter, Hermione.

Aphrodite, disregarding Helen's com-mitment to Menelaus, promised her to Paris, who had given her the beauty prize. And so it was that Paris went to Menelaus and, taking advantage of his absence, abducted Helen. It is not known whether Helen consented or not, but Paris was handsome, rich and very charming.

The foreigner

In Troy, she was welcomed by Priam as if she were his own daughter. However, Greek ambassadors came after her and demanded that she be returned. It was all to no avail. War soon broke out, and all the Grecian princes who were bound by Tyndareus's oath fought on Menelaus's side, besieging Troy for ten long years.

Helen, being a foreigner and directly responsible for this war, was hated by the Trojans. As a compatriot of the enemy, she knew them well and described them to Paris and his soldiers. However, they knew of her sympathy for their enemy and she was distrusted. When Ulysses entered the city, she recognized him but did not de-nounce him. Perhaps she even helped him.

She was the cause of all the drama and played a treacherous double game, know-ing that her beauty would always get her out of trouble.

And so Helen gave the Greeks assur-ances and helped them in their assault. When Menelaus arrived, enraged, with his sword in hand, she merely revealed herself semi-naked to him and the weapon fell from his hands.

Defended or punished

Helen became the object of much hatred. When she went to her former friend Polyxo, whose husband had been killed at Troy, she was tormented by the Furies. They were disguised as servants and frightened her to the point of suicide (*Pausanias*). It was also

*The romance of Paris and **Helen** was beautiful and moving, but also dangerous because it was adulterous. It provoked the interminable Trojan War.*

Jacques-Louis David (1748–1825): 'The Loves of Paris and Helen' (detail). 1788. Oil on canvas.

said that she was offered as a sacrifice by Iphigenia in Tauris, or that she was killed by Thetis who was angered by the death of Achilles.

Despite the havoc wreaked by her beauty, however, Helen always found defenders. After she returned to Menelaus, she became an excellent wife. Some say that, on the way home, Helen and her husband reached Argos at exactly the moment when Orestes killed his mother, Clytemnestra. He turned to Helen, claimed that she was responsible for all his misfortunes and tried to kill her. Zeus and Apollo, however, no doubt aware of her beauty and the destiny of which she was not mistress, saved her and granted her immortality.

As compensation for all the torment she had inflicted upon Menelaus, Helen also obtained immortality for him. They were honoured in many sanctuaries.

It is also said that she lived eternally on the White Isle in the Black Sea with Achilles, whom she would have married, amidst festivals and banquets.

Responsible for the war

'No, we should not be angry that the Trojans and the Achaens, with their lovely greaves, have suffered hardship for so long for such a woman. When she shows her face, she is like, in some terrible way, the immortal goddesses.' *(Iliad, III, 159–60)*

Hephaestus/Vulcan

Greek and Roman god

The blacksmith

Hephaestus was a magician endowed with remarkable skill and technique, which were unique in the world of the gods.

Hephaestus, or Vulcan, was the son of Zeus and Hera. Certain traditions say that he was the son of Hera alone, who was furious that Athena was born of Zeus alone. However, this version does not correspond with the image we have of Hephaestus cleaving the skull of his father to allow Athena to be brought into the world.

Whatever the truth, Hephaestus was a lame god, either because Hera, seeing how ugly her son was, dropped him from Olympus (*Iliad*, XVIII, 394 ff.), or because Zeus threw him down onto the island of

Hephaestus in his smithy.
Attic amphora with black figures from the 5th century BC.

Lemnos when he took his mother's side in a marital dispute (*Iliad*, I, 590 ff.).

He was brought up for nine years in an underwater cave, by Tethys and Eurynome. There he learned the work of the blacksmith, the jeweller and many other manual arts.

The artisan

Hephaestus was the god of fire. Volcanoes were his workshops and the Cyclops his assistants. He made brooches, jewellery, bracelets and automatons. He equipped the homes of the gods, forged Achilles's shield and even created, in gold, two young women servants who helped him walk (*Iliad*, XVIII, 417).

Hephaestus forged a golden throne which imprisoned whoever sat in it, and sent it to Hera to avenge himself for his fall from Olympus. Hera sat down on it and found herself trapped. Eventually, the gods called him back to free his mother (*Pausanias*, I, 20, 2).

Hephaestus fought with fire at Troy and killed the giant Clytius with a red hot bar.

The lovers of Hephaestus
Despite his handicap and his ugliness, Hephaestus was loved by the most beautiful women. Zeus gave him Aphrodite for his wife. She, however, brazenly deceived him with Ares. Hephaestus, who had been warned, set a trap for the lovers and caught them, entwined, in an invisible net.

The patrons of Athene
'Hephaestus and Athena, who have the same nature, [. . .] because their love of both science and art takes them towards the same goal, both received, as one common, single portion, this land (Athens).' (Plato, *Critias*, 109)

Hera/Juno

Greek and Roman goddess

Guardian of married women

As Zeus's female counterpart, Hera was also the sovereign of the world.

Hera, or Juno, was the daughter of Cronos and Rhea and was brought up by Oceanus and Tethys. She married her brother, Zeus, at the time of the grand festivals held in the garden of the Hesperides (which was a symbol of fertility), during an eternal springtime. This marriage was commemorated at Samos and Argos by solemn celebrations, when the statue of the goddess was dressed as a bride and taken in a procession to the conjugal bed (Hesiod, *Theogony*, 901 ff.). It was claimed that each year Hera regained her virginity by bathing in the spring of Canathus (*Pausanias*, II, 36, 2).

According to some traditions, her best-known sons were conceived by her alone, without any male assistance. She accomplished this by hitting the ground with her hand or eating a lettuce. Thus, from desire and hate rather than from love, were born Typhon, the monstrous being capable of deposing Zeus; Hephaestus; Ares, the god of war; and Hebe, Youth. Hera gave them no tenderness, as her only concern was to claim the rights due to her.

The jealous wife

As Zeus's legitimate wife, Hera had to suffer her husband's many infidelities. She pursued with a vengeance not only Zeus's mistresses, whether they had been willing or not, but also their children. She put two enormous snakes into Heracles's cradle, and she put Io under the guard of Argus with the hundred eyes. She suggested to Semele that she would like to see her lover in all his glory, knowing quite well that the mortal would not be able to bear the brilliance of lightning, and she made Dionysus's adoptive parents go mad. In addition to all that, she tried to prevent the births of Apollo and Artemis.

Zeus himself could do little against her. Sometimes he got angry and suspended the goddess from Olympus by attaching anvils to her feet, whereupon Hephaestus came to her aid (*Iliad*, I, 567). Most of the time, however, Zeus used cunning: he hid his illegitimate children by transforming them into animals or enclosing them in the earth.

The angry wife

One day, Zeus and Hera entered into a long discussion about love. He claimed that women experienced more pleasure in it than men. She claimed the contrary, so they decided to consult Tiresias who had experience of both sexes. He said that women experienced nine times more pleasure than men. Hera, furious that Zeus had been proved right with this assertion, blinded Tiresias.

Piqued at having lost the beauty competition judged by Paris, Hera hounded him vengefully and took sides against the Trojans, making herself the protector of Achilles and Menelaus.

The angry one

'Her anger rose against the women who had given children to Zeus, especially Leto, the only one who had, with him, brought into the world a son more beloved than Ares. From high in the ether, in her violent, inexpressible ire, she watched out for and closed off every refuge to Leto, who was torn apart by pain. She had two sentries watching over the earth: one guarded the continent [. . .], the other guarded the vast islands.' (Callimachus, *Hymn to Delos*, 55–65)

Heracles/Hercules

Greek and Roman hero

Strength

Although he won immortality, Hercules first led a life of achievement and superhuman suffering.

Heracles, or Hercules, was the son of Zeus and Alcmene, the wife of Amphitryon. In order to trick Alcmene, whom he knew to be very virtuous, the king of Olympus had to take on the appearance of Amphitryon. Then, in order to give the child the inordinate strength which would be his glory, he made the night of love last three times as long. (*Diodorus of Sicily*, IV, 9, 2–3)

Hera's jealousy

Zeus had great hopes for this offspring. On the day of the birth he announced to all the gods the arrival of a child who would be king. Hera, vindictive as ever, delayed Heracles's arrival. Instead, it was Eurystheus, his cousin, who came into the world, a spineless creature of no substance. Zeus, faithful to his promise, made Eurystheus a king. Heracles would only be a champion in his service. (*Diodorus of Sicily*, IV, 9, 4–8)

From his cradle, Heracles demonstrated his amazing strength by choking the serpents sent to him by jealous Hera (Pindar, *Nemean Odes*, I, 38 ff.). He was first called Alcide ('the strong'), and became Heracles ('the glory of Hera') because of the tests imposed on him by the goddess, (*Diodorus of Sicily*, IV, 9, 2)

Heracles received his education from Linus, the musician. From him he learned literature and music. However, he was an undisciplined pupil who gave his master much trouble. One day, when Linus wanted to thrash him, Heracles grabbed hold of a stool and dealt Linus such a blow that he died. At his trial Heracles was acquitted on the grounds that he only wanted to defend himself.

Amphitryon feared the rages of his adopted son and sent him to the country to look after the herds. A Scythian cattleman, Teutarus, taught him archery.

The young prodigy

At the age of eighteen, Heracles killed the lion of Cithaeron which was preying on the herds in the country. It took him fifty days to do this, and each evening of this long hunt, he came back to the palace of King Thespius. The king wanted to have the hero's grand-children, and so he put one of his fifty daughters in his bed each night. Thus Heracles had fifty sons, the Thespeiades, who would colonize Sicily.

He met the envoys of Erginus, king of Orchomenus, who had come to claim the tribute imposed on the Thebans. Heracles cut off their noses and ears and made necklaces of them, telling them to take this tribute to their master. War ensued, but Heracles won it. Thereafter it was Thebes who received a tribute, double that which they had given. As a gesture of gratitude, the Theban king gave his daughter Megara's hand in marriage to Heracles.

This marriage was not a success. Hera, still jealous, made Heracles go mad, provoking him to kill his children and threaten Amphitryon, who would have died had Athene not intervened. Heracles had to atone for his crime. He could no longer live with Megara, so he left her and put himself at Eurystheus's service.

> **Heracles's mother**
> 'I saw Alcmene, Amphitryon's wife, who, in the arms of great Zeus, conceived impassive, lion-hearted Heracles.' (*Odyssey*, XI, 267)

The Twelve Labours

Eurystheus set Heracles twelve labours, which he was to perform in the twelve years of his servitude.

He strangled the Nemean lion and made himself armour from the pelt. He cut off the many heads of the Lernaean Hydra and brought back the enormous Erymanthian Boar alive. For a whole year he hunted the hind of Artemis on the Ceryneian Hill and also captured it alive. With his arrows, he shot down the countless birds of the Stymphalian Marsh who ravaged the crops and even killed men. In one day, he cleaned the stables of Augeias by diverting the courses of two big rivers, the Alpheus and the Peneius. He brought back alive the furious Cretan Bull who breathed fire through its nostrils. He killed Diomedes, who gave his horses human flesh to eat. He seized the girdle given by Ares to Hippolyta. Using the sun's golden cup, he brought Geryon's cattle back to Greece from the Far East, clashing along the way with enemies who included Neleus, king of Pylus. From Hades he brought back the dog Cerberus, who defended the gates. Finally, he fetched the golden apples from the Garden of the Hesperides, confronting the giant, Antaeus, the Pygmies and the dragon, Ladon, and freeing Prometheus on the way.

At the end of every exploit Heracles brought back his trophies to Eurystheus, who shut himself away in a bronze jar because he was so afraid of facing the hero.

The other feats

It is impossible to describe every feat attributed to Heracles. He delivered Troy from a monster but came back to wreak havoc on the city because it did not pay his salary. He defended himself against the inhabitants of Cos, attacked the town and kidnapped Chalciope, the king's daughter. Suffering, he had to flee from Augeias who had not paid him, but he laid an ambush for Augeias's lieutenants and killed them. He fought against Periclymenus, Poseidon's son, who had the power to transform himself into any animal. Periclymenus chose, on that particular day, to turn himself into a bee so that he could crawl under the horses' yoke. Athena, however, warned our hero of this and Heracles killed the beast with one of his arrows.

His lofty deeds surpassed human limits. He went everywhere, even into hell. He stood up against forces of a different kind and succeeded in injuring Hades and Hera with his arrows (*Iliad*, V, 390 ff.). Because of his feats he was a superhuman, perhaps already a god.

But he was a man as well. He experienced suffering when he fought against Augeias. He was also reduced to slavery under the yoke of Eurystheus, a despicable creature, and under that of a woman, Omphale. Heracles joined together extremes of all sorts.

Apotheosis

Heracles won the hand of Deianeira and lived with her in Calydon. Soon, pursued by bad luck and Hera's vindictiveness, he accidentally killed one of his father-in-law's pages. He had to leave, therefore, with his wife and son, and when they crossed the River Evenus, Nessus the boatman tried to rape Deianeira. Before Nessus was killed by

---

The greatest of men

'It is Heracles, son of Zeus, of whom I would sing, the greatest — by far — among men on earth. It is he whom Alcmene brought into the world after coupling with Cronos, son of the thunder clouds, in Thebes of the wonderful dances. First he wandered over the vast earth and sea, and suffered; but he triumphed by force of valour and, by himself, he performed many bold and outstanding labours.'
(*Homeric Hymn to Heracles*, 1–8)

The death of the hero

'Iolaus and his companions made the preparations as he ordered and withdrew some distance to watch the event. Heracles then mounted the pyre and asked one of those present, then another, then another to set fire to it. None dared to obey except Philoctetes, and Heracles rewarded him by giving him his bow and arrows. The young man then lit the pyre, but thunderbolts immediately fell from the sky and the pyre was at once consumed.'
(*Diodorus of Sicily*, IV, 38, 4)

Heracles *carries on his shoulders the monstrous boar which lived on Erymanthus and devastated the land. The terrified Erystheus hides in a jar. This is one of the twelve labours imposed by Eurystheus.*

Detail from an Attic amphora, 6th cent. BC.

Heracles he had enough time to tell her that his blood was a love potion which would bring back her husband's affection should she ever lose it.

After that, Heracles went mad and went to consult Pythia, priestess of Apollo. She said that to free himself from this evil, he must sell himself as a slave. Omphale, the Queen of Lydia, bought him, and he was in her service for three years. This long separation from Deianeira led him to woo Iole, the daughter of Eurytus. Deianeira, however, was informed of this and sent Heracles a new garment which she had soaked in Nessus's blood.

Heracles, who suspected nothing, put on the tunic and was seized by incredible agony. He tried to tear the garment off, but it stuck to his skin. The love potion turned out to be poison. Heracles then built a pyre, climbed upon it, and asked his companions to set it alight.

When the flames started to leap there was a clap of thunder, and Heracles was taken up to heaven. He was immortalized. On Olympus he married Hebe (eternal youth) and was reconciled with Hera.

Hermes/Mercury

Greek and Roman god

The messenger

The distinguishing qualities of Hermes were cunning, ingenuity, knowledge and creativity.

Hermes, or Mercury, was the son of Zeus and the nymph, Maia. He came into existence almost surreptitiously, while gods and men slept. He was the one who came by surprise.

Soon after his birth in a cave on Mount Cyllene, he managed to undo his swaddling clothes and went off to steal some of his brother Apollo's herd. He led them to his cavern in Pylus and made them walk backwards to blur the tracks. He paid Battus, who had seen him, to be silent and sacrificed two of the stolen animals, dividing them into twelve parts for the twelve great gods of Olympus. The rest of the herd he hid, and then he went back to the cave. This theft won him recognition as a god himself.

However, Battus did not keep his word and revealed Hermes's hiding place. Apollo rushed to the cave and complained to Maia about her son's thefts. She showed him her son, quietly asleep in his cradle, and denied his accusations.

Nonetheless, Hermes had to defend himself before Zeus's tribunal. His speech for the defence was so spirited and skilful that the king of Olympus laughed as he listened to it. He ruled that there should be a friendly settlement of the disagreement between the two brothers.

Hermes was the god of the spoken word—the medium through which exchanges were made, gallantries and amorous raptures were expressed, and knowledge was conveyed. But he was also the god of the lying word, which disguised truth, confused lovers and discredited choices. He was, in addition, the intermediary who went from men to Olympus and from Olympus to Hades.

God of diverse powers

As the god of commerce, Hermes was the only person to achieve immortality as a result of a contract. He presided over exchanges and guided Priam in the ransom of the body of Hector (*Iliad*, XXIV, 317–330).

He was also a divine inventor and magician. As soon as he had left his cradle, he invented the lyre, made from a tortoise shell, and gave it as a gift to Apollo (*Homeric Hymn to Hermes*, 24 ff.). He also invented the flute and gave it, too, to Apollo in exchange for his golden staff (the Caduceus) and lessons in augury. He gave Ulysses *moly*, the magic plant which offered protection against enchantment (*Odyssey*, X, 307).

Zeus was particularly proud of the creative spirit of his last-born and made him his personal herald and that of the infernal gods, Hades and Persephone (*Odyssey*, V, 28). Hermes came as a messenger after the flood to enquire of Deucalion what his desires were. It was also he who gave the golden-fleeced ram to Nephele, the lyre to Amphion, a sword to Heracles, and Hades's helmet to Perseus.

Hermes in hell

'Hermes, god of Cyllene, called the souls of the suitors to him. In his hand he held the beautiful golden wand which he used at will to close the eyes of humans or to waken them from sleep. With his wand he led the troop and the souls followed, emitting little squeaks. In the depths of the caves, bats flew away with little squeaks when one of them, hanging from a rock, lost his grip.' (*Odyssey*, XXIV, 1, ff.)

103

***Hermes** wears winged sandals and his travelling hat, the petasus. He drives Aphrodite's chariot, which is drawn by Eros and Psyche.*
Bas relief in moulded terracotta from Locri (Southern Italy).

As god of travellers (*Odyssey*, XIV, 1–22), his image was at all crossroads in the form of a pillar surmounted by a bearded head and a protruberant phallus. He also guided Dionysus in his flight from Hera.

As a divine benefactor, Hermes performed many tasks. He saved Ulysses by ordering Calypso to let him go (*Odyssey*, V, 145). He protected Heracles by preventing him from fighting the ghost of Medusa, and when Heracles had to become a slave, provided him with a mistress in the form of Omphale. He freed Ares from the bronze jar in which he had been enclosed by the giants. Finally, he protected Zeus himself by tearing Io, his lover, from the hands of the monster Argos, and by giving Zeus back his sinews, which Typhon had stolen.

As the god of thieves and brigands, however, he was cunning, ambiguous and deceitful. The Greeks referred to a 'stroke of Hermes', meaning a stroke of luck that was ambiguous. He escorted the three goddesses—Hera, Athena and Aphrodite—to the beauty competition which caused the Trojan War, carried Hades's helmet which made him invisible, killed Hippolytus and knew which road led to hell (*Odyssey*, XI, 626).

His descendants

Hermes loved Chione, daughter of King Daedalion. By her he had Autolycus, the grandfather of Ulysses. Among his other children were Erytus, the Argonaut; Abderus, Heracles's lover; Cephalus, grandfather of Danae; and finally, according to post-Homeric traditions, the god Pan, the son conceived by Penelope when she was unfaithful to Ulysses.

Heroes

Mythical supermen

Models

Heroes gave form to the most extraordinary dreams.

Heroes were men of the past or of a mythical age who possessed exceptional strength and powers. As such, they were demi-gods. The renditions of their births were often marvellous and their education exemplary. They were pioneers and creators. They were not greater than the gods, the masters of the world, but neither were they mortals. They make up a separate category altogether.

Exceptional beings

Glory came easily to heroes. They accomplished lofty deeds, winning difficult battles, undertaking perilous adventures, and experiencing extreme—though never crude —emotions. They lived very full lives and achieved eternal renown. They were clear-cut characters, paragons of some particular virtue, quality, or gift, sometimes even of a vice. Whatever the quality, it was a singular trait and they were the most extreme expression of it. Ulysses was cunning personified, Achilles speed and Hercules strength.

An ideal image

Heroes represented values. They embodied ambitions and furnished the illustration of impossible dreams. They were the expression of the ideal of a civilization, and they showed both how close that was and how far away. Heroes were the driving force of evolution: they pointed in one direction and inspired attitudes and actions.

Demiurges

In many civilizations, ranging from North America to Siberia and from black Africa to the Far East, we find civilizing heroes: mythical ancestors, founders of institutions, bestowers of culture. They reassembled the world after the flood, changed the nature of the landscape, and stole from the 'other world' fire, light and water. They killed monsters and rescued humanity from great plagues.

Tricksters

Tricksters were a particular kind of civilizing hero belonging to the American Indians. They were really neither man nor god. They had affinities with certain animals — such as the coyote, the crow, the mink, and the jay or magpie — and they shared the animals' characteristics.

They were always in search of adventure, ready to use their magic powers. They did not concern themselves with either good or evil but were at the root of suffering and joy. They died and were resurrected. They were capable of all sorts of pranks; however, they were rather stupid and were duped themselves as often as they duped others.

Enthusiasm

'In every great epoch of history, men throughout the world have had many different causes in which they have based their actions. Those who in bygone centuries were called heroes had the civilization of the earth as their goal . . . then came enthusiasm for their native land, and this inspired everything great and beautiful which the Greeks and Romans made.' (Mme de Staël, *De l'Allemagne*, t. 4) .

Hestia/Vesta

Greek goddess

Hearth and home

The steadying factor of the family and the city, Hestia was the hearth around which all life was organized.

Hestia was the daughter of Cronos and Rhea and thus the sister of Zeus and Hera. From the king of Olympus she obtained the privilege of keeping her virginity for ever.

As goddess of the hearth she never left the 'lofty abode of the eternal gods' (Hesiod, *Theogony*, 454 ff.) and never intervened in the stormy history of the gods. She was the central point, the meeting place.

She received particular honours in the home where her symbol, the fire, was never allowed to go out. Also, the young bride and the newly born child were presented to her and she was invoked before each meal. In addition to these honours she received the first part of every sacrifice.

She was the centre of the city, where her flame burned ceaselessly. In Rome, the temple of Vesta (the Roman goddess corresponding with Hestia) was served by the young vestal virgins.

> **Prayer**
> 'Hestia, in all homes, earthly or heavenly, you are the first to be honoured; sweet wine is offered to you, before and after the feast. Gods and mortals can never sit down to eat without you.' (Prayer before a meal)

Horus

Egyptian god

King of the sky

Horus was the champion of light against darkness.

Horus was considered to be the son of Re. He was the husband of Hathor, the brother of Seth and the ancestor of the dynasties of the pharaohs.

Horus had two faces. Harsiesis the great and Harpocrates the child (a child sucking his finger). He had a falcon's head and ruled the air. His eyes were the sun and moon, and he watched over the application of the law. He was also the 'shepherd of the people'.

Later, Horus became the son of Isis and Osiris. Osiris was killed by his brother Seth, who seized power. Isis succeeded in fertilizing herself by the dead Osiris. Horus was born and undertook to regain his father's heritage and pursue his murderer. It was a hard battle; he lost an eye (the moon) which was given back to him by Thoth, but he managed to castrate his enemy. It was acknowledged that Horus had won the delta, with Seth remaining the master of Upper Egypt. However, Horus was soon made the universal king of the earth, and Seth was no more than the god of the barbarians. Horus represented light and Seth, darkness. (*Texts of the Pyramids*, 1463 ff.)

Huang-ti

Chinese cultural hero

The Yellow Emperor

Legendary emperor of China, patron of alchemists, doctors, and seers, Huang-ti was one of the fathers of Taoism.

The emperor's birth was miraculous, as his mother was made pregnant by lightning from the Great Bear.

Sovereign

Huang-ti was a perfect example of a sovereign. He wielded his spear and shield, tamed wild beasts and used them to subjugate the lords in his entourage. He made a drum which could be heard from far away and forced the whole empire to respect him.

Huang-ti was also the founder of civilization and the patron of alchemy, sexuality and medicine. He wrote the book of medicine called *The Book of Huang-ti*. He invented chariots, ships and houses. As a model emperor, he understood that every activity in the world (macrocosm) had to be preceded by putting the individual body (microcosm) in order.

While his subjects were living quite happily, Huang-ti enjoyed the use of all his senses, but his sensitivity was dulled. After a reign of 30 years, he felt wasted and tired. He said to himself, 'If I am incapable of doing good to myself, how can I do it to everyone else?' So saying, he gave up the cares of government, withdrew to a secluded room and for three months, applied himself to ordering his thoughts and refreshing his body.

One day, he dreamed that he was walking in the land of Hoa-su-cheu. One could not travel to this land in a chariot or ship; only the soul in flight could reach it: 'There is no leader. Everything works spontaneously. The people have neither desire nor lust, but only their natural instinct. No one there loves life, or fears death; each lives out his time. There are no friendships and there is no hatred; no gains and no losses; no interest and no fears.'

Waking up, Huang-ti called his ministers together and showed them the way of the Tao: 'The Tao cannot be looked for with the senses. I know it, I have found it, but I cannot tell you about it.' For the next 28 years of his reign, Huang-ti applied the method of letting everything run itself, and the empire became almost as prosperous as the land of Hoa-su-cheu. Huang-ti then rose into the sky like an immortal, and the people wept for him without stopping for two hundred years (Lie-tseu, II).

The search for immortality

Huang-ti went to the master of wisdom, Koang-tch'eng, and asked him how to conduct himself and how to keep himself. The master answered him, 'When one looks at nothing, listens to nothing, when one focuses the spirit in meditation, then the body spontaneously rights itself. Be contemplative, be detached, do not tire your body, do not upset your instincts and you will be able to last for ever.' (Tchouang-tseu, [Zhuangzi] XI)

The wise government

'The empire can be governed as I govern my horses, said the boy. — Huang-ti asked him to explain and the boy replied: I keep away from my horses anything that might do them harm. As for the rest, leave them to it. I think that, in governing men, an emperor should limit himself to that.' (Tchouang-tseu, [Zhuangzi] XXIV, C)

Huitzilopochtli

Aztec god

The sun at its zenith

Huitzilopochtli, the god of war and the protector of the city, was the blazing midday sun.

Huitzilopochtli was represented with hummingbird feathers on his head and left leg, his face black, and brandishing the *xiuhcoatl*, a serpent made of turquoise or of fire.

Coatlicue, the ancient goddess of the earth, 'she who has a skirt of serpents', was the mother of Coyolxauhqui, nocturnal darkness, and of the four hundred southerners who were stellar divinities. One day as she was praying, a bunch of feathers fell from heaven and she placed them in her bodice. Shortly afterwards, she discovered that she was pregnant. Her children reproached her for this belated pregnancy and contemplated killing her. But Huitzilopochtli emerged fully armed from his mother's womb, wearing blue armour and carrying a blue javelin, and massacred his brothers and his sisters—just as sunlight scatters the stars.

Huitzilopochtli became the supreme authority. As a soothsayer he communed with the priests at night. As a cruel god he tore out the hearts of those who disobeyed him. Great feasts were organized in his honour with mock battles, processions advancing at the double, banquets and sacrifices. During these ceremonies, the priests chanted, 'The sun has risen, thanks to me'.

The 'warrior who died in battle'

The name Huitzilopochtli derives from huitzilin, 'hummingbird', and opochtli, 'on the left', which means 'the warrior who died in battle'. The Aztecs believed that at the time of death a warrior was changed into a hummingbird, and that the left hand side was the southern direction, the abode of the dead.

Inanna

Sumerian goddess

Lady of the sky

Cunning, wilful and vindictive, Inanna protected Uruk and brought civilisation to her city.

Inanna was the patron of Uruk. As goddess of love and war, she had command over life and death.

She was called Inanna because she was the 'lady of the sky': *In* means 'lady' and *An* means 'sky'. She was associated, sometimes as wife and sometimes as daughter, with Anu, the master of the heavenly domain and patron of Uruk. Anu, however, was a distant god and left the affairs of the city to Inanna.

Guardian of Uruk

Enki, the demiurge, was the possessor of the *me*, meaning everything which makes up civilization. He made sure that his city, Eridu, took advantage of this to live in prosperity and wealth. Inanna undertook to steal the *me* from him, for her own city's benefit. To accomplish this she invited Enki to a banquet and managed to get him drunk. She was then able to steal the *me* while Enki slept peacefully. The theft did not deprive Enki, but thereafter, Uruk had progress and civilization. (*Inanna and Enki*)

A curious love story

Inanna married Dumuzi, who thus became the ruler of the city. She was very much in love and loudly proclaimed, 'I walk in joy! ... My lord is worthy of the sacred bosom.' However, her marriage and her happiness did not prevent her from being active, and she decided to go down to the underworld to seize power from her sister, Ereshkigal,

who governed it. She managed to pass through the seven doors, but at each one she had to take off one of her garments. She therefore arrived before her sister completely naked and stripped of power, as if lifeless.

Enlil, warned of Inanna's misfortune, sent messengers to take her the 'food of life' and the 'water of life', and they succeeded in resuscitating her.

However, a harsh law was then imposed on Inanna. If she wanted to leave the underworld, she had to find a replacement. Escorted by demons, the *galla*, she went back to earth to look for someone to take her place. She went to Umma, in Bad-Tibira, and there the guardian divinities threw themselves at her feet to beg for pity. She was aware of their terror and so went away again. Eventually, she found herself back in her own city of Uruk.

In Uruk, Dumuzi sat on his throne, richly dressed and leading a great life. He was having a wild time and enjoying his power as if there was nothing wrong, and he did not show the slightest concern for Inanna's tribulations. She noticed all this and, incensed, she fixed him with a deathly look and cried, 'Take him away!' And so the demons seized him, tortured him and took him down to take Inanna's place in hell, where he had to stay for half of the year.

The salvation of Dumuzi

'In all likelihood, it was Ereshkigal who, moved by Dumuzi's tears, made his sad fate easier by deciding that he should only stay for one half of the year in the lower world, and that her sister Geshtinanna, would take his place during the other half.' (S. N. Kramer, *The Sacred Marriage*, p. 69. Indiana University Press, 1969)

Indra

Indian god

The invincible

An exemplary warrior, Indra was the personification of the exuberance of life.

Indra was an athlete. The nape of his neck was very powerful, his jaw was made of gold and he wore a full beard. His power could also be seen in his heavily muscled arms and huge hands. His vitality showed itself further in his thousand testicles and in his throat, which resembled a river. He also had an enormous appetite and an unquenchable thirst for soma. Indra was a young adult with a violent and courageous nature, but he had the wisdom and intelligence of maturity. He was a magnanimous lord and a man of action. His golden chariot was drawn by two horses. His jet club had a thousand points. He was the supreme fighter, the leader.

As a divine power involved in everything that was positive, Indra gave life and light. He created the ox and the horse, gave the cow milk, made all the women fertile and had many adventures with mortal women. He was the benefactor of the whole world.

Indra fought all the enemies of his faithful followers, overthrew the rebel Pipru by destroying his fortifications (*Rig Veda*, IV, 16, 13), hurled Cambara from the top of the mountain (*Rig Veda*, IV, 30, 14), and drove out the gang of the robber Varcin. He fought against bandits, the irascible, the avaricious and sorcerers.

The god 'born to kill Vrtra'

Vrtra was a demon, the son of Tvastar. He was the symbol of the obstacle, of closing. He was completely evil and closed the great space between the sky and the earth (*Catapatha-brahmana*, I, 1, 3–4). He was an immense serpent without feet or hands and lay on the mountain, sure of his power, opposing everything that lived or moved. He stemmed the flow of water in the streams, the rivers and even the rain from the sky. He personified universal disorder.

Indra, however, crushed him with his club. He thrust his weapon into the nape of his neck and split open his head, thus freeing the waters which all rushed towards the sea. It was a complete victory which would last forever. It allowed the dawn and the sunrise to be created and the sky and earth to be strengthened (*Rig Veda*, I, 80, 4). The order of the world was re-established and the earth became habitable again.

The Maruts

In combat Indra was accompanied by the Maruts who were young, handsome and clothed in gold. They sang his praises unceasingly, strengthened him and surrounded him at the time of sacrifice. Powerful and fearsome, Indra's companions flew above the mountains and made the land tremble. They gave birth to the winds, to lightning and rain. They inspired artists and were beneficent for everyone, producing food and wealth and promoting victory.

Trita Aptia was also at Indra's side. He too was a warrior. He killed the three-headed Vicvarupa, took part in the battle against the demon Vrtra, and made food available by freeing the cows who had been

The Asvins were twin gods, handsome and ever youthful. Every day they travelled the world, seeking to do good for the sake of mankind. They were miracle-workers and doctors. They gave Indra the particular strength of which Namuci robbed him, and they were often compared to the Dioscuri, Castor and Pollux.

Indra on his elephant and Vishnu on his eagle survey the battle of the animals, in which garudas and eagles fight against serpents. In the foreground and behind, elephants and demons fight against tigers and leopards.

Gouache on paper, Pahari School, early 19th cent., illustrating a manuscript of Shiva-purana.

shut away by the demon Vala (*Rig Veda*, I, 187, 1).

The fight against Namuci

Namuci was the demon 'who would not let go what he had'. Indra did not get the upper hand immediately and was obliged to make an agreement whereby he could not kill the demon at night, during the day, or with anything dry or wet.

Namuci, who was wily and full of venom, managed to reduce Indra to impotence by getting him drunk on a mixture of alcohol and soma. The god received aid, however, from the Asvins and the goddess Sarasvati, who freed him from his drunkenness. He then surprised Namuci at dusk and decapitated him with foam (*Rig Veda*, 14, 13).

Indra was a very ancient Indo-European god. His essential function as 'breaker of obstacles and god of victory' is described in the Iranian *Avesta* and in the Armenian *Vahagn*.

A great god

'Indra is king, the most important of the gods. This is the teaching. His strength and energy are without measure for he is endowed with vigour and his radiance is infinite.'
(*Mahabharata*, I, 123, 4769–4776)

Ishtar

Mesopotamian goddess

The passionate lover

As the star of the morning, Ishtar personified war. As the star of the evening, she personified love and sensual pleasure.

Ishtar was always a virgin, not because she abstained from sexual relations but because she periodically regained her virginity by bathing in a lake. She was always followed by two musician-servants, Ninatta and Kulitta.

She was often identified with Inanna and Astarte and was the sister and wife of Tammuz, the Sumerian Dumuzi. Every year Tammuz died, descended into hell, came back to life, and returned to the earth with the vegetation in springtime. And so, every year his mourning and his return to life were celebrated. Ezekiel talks of 'women sitting and waiting for Tammuz.' (*Ezekiel* 8, 14)

Goddess of love

Ishtar was a great lover and sang passionately of her love for Dumuzi. She also loved Gilgamesh who, knowing how dissolute her life was, insolently rejected her. She was the goddess of love, and her temples were places of prostitution. Every woman in Babylon had, at least once in her life, to sit within the temple and wait for a stranger to pass by. She would then throw money at him, saying, 'I call upon you in the name of the goddess.' Then she would follow the man and fornicate with him (Herodotus, *History of the Persian Wars*, L, 2).

As a benefactor, she came to the aid of those who were sexually impotent. To attract Ishtar's attention, her devotees offered her sacrifices of sheep, tributes of incense, libations of beer and cremated figurines of wax, tallow, bitumen or wood.

Goddess of war

As a hostile warrior, Ishtar was cruel and determined. She was depicted with a bow and quiver, commanding the forces in battle. She established the fame of Assyria and was responsible for the cruelty of its kings. Assur-Nasirpal (883–859 BC) became famous for the barbarity with which he treated vanquished enemies. He often had them flayed alive or their hands cut off.

Goddess of War

'Irnini, you are the most haughty, the greatest of the Igigi (here taken to be celestial gods, as opposed to the Anunnaki, considered to be infernal gods), you are powerful and sovereign, and your name is sublime! You, you are the light of the skies and the earth. O heroic daughter of Sin, who makes arms to clash and provokes battles, you who concentrate within yourself all powers, and carries the sovereign crown.' (L. W. King, *Seven Tablets of Creation*, II, pl. LXXV)

Astarte

Astarte or Ashtart was a Phoenician goddess who combined the qualities of Aphrodite and Eros, representing seduction and sexual abandon. As the goddess of love she was worshipped in many eastern countries. Her temples can be found at Tyre, in Carthage and in Cyprus. The Bible calls her the 'Sidonian goddess' because the kings of Sidon were priests of Astarte. She was also, however, a lustful goddess, and sometimes orgiastic rites were part of her cult. She has sometimes been identified with Anat, the sister and/or lover of Baal; with Athirat, wife of the god El; and with Inanna, the daughter of the god An.

Isis

Egyptian goddess

The great magician

As a great benefactor, Isis placed her magic powers at the service of life, Osiris's life and the lives of all men.

Isis wore a solar disc and the horns of a cow. She was the daughter of Geb and Nut, the faithful and devoted wife of Osiris and the attentive mother of Horus. She was the mother, protectress of love and mistress of destiny.

Her power was obtained by trickery. She created a serpent which she placed in Re's path. The sun-god was bitten, and she told him that unless he announced his secret name, he would not be cured. As he became more and more poisoned by the venom in his veins, Re was obliged to speak. Isis then appropriated a portion of the god's power.

Isis tried to find the body of her husband, whom Seth had shut up in a chest. She found it in Byblos and hid it, but Seth seized the body, cut it into fourteen pieces and then scattered the pieces. Isis managed to put thirteen of them back together and to make herself pregnant by them. The child who was born was called Horus.

As a magician Isis also cured her son, who had been bitten by a snake. The cult of Isis and Osiris spread from Egypt throughout the whole of the Middle East.

Love charm

'Make her blind, so that she does not know where she is. Put fire in her backside (such vulgarity!), enough to make her come to me, to make her love me always. Make her unable to eat or drink until she comes to me and loves me always.' (*Love charm*, British Museum)

Itzamma

Mayan god

The lizard

God of heaven, Itzamma was the creator and civilizer of mankind.

Itzamma, the son of Hunab Ku, had the appearance of an old toothless man with sunken cheeks and a prominent nose. He was the lord of day and night and was the inventor of the hieroglyphic writing system. He gave places their names and distributed the land between the different tribes.

Sometimes he was depicted as an enormous serpent which represented the sky. From his mouth fell both the fertilizing rain and the flood. Itzamma was an ambivalent god, sometimes fearsome and sometimes benevolent. He was a doctor and gave his knowledge to warriors.

At the beginning of each year followers of his cult would sacrifice a dog, or even a human victim, in his name. The sacrificial victim was thrown from the top of a pyramid onto a pile of sharp stones. Once the object of sacrifice had landed on the ground, its heart was torn out as an offering to the god.

Janus

Roman god

He who knows

'Janus presides over all that begins, and Jupiter over all that ends.'

Janus was the two-faced god. He looked in front and behind, inside and out, right and left and high and low. He knew all the arguments for and against and personified absolute clearsightedness.

The god of transitions

Janus was the god of beginnings. He presided over the beginning of all undertakings; at the start of war and the succession of a kingdom. The month which bears his name is the first of the year.

As the god of gateways, he made the transition between savagery and civilized life, war and peace, and town and country (his temple was at the gates of Rome). He protected the passage which gave access to the street and presided over the initiation of

Janus, the two-headed god, omnipresent and enigmatic.

Head from the Celto-ligurian sanctuary of Roquepertuse, 3rd–2nd cent. BC.

young people entering adult life.

Originally from Thessaly, Janus was welcomed by Camese, with whom he shared a kingdom in Latium. He settled on the hill which was to bear his name, Janiculum and his wife, Camise or Camasené bore him children. One of them was Tiber, who would give his name to the river. After the death of Camese he reigned alone in Latium and took in Saturn whom Jupiter was hunting.

The golden age

As the first king, Janus made order reign. It was truly a golden age: men were good, there was wealth in abundance and the country lived in peace. Janus invented money, the cultivation of soil and legislation.

After his death, Janus was deified and assured Rome of his protection. When Romulus and his friends kidnapped the Sabine women, the Sabine men attacked the city. The daughter of the guardian of the Capitol betrayed her compatriots and let the enemy through. They began to scale the heights of the hill. Just as they were about to capture the temple, Janus made a spring of hot water gush forth, which terrified them and made them turn back.

From that day on, the temple of Janus stayed open in wartime so that the god would be able to act. It was closed in peacetime.

After the foundation of the republic, one of the royal functions was preserved, that of *rex sacrorum* or *rex sacrificulus*. The invested priest regularly offered sacrifices to the god.

> **Guardian of the world**
> 'Whatever your eyes let you see — sky, sea, cloud, earth — these are my domain and remain in my hand. It is my function to look after the vast world.' (Ovid, *Fasti*, I, 117)

Jason

Greek hero

The quest for the Golden Fleece

*Long, hard and perilous adventures
showed Jason to be courageous yet
fickle.*

Jason was the son of Aeson, the king of Iolcus. The latter found himself deposed by his half-brother, Pelias. Therefore, he asked the centaur Cheiron to look after Jason's education on Mount Pelion. It was a hard upbringing for Jason; he learned the art of war, hunting, music and medicine.

One day, Pelias organized a great sacrifice in honour of Poseidon, and Jason came back to Iolcus for the ceremony. He was dressed in a panther skin, as he would have been in the mountains, and he carried a spear in each hand. On the way, he crossed a river and lost a sandal. In Iolcus, he stayed for a few days with his father and then presented himself to Pelias, the king. Pelias grew frightened at the sight of him, for an oracle had once predicted that his downfall would be brought about by a man wearing only one sandal.

The Golden Fleece

Jason claimed the power usurped by Pelias. Without opposing him, the king set him a test which would show if he was worthy of the crown: to bring back the Golden Fleece from Colchis. The fleece was that of a ram which had previously transported Phrixus through the air. It was dedicated to Ares by the king of Colchis, Aeëtes, and was guarded by an ever-wakeful dragon. Secretly, Pelias hoped that Jason would never return from this impossible mission.

Jason called for companions. The bravest men in Greece, always ready for adventure, came running to him. Athene helped them build the *Argo*, the ship which

was necessary for the expedition. They left on the voyage, during which they would overcome a thousand obstacles and take part in a thousand battles. The passage through the Symplegades was infamous. It meant going through massive rocks which were constantly moving, sometimes opening apart and sometimes crashing together. Athena intervened to help them, holding back a rock with one hand while pushing the *Argo* through with her other hand. Only the stern of the ship was touched by the rocks during the passage, and the Argonauts were safe and sound.

When they had arrived in Colchis, Jason asked Aeëtes for the Golden Fleece. It was promised to him if he could succeed in yoking the brazen-footed, fire-breathing bull. Luck smiled on our hero. Medea, Aeëtes's daughter, conceived a great passion for Jason and used magic to make it possible for him to accomplish the tasks set for him. The king, however, was still opposed to Jason and did not want to keep his promises. So, weary of war, Jason stole the fleece and left. He took Medea with him and married her.

Jason and Medea

Medea was Jason's salvation. In order to delay Aeëtes—who, in his rage, was pursuing them—she slit her brother's throat, dismembered him and, one by one, threw the pieces overboard. The king was so busy retrieving the pieces and burying them that he soon lost track of the Argonauts. When they arrived in Iolcus, Medea persuaded Pelias's daughters to kill their father and boil him in a cauldron. 'Thus', she said, 'he will find new youth'. Once the crime had been committed the way was clear, and Jason took the throne.

Jason and Medea lived happily, first in Iolcus, then in Corinth. After some years, Jason realized that his children were not

Jason and his friends are scared when they come face to face with a menacing dragon and fire-breathing bulls. Jason and the Golden Fleece. Anonymous engraving, 1655.

accepted as heirs to the throne because their mother was a barbarian. He divorced Medea and married Creüsa, the daughter of King Creon of Corinth. Medea was true to her evil past. She sent a robe as a wedding present to Jason's new wife; the robe was impregnated with a deadly poison, which killed Creüsa as soon as she put it on. When Creon rushed to help his daughter he too was poisoned. In her rage, Medea also killed her two children by Jason before escaping in an airborne chariot. As Jason in total despair sat brooding on his misfortune under the hulk of the *Argo*, with which he had won all his glory, a beam fell from the ship and killed him.

Medea's decision

'My friends, I have reached a decision: my sons must be killed as quickly as possible and I must depart from this country. I do not want any delay on my part to result in my children being delivered to murderous blows from hostile hands. Either way they must die and it is better that we who gave them life should now take life from them. I must steel my heart.'
(Euripides, *Medea*, 1236–1243)

Kama

Indian god

Love

Kama was the personification of desire: both sensual pleasure and, more particularly, sexual pleasure.

Without a doubt the most ancient of the gods, Kama gave rise to the creator's desire for other beings. He was given different names: Dipaka ('Igniter'); Gritsa ('he who penetrates'); Mayi ('Deceiver'); Mara ('Destroyer'); Ragavrinta ('the way of passion') and Titha ('Fire'). His wife was Rati ('Voluptuousness').

Kama was a handsome young man, mounted on a parrot and armed with a bow made from sugar-cane and arrows made from lotus buds. As soon as he was born, he looked around him and asked who he was going to 'set on fire'.

The 'bodiless' god

Kama was always ready to initiate love, either in men or in the gods, as the following episode shows. Sati could not bear the scornful attitude of her father, Daksa, towards Shiva, her husband. Consequently, she killed herself by throwing herself into the fire. Shiva, shocked, retired to the Himalayas and resigned himself to meditation and the observation of complete celibacy and profound asceticism.

Then a woman came to him. It was Parvati, the mountain woman. She was rather retiring, humble and respectful. In silence, she took up the same position as his, performed the same exercises and followed the same rules. In this way, she hoped to attract his attention and win his love. Sati, who was still in love with Shiva, was reincarnated in her.

During this time the world was threatened by Taraka, a demon on whom Brahma had bestowed invulnerability. He could be brought down only by Shiva's offspring. But this seemed impossible, as the god was enjoying total abstinence and would not even deign to look at the woman who presented herself to him. The gods spoke to Kama. He went with his wife, Rati, to Shiva and tricked the 'guardian of the door' by turning himself into a perfumed breeze. Then, returning to his usual form, he watched Shiva intently, waited sixty million years and then shot his first arrow.

Shiva opened his eyes, saw Parvati and was filled with desire. He understood immediately that Kama had brought him out of his deep meditation. He found Kama and reduced him to ashes. Then he turned to Parvati and, admiring the purity of her bearing, promised to fulfil her dearest wish. 'Let Kama live and warm the world', Parvati replied. Kama lived, but without a body. This incident earned Kama the name *Ananga*, meaning 'bodiless' — the worst thing that could happen to the god of desire! However, it also explains his hidden and perpetually active presence in the world.

Shiva and Parvati were joined. A son, Kaumara, was born to them, and he put the demon to death. (*Kumara-sambhava*)

> 'Make Kama live and make him warm the world. Without Kama I desire nothing.'
> (*Kumara-sambhava*)

The 'guardian of the door'
Hindu mythology has a certain number of 'guardians of the door'. Their function was to protect a secret from the indiscretions of others. Ganesha and Nandin, the bull, were part of Shiva's retinue. The former protected Parvati's privacy; the latter protected Shiva's sexual relations or his asceticism.

Kami

Beneficent Japanese spirits

The powers of nature

The kami were manifestations of natural forces and superior to men.

Everything that was big or inexplicable was kami. There were eighty million of them. Ancestral kami were simply deified ancestors. There were frontier kami, art kami, kami of the seasons, or rain, of good weather and storms and, even, foreign kami. The list was never-ending.

It was a time when the trees and the grass talked (*Nihongi*, 2nd month, 16th year of Emperor Kimmei). Even stones were sometimes great deities (*Kojiki*). They were prayed to and, in times of drought, rain was obtained from them (*Izumo Fudoki, Tatenui no kôri*). Animals, rivers, lakes and seas were objects of veneration. They were personified forces, living beings, who had a strong influence on man. Such were kami, to whom human sacrifices were sometimes made (*Nihongi*, 10th month of the 40th year of Emperor Keiko).

The holy mountains

Mountains were particularly venerated. Some of them were considered to be the bodies of divinities, such as Miwayama. Others were the homes of the gods who sent spring water from their summits. The mountain deity usually showed itself as a hideous and terrifying serpent which was said to be female. When it descended to the plains, it became *ta no kami*, the divinity (or spirit) of the fields who fertilized all plants.

Anything at all can be declared to be kami. It is told how a certain Oube No Oshi said that such-and-such an insect was the god of the beyond. People believed him and started to worship the insect, praying to it in order to obtain wealth and long life. They also organized festivals and ceremonies in its honour. A place was dedicated to it, offerings were made, and it was honoured in song and dance. This went on for a long time . . . until a sensible man declared that nothing was happening and ridiculed Oube No Oshi (*Nihongi*, XII).

Saké, a drink considered mysterious because of its intoxicating effect, was the offering preferred by the kami.

The kannushi

The kannushi were powerful people, masters or possessors of a divinity. They spoke for the divinity, acted in its name and exercised its authority. They relayed prayers to the kami and were even capable of making them act. The *Wei-chich* speaks of the queen of the Wa (Japanese), Pimiko, who knew how to enchant people. She did not get married and rarely appeared in public. She was the intermediary between the spirits and the world of men. Her younger brother actually exercised the power, but at her command. Pimiko was a kannushi.

The world of the innumerable kami

. . . from there, this multitude of kami, of which the classic texts say that they are *ya oyorozu*, "eight hundred myriads", or, to put it differently, innumerable. Under these circumstances, it is doubtless inadequate to translate kami as gods . . . It would be better to talk of *numina*, as the Romans did.' (R. Sieffert, *Les Religions du Japon*, (Japanese Religions) Paris, 1969, p. 12)

Krishna

Indian god

The avatar of Vishnu

Krishna, or Krsna, was the lovable child and merciless warrior, adored by shepherdesses and inaccessible.

Krishna was born at Mathura, in the north of Agra, at the end of the third age of the world. His mother was Devaki and his father, Vasudeva. He was dark-skinned and his name means 'the Black One'. Hindu houses often have a picture of Krishna as a child stealing butter or as a shepherd playing the flute.

At the time of Krishna's birth, Kamsa, the brother of Devaki, ruled on Mathura. From an oracle, he knew that one of his nephews would kill him. Consequently, he held his sister prisoner and killed her children. Balarama was the first to escape from him. Krishna was then saved; the daughter of Nanda and Yasoda, who was born at exactly the same moment, was substituted for him at birth.

Krishna was endowed with exceptional strength and intelligence and made light of the enemies who opposed him. When Putana breast-fed him with poisoned milk, he drank so much that he exhausted even the substance of the demon's life. He killed Trinavarta, who wanted to carry him off into the sky. When Kamsa decided to destroy all the children in the region who were rather unusual, Nanda took Krishna away with Balarma to Gokula, where they hid for seven years.

At Gokula, Krishna continued to be an extraordinary child. He killed the monster Baku who had taken the form of a crane, just as Arista took that of a buffalo and Kesin a horse. He fought with Kaliya, the king of serpents, who had poisoned the waters of the Yamuna; he danced on Kaliya's head, but since he recognized that Kaliya was only obeying the laws of his species, he spared his life and sent him into the ocean.

***Krishna** lifts up Mount Govardhana to protect the shepherds who are threatened by thunderbolts.*

Wood with traces of polychrome. 18th cent.

The beneficent

'Life is unbearable without you, Krishna; like a lotus without water, like a night with no moon, so am I without you, my beloved.'
(Mira Baï, in A. N. Basu's *Mira Baï*, London, 1934)

Shepherds had celebrations for him, and he invited them to replace the ceremonies in honour of Indra with sacrifices offered to the deities of mountains and forests. Indra became angry and caused a terrifying storm, so Krishna had to protect his friends by holding Mount Govardhana above their heads like a kind of umbrella. Indra then recognized in Krishna an incarnation of Vishnu.

The great lover

Krishna was cherished by shepherdesses, and he danced with them and accompanied their songs with his flute. One day while they were bathing, he hid their clothes so that they had to come to him naked, one by one, to ask for them back. He married a thousand of them, but his favourite was Radha, 'she who pleases' (*Gitagovinda*).

He eventually killed Kamsa and became master of the kingdom. Very quickly, though, he left and founded Dvaraka, the mythical city where his own came to join him. There he married Rukmini-Lakshmi, the daughter of the king of the Vidarbha, and settled down into a luxurious existence with his sixteen thousand wives and his one hundred and eighty thousand children. His life was nevertheless interspersed with numerous battles against demons, a duel with his cousin, King Cisupala, and the war of the Bharata (the subject of the vast poem entitled the *Mahabharata*).

Krishna was full of tricks. In the battle between the Pandavas and the Kauravas, the former found themselves faced with a particularly invulnerable captain. The only thing which would make him lower his defences would be some distressing news. Krishna had the idea of telling him that his son, Asvatthaman, was dead and, so that there would be no lie involved, they gave the name of Asvatthaman to a dead elephant. The trick worked and the enemy was killed (*Mahabharata*, VII, 8694–8892).

Arjuna's driver

Krishna was then reincarnated as the character of Arjuna, who was fighting in the ranks of the Pandavas. Krishna was a skilful charioteer and Arjuna's friend, counsellor and instrumental supporter. Long discussions took place between them. Arjuna spoke of his uneasy conscience and doubts about engaging in a fratricidal war.

*Kama, god of love, fires a lotus blossom arrow at **Krishna**.*

Gouache. 17th cent.

Krishna plays his flute, and women, animals and nature are all under the spell of his melodies.

Mural painting, 20th cent.

Krishna offered guidance to ease his friend's troubled mind and strengthen his courage.

Krishna was a wise man, but not a warrior. Once, however, he advanced before the enemy, and it was Arjuna who hesitated, fearing for his life and doubting the justification for the battle. Krishna, taking Arjuna's place, got down from the chariot and walked, step by step, towards Bhisma, the enemy. At the tenth step, Arjuna stopped him and said, 'This is my responsibility, it is I who will kill'. He had found the resolve which he had been lacking (*Mahabharata*, VI, 2597). When the enemy acquired the ultimate weapon, which could be made simply by blowing on something and saying a mantra, Krishna was there to warn and give counsel. On one occasion Asvatthaman used the ultimate weapon. Krishna cried out and told Arjuna to throw 'the weapon to disarm weapons'. Two great *rsi* came between the two weapons, and they asked each fighter to recall his dart. Arjuna, who was pure, did so without difficulty, but Asvatthaman, who was not, could not do so. Instead, he turned it on the children-to-be of the Pandavas. The only child who was saved was the one whom the daughter-in-law of a

Pandava was expecting, and Krishna declared this. Asvatthaman was furious and tried to aim at that embryo too. It was, in fact, still-born. However, Krishna, showing himself here to be a great god, brought it back to life immediately and so saved the race. Without pausing for rest, he sent the enemy into three thousand years of solitude (*Mahabharata*, X, 729).

A quarrel within his clan, the Yadavas, sparked off a furious battle in which everyone perished. Krishna withdrew to the forest, where he was brought down by a stray arrow. He was wounded in the heel, his only vulnerable spot. He died of it and rose to the gods' heaven, where he regained his divine form.

Krishna was the incarnation of Vishnu. He was the supreme god, the object of worship known as *bhakti*. Bhakti, as Jan Gonda says in *Die Religionen Indiens*, consist of a relinquishment, deep devotion, personal and passionate affection, and a need to unite oneself with the object of worship. The love of the shepherdesses for Krishna is an example of this sort of attachment to the god, and the songs of the *Gitagovinda* are the 'Song of Songs' of India.

Krishna has become the only god in many Hindu sects.

Kumarbi

Hurrian god

The rival

The last sovereign of the gods of antiquity, Kumarbi was himself deposed by the young god, Teshub.

For nine years the divine throne was occupied by Alalu, but the powerful Anu considered himself above him. In the ninth year, Anu engaged Alalu in battle and defeated him, thereafter taking his place on the throne. Kumarbi, the powerful, bowed down at Anu's feet, but rivalry came between this servant and the new sovereign. Anu, unable to tolerate Kumarbi's brilliance, escaped by taking flight like a bird, up into the sky. Kumarbi pursued him in order to pull him down from the sky, and 'he bit Anu's knees and swallowed his manhood'.

Kumarbi rejoiced. Anu recovered, however, and said, 'I have laid a heavy burden on you. I have impregnated you with three powerful gods: Teshub, the god of the storm; the river-god, Aranzah (the Tiger); and the great god Tashmishu.' Kumarbi spat in reply, and his saliva fell on the ground carrying Anu's semen. From this semen were born the gods who had been predicted.

And so Kumarbi was deposed by Teshub, the storm-god (*The Heavenly Royalty*).

Kumarbi's revenge

Kumarbi, now dethroned, plotted against the storm-god.

He took his staff in his hand, and 'wearing the wind on his feet like swift sandals, left his town and went towards a very large stone of three thousand (?) in length and one and a half thousand (?) in width.' He dreamt of creating a monster who would crush his rival, and he slept with the stone as if it were a woman.

The son of Kumarbi and the stone was born. Kumarbi called him Ullikummi and said, 'May he rise into heaven and take over the kingship . . . May he bring down the god of storms, crush him like salt, and trample him underfoot like an ant.'

Ullikummi

Ullikummi was like a rock, as his body was made of diorite (greenstone). He was entrusted to the Irshirra, the servant goddesses of Kumarbi, and they set him like a spire on the right shoulder of Upelluri (the world). The stone grew and reached the height of the temples and the kuntarra of the heavens (the dwelling-place of the gods).

The sun and the god of storms took counsel together. Ishtar, the goddess of love, tried out her charms on Ullikummi, the monster, but without success. He remained impassive. The fight began, but Teshub, who could not restrain his enemy, was beaten. Ullikummi continued to grow. He made the heavens shake and forced Hebat, Teshub's wife, to leave her temple.

The gods met together and decided on a new strategy: they would cut off Ullikummi's feet. Thus, Ullikummi was defeated; he could no longer go on. Kumarbi, who had made him, was defeated as well. (*The Song of Ullikummi*).

Although he was a fallen god, Kumarbi was not rejected by the infernal gods. His cult was kept alive within the Hurrite and Hittite religions for a long time.

Lakhsmi

Indian goddess

The energy of Vishnu

The gifts of Lakhsmi were happiness, beauty, wealth, and prosperity.

Lakhsmi lived in sumptuous surroundings consisting of precious fabrics, jewels, musical instruments and domestic animals. She was mounted on a peacock or on a lotus blossom and was beauty personified.

As the wife of Vishnu, she was the incarnation of the great god's strength and power. She was active while Vishnu, indifferent and impassive, dozed on his serpent. In another incarnation as Radha, she was the favourite of Krishna.

She was kind and distributed her favours without explaining why one person was chosen and another not. She was fortune, with all its implications of randomness and unfairness.

When a young husband brought his wife into the house, he brought Lakhsmi. The bride had to wear jewels and be dressed in a robe which, at the very least, had gold brocade. Gold was the symbol of the goddess. Jewels were the sign that Lakhsmi was present.

Lares

Roman gods

Guardians

The Lares protected inhabited places.

Jupiter loved the nymph Juturna and used every possible means to approach her, but she refused him and fled. The god then assembled all the nymphs and asked them to help him. They agreed, but one of them, Lara, reported all this to Juno.

Jupiter was furious, tore out Lara's tongue, and gave her to Mercury to take her down to hell. On the way, Mercury raped her and she gave birth to twins, the Lares (Ovid, *Fasti*, II, 583 ff.).

The Lares were deities who protected the land. They were depicted as two boys accompanied by a dog. We can distinguish between two types of Lares. The *lares compitales* were found in the country, at crossroads, and in popular meeting places, and they were worshipped at the *Compitalia* in January. The *lares familiares*, were guardians of the family home, to whom the master of the house offered a wreath saying, 'May this dwelling-place be for us a source of goodness, blessings, joy and good luck.' (Plautus, *Trinummus*, 40–41)

The lares familiares

'Among the souls of the dead (or human souls) there are those who have been entrusted with the mission of watching over their descendants, and their peaceful and calming power held sway over the house. They were given the name *lar familiaris*'. (Apuleius, *De Deo Socratis*, 152)

Leviathan

Phoenician monster

Hostile power

*As the personification of evil,
Leviathan had to be conquered for the
arrival of the new age.*

Leviathan was a ferocious monster, and just a look from him was enough to knock someone down. His strength had no equal. He wore a double breastplate, and his back was like a row of shields, so close together that not even a breath of air could pass between them. Sparks of fire shot from his mouth and smoke poured from his nostrils. His breath could even kindle coal. 'When he raises himself, strong men take fright' (*Job* 41, 25). His heart was as hard as stone. 'Iron he counts as straw, and bronze as rotting wood.' (*Job* 41, 27)

In Phoenician mythology, Leviathan came out of the primal chaos. Vanquished by the creator at the beginning, he took refuge in the sea where he could still demonstrate his wickedness. Like a beast lying in wait, he made himself forgotten, feigned sleep, and waited for just the right moment to leap up and skin his victims. 'How fierce he is when he is roused! Who is there to stand up to him?' (*Job* 41, 10)

He was Egypt for the Hebrews held prisoner there, Babylon for those who were in exile there and Rome for those colonized by the Empire. He was power for those who were enslaved and silver for those who were slaves to it. Leviathan personified fetters, handicaps and paralysis. He was contrary to the proper order, the good running of things, the salvation of men and the reign of God.

Leviathan was chained up for a thousand years and then released, whereupon he undertook to consolidate his power. As a seducer, he knew how to conquer kings and peoples 'in the four quarters of the earth',

and his followers were as 'countless as the sand in the sea' (*Revelations* 20, 8). He even laid seige to the camp of the saints.

'The fleeing serpent, the twisting serpent' (*Isaiah* 27, 1), Leviathan came from the beginning of time and the depths of being. Leviathan was the instinct in everything undisciplined and savage, hostile to the law or to God. He was always present, hidden in each individual, in social structures and in the inventions of man. He acted in an underhand way, without being noticed, but nonetheless was very effective. He always appeared where he was least expected.

He was the enemy which had to be overcome, the beast who had to be got rid of, the animal nature which one had to get beyond. He was the monster who opposed God and the friends of God. He was the primal force, a protagonist in the cosmic battle which has raged since the beginning of time and will finish only when everything has been consumed. Leviathan personified evil.

Only god, 'who didst crush Leviathan's many heads and throw him to the sharks for food' (*Psalms* 74, 14), and the angels of God, who 'seized the dragon, that serpent of old' (*Revelations* 20, 1) could crush him forever and thus make way for the coming of the Holy Jerusalem.

The unapproachable

'And Leviathan [. . .]. Will he make many supplications to you, will he speak soft words to you? Will he make with you a covenant to take him for your servant forever? Will you play with him as with a bird, or will you put him on a leash for your maidens? Will traders bargain over him? Will they divide him up among the merchants? Can you fill his skin with harpoons or his head with fish-hooks? If ever you lift your hand against him, think of the struggle that awaits you, and let be.' (*Job*, 41, 3–8)

Loki

Norse god

Disorder

Loki's characteristics were deceit, disorder, malevolence and perversity.

Loki was the son of Laufey and Farbauti, a giant couple who were part of the primal world. He was extremely handsome and seductive and was the spirit of air and fire. He fathered the most horrible monsters: Hel, a hideous goddess who was guardian of the empire of the dead and whose body was half black and half blue; and Fenrir, the great evil spirit. It was Loki who put obstacles in the way of everything and forbade the world to be happy.

Loki was a trickster. He never stopped making jokes which were amusing or cruel to himself or to others. He was a malicious, little imp who applied himself to thinking up the worst tomfoolery to make fun of the giant, Skadi, and terribly cruel, coarse jokes to make Thor disguise himself as a woman. He had no sense of moderation, took risks while he amused himself and found himself in the middle of inextricable adventures from which he could escape by cunning and treachery.

The amoral one

Loki had no moral sense. He put his prodigious talents at the service of good just as much as evil. He had no friends, no goal to reach and no cause to defend. It seemed that nothing was forbidden to him. He was 'of bad spirit and very unstable in his ways' (*Gylfaginning*, XXXII) and the spirit of evil in all its forms. He was thief, adulterer and murderer and caused the final war in which all the gods and he himself would be annihilated.

As a magician, Loki had the power to transform himself. He became a mare in order to seduce the stallion who was taking part in building Asgard. He also became a falcon to kidnap Idunn, a fly to steal Freyja's necklace, a sorcerer to prevent Balder from leaving Hel's abode, and a seal to fight against Heimdallr.

The abduction of Idunn

One day, Thor, Loki and Hoenir were travelling, and they ran short of food. Seeing a herd of oxen, they killed one of them and started to cook it in a pit. The meat, however, would not cook. The giant, Thjazi, appearing in the form of an eagle, demanded his share of the feast. After waiting for the meat to be cooked, he made off with the best bits: the leg and shoulders. Loki was furious and attacked him with a stick, which stuck to the eagle's back and to Loki's hands. The eagle then took flight with Loki still attached to him.

Loki begged his abductor to release him. Thjazi agreed to do this on condition that Loki promised to bring Idunn and her apples of youth out of Asgard. When Loki had been freed, he lured Idunn into a forest, saying to her that he thought her apples were wonderful and wanted to compare them with his own. Thjazi, again in the form of an eagle, then swooped down and seized Idunn.

The Aesir, however, suffered because of Idunn's disappearance. They aged quickly and became grey. They met together and realized that the last time they had seen

---

Asgard was the stronghold of the gods.

Idunn was the wife of Bragi, the god of poetry. She kept the apples of youth which allowed the gods to remain eternally young.

Sif was Thor's wife.

Idunn was in the company of Loki. They demanded that Loki give the goddess back. He then asked Freyja to lend him her falcon shape. Thus disguised, he took advantage of Thjazi's absence to carry Idunn away.

The giant was angry and rushed to look for the goddess. He reached Asgard after Loki. The Aesir made a pile of wood shavings, set fire to it and burned the eagle's wings. Skadi, the daughter of Thjazi, wanted to avenge her father, but the Aesir offered her compensation and authorized her to choose a husband from among them. In return, she asked for an assurance of conciliation — to make her laugh. She thought that this was something they were incapable of doing, but she did not know Loki. He started clowning around so much that she burst out laughing, and peace was concluded (*Skaldskaparmal*, I).

The bet

Another time, Loki spitefully cut off Sif's hair. Thor was very angry and would have killed him there and then had Loki not promised to get hair made of gold for Sif. Loki got dwarves to make hair which would grow steadily from the moment it was on Sif's head. Then they made a ship called *Skidbladnir* which would have the wind at its stern as soon as the sail was hoisted.

The festival of trouble

'I must go into the hall of Aegir to see this banquet. I bring discord and dissension to the sons of the Aesir, and I will mix evil spells with their mead.' (*Lokasenna*, II)

A trap for Loki

'When Kvasir noticed the burned net in the ashes left by the fire, he thought that it must be a tool for catching fish and he said so to the Aesir. They then made a net like the one made by Loki that they had seen in the ashes. When the net was ready, they went to the river and threw it into the waterfall.' (*Gylfaginning*, XLIX)

The ship, Skidbladnir, was pliable and could be dismantled, rather like the ones carried in processions at the time of the cults.

Finally, they made a spear which could never be stopped when it was used to strike a blow.

Loki had made a bet with Brokk, the dwarf, that he could not make such precious objects as these. Brokk then set about making a boar which could fly through air and water, night and day, faster than any horse. He also made a ring of gold from which every nine nights, eight rings fell, weighing just as much as the original. Finally, he made a hammer which dealt the most powerful blows without the handle loosening at all.

The Aesir decreed that the hammer was the most precious of all the objects, and so declared the dwarf to be the winner.

Loki offered to pay a ransom to save his life, but the dwarf did not see things the same way and tried to cut off his head. 'My head, yes,' said Loki, 'but not my neck.' The dwarf then pierced his victim's lips and sewed his mouth closed. Loki, however, ripped the stitches open (*Skaldskaparmal*, XXXIII).

Sarcasm

Loki came to provoke the gods who were gathered together for a banquet. One by one, he insulted and offended them and told them their faults. Each tried to match him in and stem the flood of insults, but to no avail. Thor then took out his powerful hammer and threatened to strike Loki down. He replied with renewed insults and went away, saying, 'For you alone will I leave. For I know that you will strike me.' (*Lokasenna*)

Loki had really gone too far. The gods were very angry and banded together against him. They pursued him to the waterfall where he changed himself into a salmon. They made a net, just like one Loki himself had made one day, caught him and then took him to a cave.

The gods tied Loki to sharp rocks with the intestines of his son, and Skadi caught a poisonous snake and tied it above his face. Sigyn, Loki's wife, held a bowl under the venom. However, when the bowl was full she went to empty it and venom spilled over Loki, who writhed so violently that the whole earth shook. This was the origin of earthquakes (*Gylfaginning*, XLIX).

Lug

Irish god

Skilled in many arts

Lug was an exceptional god, beyond any particular office because he fulfilled them all.

Lug was the son of Delbaeth, a Fomoiré or evil spirit, and Éri. He was warrior, sage, magician, musician, master of all crafts and the leader of the Tuatha Dé Danann.

The Fomoiri were hideous, evil beings who occupied Ireland and oppressed its inhabitants. The king of the Tuatha Dé Danann, Nuada, had lost an arm in the course of battle, and this handicap made him unfit to rule. In order to win the favour of the occupiers, the Tuatha Dé Danann elected Bres, the Fomoiré, as king; Bres, however, turned out to be a bad king who exploited his subjects.

After some time, Bres was forced to give his power back. Dian Cécht, the god of healing, made a silver arm for Nuada, which had all the characteristics of a real arm. Bres was afraid at first and fled to his father, the king of the Fomoiri, but then recruited a vast army and invaded Ireland.

Then Lug, a young warrior, presented himself. He claimed to possess every talent and went on to prove it. On the harp, he played the three Irish melodies (the melody which brings tears to the eyes, the melody which makes one fall asleep, and the melody which brings joy); he put the stone of Fal back in its place (it could be moved only by 80 oxen); and finally, he won a game of chess against the king. The king proclaimed Lug to be the wisest of the wise, gave him the throne for 13 days and put him in charge of organizing the battle against the Fomoiri.

Lug allotted the different tasks. The druids were to join the waters together to hinder the Fomoiri, sorcerers were to cast spells on the enemy, craftsmen were to make weapons, champions were to lead the fighting, healers were to tend the wounded . . . Everything was so well organized that the Fomoiri were conquered, and Bres was taken prisoner. He was allowed to live on condition that he tell the secret of prosperity.

Lug took very little part in the fighting. His abilities made him too precious to lose, and he stayed out of the mêlée. Crossing from one side to the other, he announced the 'supreme curse' and so brought about victory. He performed one splended deed, however: with a stone from his sling he pierced the eye of Balor, whose gaze could paralyze men and whose eyelid had to be raised by a hook.

Another version of the same text demonstrates the rivalry between Nuada and Lug.

The many-skilled artist

'When Nuada saw the many talents of Lug, he started to think and asked himself if such an able man could not free the people of the goddess Dana from the servitude imposed on them by the Fomoiri. He deliberated on this with his counsel and this is the decision he came to: he would change places with Lug. Lug, the master of all trades, went and sat on the king's throne and the king sat before him. This honour was given to Lug for 13 days.' (*The Battle of Moytura*, I, 74)

Dagda

Another Irish god, Dagda, was a glutton bursting with sexuality (*Cath Maighe Tuireadh*). He had a club which killed with one end and brought back life with the other, a magic harp which played wonderful tunes by itself and a cauldron 'which no troops would leave without recovering their strength'.

The latter was tied to a pillar by the king, who wanted to keep the glory of battle for himself. Lug, however, burst his chains and won the battle virtually by himself (*Cath Maighe Tuireadh*).

Llud, king of the island of Britain

Lug was confused with Llud, the king of the island of Britain, who was a builder and warrior. Three scourges devastated his kingdom: invaders appeared who could hear every conversation throughout the island; every first of May, two terrible dragons duelled and uttered such cries that all living beings, men and animals, were stupefied and made barren; and finally, a magician came by night to steal the stocks of food the king had put by.

When Llud reached the end of the three scourges, however, he found that he possessed three benefits. He had a magic drug which was powerful enough to triumph over any invader who was more knowledgeable than he; the two dead dragons turned out to be a talisman against enemies; and finally, the thief was overcome and gave back the vast quantity of stolen provisions (*Cyfranc Llydd a Llevelis*).

The cult of Lug spread far beyond Ireland. This can be seen in the names of the towns of Lyon (*Lugdunum* = citadel of Lug), Laon (Aisne), Laudun (Gard), Loudon (Vienne), and so on. In Lyon, the god was worshipped on the Fourvière hill.

Maat

Egyptian goddess

Balance

Maat represented the social and cosmic order and was the guardian of ethics and rites.

Maat was the daughter of Re, the sun-god. The gods loved her because she was necessary to their existence and functions.

Maat was the offering made by kings to the gods, in the form of a statuette held in the hollow of the hand. She was the perfect offering because she encompassed all the others. She was justice and truth, the weight by which the hearts of the deceased were judged and the regulator of religious rites. Judges wore effigies of her next to their chests, and the vizir, supreme head of the tribunals, was said to be the 'priest of Maat'.

Maat personified order. She arranged the proper development of individuals' lives, presided over social relationships and authenticated deeds of power. Maat was present wherever a decree was accomplished. Everyone, from the king to the most humble subject, was responsible for ensuring her reign. She represented the philosophy of Egyptian society.

She was there at the beginning of the universe, watching over the balance of everything and making sure that there was a harmonious rapport and a necessary cohesion between human beings. She maintained order in heaven just as she did on earth. She was responsible for the seasons, for night and day, for the movement of the stars and for rainfall. Her role was both cosmic and social.

Maat's continuous work
'Maat is great and her work is continuous. She has never been in trouble since the time of her creator . . . While there is punishment for those who transgress her laws. She is the path before the inexperienced'. (The vizir Isei to his son, in *Mythes et Croyances du monde entier* (Worldwide Myths and Beliefs), Paris, 1986)

Marduk

Babylonian god

The sovereign

The child of a new generation of gods, Marduk became ruler of the universe at the same time as he became its champion.

Marduk, the son of Ea and Damkina, was given a two-fold divine essence and a four-fold understanding at his birth. His wife was Zerbanitu and his son was Nabu, the god of scribes.

Marduk was the champion of a new generation of gods, those who represented life, civilization and progress, as opposed to the primordial gods, who represented primitive chaos, disorganized nature and brute force without intelligence.

Marduk created the winds and raised the tempest. The first-born gods were distressed by the wind and pondered evil in their hearts, saying to Tiamat, 'avenge Apsu, your husband, and Mama who has been put in irons. Go to war.' 'Tiamat gave terrible dragons a frightening appearance and imbued them with supernatural brilliance . . . she created eleven species' (*Enuma Elish*, tablet I, 135–140). She put Kingu at the head of her army.

The gathered gods suggested to Marduk that he defend them. He agreed to on condition that he would then acquire supreme power. At first Kingu wavered, but Tiamat stood up straight and did not turn her head. Tiamat and Marduk went for each other. The lord enveloped his adversary in a net and sent an evil wind.

Tiamat opened her mouth to swallow it, and the wind inflated her body and her belly swelled up. Marduk threw an arrow which tore her entrails and pierced her heart. He then stood on top of her corpse and everyone ran away. He trampled his enemies underfoot, and Kingu was sent to join the ranks of the dead gods.

The creation of man

Marduk examined the cadaver and cut it in two like a dried fish and. From one half he made the heavenly vault where he built the palace of Eshara which was heaven, and there lived Anu, Enlil and Ea. From the other half he made the earth, gathering the mountains on his head, starting the Euphrates and the Tigris from his eyes, and creating great hills and founding sanctuaries on his breast. At the sight of all these marvels, the gods were full of admiration. 'I want', said Marduk, 'to make a network of veins full of blood and a frame of bone in order to produce a species of being whose name will be man' (*Enuma Elish*, tablet VI, 1). His 'will be the duty of serving the gods for their relief' (*Enuma Elish*).

He caught Kingu who had stirred up the war, slit open his veins and from the blood, created humanity. Marduk remained responsible for order in the world. When Erra, the god of death, succeeded by a ruse in making Marduk rise from his seat, the world was turned upside down. The light of the sun changed into darkness, the roads became infested with brigands and man ate man. Order was re-established only when Marduk took his place again.

Minos

Greek hero

Protected by the gods

With the help of the gods, Minos was the inventor of a just and austere civilisation.

Minos was the son of Zeus, who had taken the form of a bull in order to impregnate Europe. He was brought up by Asterius, the king of Crete, His wife was called Pasiphaë and his brothers were Sarpedon and Rhadamanthys. Phaedra was to be his daughter. Minos was a hard man, just and haughty. Since he knew he had the support of the gods, he was sure of himself and intractable. His ambitions were great and his courage exemplary.

Minos was handsome, strong and attractive. Women fell into his arms wherever he went: Scylla, the daughter of the king of Megara was one; Periboea, an Athenian who was fated to be sacrificed was another; and there were many more. He was also interested in young boys, and he was the inventor of pederasty. Pasiphaë was furious about his indiscretions and decided to take her revenge by casting a spell on him. From that day on, all his conquests would be devoured by scorpions and serpents which would come from his sperm.

When Asterius died, Minos ousted his brothers, sent them into exile and claimed power, saying that the gods had decreed that it was his destiny — the proof being that his prayers were always granted. Thus he prayed to Poseidon to bring a bull out of

the sea so that he could sacrifice it to him. His prayer was immediately granted, and so the throne was given to him without discussion. The bull remained the talisman of Cretan royalty.

The Minotaur

Poseidon's bull was a handsome beast. He charmed Minos, who did not want to lose him. He put the bull into his herd and hastily sacrificed another animal which was more ordinary and of far less worth. Poseidon was angry and gave the bull an alarming streak of savagery and made it the object of Pasiphaë's insuppressible desires.

She did not know how to satisfy her passion and asked Daedalus for help. He made her a heifer of wood and leather into which she could climb and thus present herself to the bull. The fake was so perfect that the bull was fooled and they mated. From this union was born the Minotaur, a monster with a bull's head and a man's body.

Minos was frightened. What was he to do with this mad and violent animal in the city? He decided to shut it away. He had Daedalus build an immense palace, made up of such a great number of rooms and linking corridors that no one could ever find the way out. The Minotaur was master of this labyrinth and guarded its secrets. He ran the length of its long paths and exercised his cruelty there.

Each year Minos gave the monster a sacrificial offering of seven young women and seven young men to eat, but Theseus managed to put an end to this carnage.

Sovereignty of the seas

Minos had the reputation of being a good, gentle and just king. He was a respected and feared master. His decisions were irrevocable and his notable laws were cited

---

Knossos the Great

'Knossos, a great city where Minos, who was the close friend of great Zeus, ruled for nine years.' (*Odyssey*, XIX, 178)

*The palace of Knossos in Crete, the kingdom of **Minos**. The bull is the national emblem there. Its imposing symbolic horns, which are very much in evidence throughout the country, can be seen.*

South propylaeum, late Minoan, 1700–1400 BC. The horns are a reconstruction.

in many lands. It is true that they were directly inspired by Zeus, whom Minos consulted every nine years in the cave of Ida, where the king of Olympus was brought up. His royalty was of divine origin and his exercise of it also bore the stamp of the gods. Minos cleared the region of the pirates who infested it. He had a powerful army, a recognized authority and an uncontested supremacy. He imposed his laws and his peace on the islands of the Aegean Sea and spread Cretan civilisation far beyond the frontiers.

His reign was marked by various military expeditions. He went away to avenge the murder of his son Androgeus; he captured the town of Megara because of the betrayal of the king's daughter, Scylla, whom he had seduced; and he ruthlessly subdued Athens following an epidemic of plague which the city had suffered. He made the Athenians responsible for the delivery of the seven young women and seven young men demanded by the Minotaur.

Meanwhile, Daedalus, the ingenious builder, had fled Crete and gone to hide

with King Cocalus of Sicily. Minos came after him with his entire army. He met the king but did not find Daedalus. He then had the idea for a trick: he challenged everyone to pass a thread through the spiral of a snail's shell. No one could do it. The king, however, said that someone in his palace would manage the feat. It was Daedalus who attached the thread to an ant, which he sent round the spiral of the snail's shell.

Daedalus was discovered. In order to escape from Minos he suggested to the daughters of Colacus that they prepare the Cretan king a bath. They did so and drowned Minos while he was in it. Thus, the first king of Crete died, and it was said that he became a judge in hell.

The judge of Hell

'I saw Minos, the illustrious son of Zeus, sitting on a throne, a golden sceptre in his hand, giving judgment to the dead.' (*Odyssey*, XI, 572)

Mithra

Indo-European god

The friend

Mithra was a sovereign god. His mission was to reward men and distribute favours.

Mithra (or Mitra in the Vedas), held the sovereignty with Varuna. Serenity was one of his qualities while coercion and violence belonged to Varuna. Mithra personified friendship, benevolence and non-hostility. He watched over contracts and agreements and opened the way for compromise. The harmony in the world was due to him.

In the *Avesta*, Mithra is closely associated with the sun. He rose before it, standing in his chariot to which were harnessed two white horses. As the god of a thousand eyes and a thousand ears, he embraced the universe. Nothing escaped him. As a fighting god he was to be seen at the head of armies, armed with a long spear and swift arrows, or even as a judge in hell. He was also, perhaps, represented as bringing the dead back to life at the end of time.

The mysteries of Mithra

In the brand of Mithraism which spread across the Roman Empire during the first centuries of our own era, Mithra appeared as a 'killer of the bull'. He was invincible and was depicted subduing a bull by holding its nostrils and plunging a sword into its body. A dog and a snake drank the blood which poured from the wound, while a scorpion gripped the beast's testicles. 'From the dying body of the victim were born all the herbs and beneficial plants. From his spinal chord grew the wheat which would become bread and from his blood came the vine which produced the sacred beverage of the mysteries' (*F. Cumont*).

Mithraism was a religion of salvation, for Mithra did not die. Certain pictures of him show him behind the sun's chariot, rising up to heaven to perform the last judgment and the resurrection of the body.

Mithraism was a religion of small groups. The faithful would gather together in caves or in buildings like caves. There they celebrated the cult, which consisted of a meal commemorating the feast eaten by Mithra and the sun after the creation of the world. A bull may have been sacrificed at this meal.

As an initiatory religion, Mithraism consisted of seven levels through which its followers must pass: the crow, the griffin, the soldier, the lion, the Persian, the courier and the father. At each stage there were corresponding masks, insignia and functions such as serving the drink or burning incense.

Mithraism was enormously successful in the Roman Empire. It was introduced by soldiers and reached the highest ranks of society. Emperor Commodus was himself initiated.

The religion of Mithra flourished until the 5th century and spread from Rome as far as the north of England, the shores of the Rhine and the Danube, and Syria and Egypt.

Guardians of the earth
'Mitra [. . .] makes men organize themselves. Mitra has borne the earth and sky for all time. Mitra observes [. . .] human establishments'. (*Rig Veda*, III, 59, 1)

The Avesta
The *Avesta* is the holy book of Mazdaism and has texts which, without a doubt, date back to the 5th or 6th century BC. Along with the Hindu Veda, it is one of the most important accounts of Indo-European tradition.

Modimo

African god

Supreme being

Modimo was invisible and inaccessible as well as being ambiguous.

Modimo, originally from Zimbabwe, was the creator. He distributed good things, appeared in the east and belonged to the element of 'water'. At the same time he was a destroyer, a terrifying monster responsible for drought, hail, cyclones and earthquakes. When these things happened he appeared in the west and was part of the element 'fire'. Modimo was also sky and light, earth and root.

Modimo was unique and singular. He had no ancestors, no past or future. He pervaded the whole of creation. His name was taboo and could be spoken only by priests or seers.

Modimo could be reached only by imperfect beings, called the Badimo. They, however, were very volatile and, if they were forgotten, became very malicious. Small children, imperfect because they were still incomplete, were also able to talk to Modimo.

Moerae/Parcae

Greek and Roman goddesses

The Fates

The Moerae were the personification of inflexible law.

There were three Moerae—Atropos, Clotho, and Lachesis—all daughters of Zeus and Themis. Their authority was over everyone, from the greatest to the most humble, from the most ancient to the youngest, and from the strongest to the weakest.

The first spun a thread which signified birth. The second unravelled the thread, symbolizing the unravelling of life. The third cut the thread, and this was death. They were resolute and blind, and they determined the hours of beginning and ending. They were the destiny which constituted the history of each day.

They also signified the limit which could not be overstepped. They were connected with their sisters, the Erinnyes, who punished crime. They represented violent death and punishment. They followed the fortunes of war, as well as accidents and illnesses, and imbued them with their own wishes.

In Rome they were assimilated to the Parcae, who were originally birth demons. They were represented in the Forum and called the three Fates.

> **Fate**
> 'This is the ancient law, the law of Cronos [. . .]. Divine woman, what has been done cannot be undone. The Moerae gave your son such a destiny on the day itself when you gave birth to him.' (Athena's words to a woman whose son went blind, *Hymn for the Bath of Pallas*, 100–105)

Monsters

Fantastic beings

The unyielding ones

Monsters, opposed as they were to order, were enemies to be vanquished.

Polyphemus, Geryon, the Minotaur, Leviathan, the Sphinx, Hydra, the Unicorn, Python, Centaurs, the Cyclopes, Gorgons, Titans, dragons, sirens and vampires — were all kinds of monsters. They came in all shapes and with every imaginable degree of strength. They are found in all mythologies as wild, unmanageable forces destined for lowly tasks and clinging to that despite every difficulty.

In general, they were a mixture of two living creatures. In the case of the Minotaur, the mixture was bull and man. It was horse and man for the Centaur and woman and fish for the sirens. Dragons had the claws of a lion, the wings of a bird and a serpent's tail. Sometimes they had only one unusual characteristic: a Cyclops, for instance, had only one eye in the middle of its forehead,

and the unicorn had only a single horn on its forehead.

A primitive force

Monsters represented irrational forces. They were misshapen, close to primal chaos and possessed something of the initial power which preceded creation. The first life often came from a monster, and it seems to be there to remind us that there is still much to do to ensure the reign of order.

Guardian

Since they were stubborn, monsters were often made guardians of treasure, in the knowledge that they would never shy away from their task. They guarded such treasure as the Golden Fleece, the gold of the Nibelungen or immortality. They were there to measure and to stimulate the effort necessary for the acquisition of property, whatever its importance.

Death and resurrection

Finally, as a sign of resurrection, monsters symbolized the death necessary for new life, destruction before paradise, night before day. They were the rough, painful and anarchical energy which preceded and produced creation and order.

Fafnir

Fafnir, a Scandinavian dragon, was the personification of lust for gold, which is stupid and profitless.

Fafnir killed his father, Hreidmar, and drove away his brother Regin, in order to get hold of the 'Rhinegold'. He loved this treasure dearly and lay down on it, turning himself into a dragon to frighten anyone who dared to come near.

Regin, however, incited Sigurd to fight and kill Fafnir. Before he died, the monster told his killer magic secrets: the dragon's blood gave him the power to understand the language of the birds and, through them, to find out about the evil intentions of Regin rowards him. Sigurd killed Regin, drank the blood of the two brothers and ate Fafnir's heart. (*Fafnismal*)

The raging dragon

'The wave approaches, breaks and pours into our eyes,

Among the foaming waves, there is a furious monster.

His forehead is wide and armed with menacing horns

His whole body is covered in yellowing scales;

Untameable bull, raging dragon,

Its hindquarters bend in twisting curves'.

(Racine, *Phèdre*, V, 6)

Muses

Greek goddesses

Divine singers

The Muses' vocation was to inspire poets and promote the arts.

There were nine Muses, the daughters of Zeus and Mnemosyne (Memory). Each of them had her own domain. Calliope's was epic poetry, Clio's history and Polyhymnia's mime. Euterpe's was the flute, Terpsichore's dance and Erato's lyric art. Melpomene's was tragedy, Thalia's comedy and Urania's astronomy.

They delighted the gods and inspired poets. They favoured communication and gave birth to dialogue.

The Muses created what they sang about. By praising the gods, they completed their glory; by boasting of valiant warriors, they wrote their names in history. In this way they collaborated in the ordering of the world and discredited those they forgot.

The disciples of Pythagoras celebrated the Muses as the keepers of the knowledge of harmony and the principles of the universe which allowed access to the everlasting gods.

Apollo's companions

[. . .] 'Jupiter gave them to Apollo as companions so that they would constantly surround him and direct their concerts on Parnassus, their usual residence.' (Emile Henriot, *Mythologie légère* (Light Mythology), Paris 1957)

Narcissus

Greek hero

The love of self

Narcissus was the symbol of self-love.

Narcissus was the son of the god Cephisus and the nymph Leiriope. The seer Teiresias foretold that the child would live to a ripe old age as long as he never looked at himself.

Narcissus was exceptionally handsome and boys and women all stared at him. He was unaware of all this and continued on his way without even turning his head. He spent his time hunting and cared for no one but himself. Ameinias, his friend, killed himself in despair, and those who were in love with him were disheartened and cried for vengeance. Even the nymph Echo faded away.

Nemesis decided to avenge the victims of this handsome but indifferent man. One very warm day, Narcissus, who was worn out and thirsty, leaned over a spring to drink from it. Seeing his reflection in the water, he immediately fell madly in love with what he saw; he went closer to the object of his love, he lost his balance and drowned. From his body was born the flower which bears his name (Ovid, *Metamorphoses* III, 339–510). Narcissus died because he did not want to give himself to others.

Nemesis

Greek goddess

Moderation

As the instrument of divine vengeance, Nemesis fought against **hubris**, *(excess of every sort).*

Nemesis was the daughter of Night. From her union with Zeus were born the Dioscuri and Helen, the cause of the Trojan War.

Nemesis ruled over the distribution of wealth. She looked after balance, took revenge on arrogance and punished excess. She also condemned excesses of happiness, riches and power — indeed, of everything which threatened the equilibrium of the world and upset the order required by fate.

She put people in their place and led Croesus, who was too happy and powerful, into an ill-fated expedition against Cyrus.

Rhamnus kept the most famous of the temples dedicated to Nemesis. He testified to the immoderate behaviour of the Persians, who were very confident of a victory over the Athenians. Nemesis prevented them from seizing the city, and, in a block of marble brought to celebrate the victory, Phidias sculpted a statue of the goddess.

> **Moderation**
> 'Know your human state and its limits, do not expose yourself by excess to the venegeance of divine Nemesis.' (Socrates)

Nephthys

Egyptian goddess

Sterility

Nephthys cared for the dead and protected them.

Nephthys, the wife of Seth, god of evil and the sworn enemy of Osiris, was also the sister of Isis, Osiris's wife. She took sides with Osiris against her own husband. When he was vanquished, killed and torn to pieces, the pieces were scattered throughout the world. Nephthys helped to find the bits of his body, put them back together again and bring him back to life. She took part in the funeral lamentations required by his death and performed the ritual acts which made the miracle take place.

She was very close to Osiris and Isis. She was said to be the mistress of Osiris, an inconstant husband. Isis, the goddess of love and charm, complained bitterly about this. Nephthys's history is mixed up with theirs, and her name is always associated with theirs.

With Isis, Nephthys was the guardian of the tomb. One was placed at the head of the dead person, the other at the foot. She was called 'the lady of the castle'. Since she was always associated with other goddesses, Nephthys does not appear to have had her own cult. She was worshipped in Kôm Mer, in Upper Egypt.

Nergal

Babylonian god

Master of hell

Nergal presided over war, epidemics and disasters, all of which brought him new subjects.

Nergal was the son of Enlil, the god of heaven. His father gave men to him, and he determined their fate. He was a fearsome warrior and carried a bow and arrows. His ambition was to be the strongest wherever he was.

Arrogant, violent and impetuous, Nergal was likened to a wild bull. He loved catastrophes, epidemics and war and was compared to a hurricane or flood. Death was his kingdom, so he looked for it, caused it and spread it. He made death his personal territory.

The mastery of hell

Ereshkigal, the daughter of Anu, built herself an independent and terrible kingdom in hell. The gods themselves could enter it only after being stripped of their dignity. Because of this condition, they became her subjects and took the risk of being kept prisoner.

In this way, Ereshkigal had cut herself off from her peers to the extent that she could not take part in the celestial banquet. She did send a messenger, however, to fetch her share. Nergal refused to sit down in the assembly of the gods with this emissary from beyond the tomb. Ereshkigal was angered by this, demanding an apology from the insolent god.

Nergal, however, did not shy away from this. He went to hell, escorted by fourteen demons who allowed him to pass safely through the seven gates of the infernal world. When he reached the mistress of this place he showed himself in all his radiance:

he was courteous, likeable, amusing and well behaved. He did this to such an extent and so well that he charmed the beautiful woman, seduced her and then, without any warning, returned home.

Ereshkigal did not take kindly to this. She had been misled and wanted to punish the despicable creature. She sent a missive to Anu and demanded that Nergal return so that he could be put to death. She threatened the world with the greatest calamities if she did not obtain satisfaction.

And so Nergal went once again to hell; this time, though, he had no hope of returning. This state of affairs, however, stimulated his violent streak and his strength: if he had to stay in hell he would be master of it. When he reached Ereshkigal he seized her by the hair and threw her to the ground. She asked for mercy and promised to marry her aggressor if he would let her go. Through this marriage, Nergal would acquire Ereshkigal's power had in the underworld.

Nergal accepted the bargain and from being cruel, he became tender. He took the queen in his arms, married her and became the king of hell. He was a terrifying leader, in command over the infernal gods and reigning over the people of the dead— twilight creatures clothed in feathers and feeding on earth (*Nergal and Ereshkigal*).

Erra

We next see Nergal under the name of Erra, a satisfied husband resting on the conjugal bed. Tired from lack of sleep, tempted by drunkenness and incapable of taking a decision, he let his presence be forgotten and the world lived in complete calm. Men and animals multiplied to excess. Nature could not supply enough food for everything that lived. Everywhere there was excess and immoderation.

However, there were still the Sibitti.

Nergal, a solar deity, became the god of the underworld and the dead. His breath was the wind in the desert, and the bull of the skies helped him in his work of destruction. Relief in terracotta from Kish. Babylonian art. 2000 BC.

They were infernal gods, faithful servants of Erra, always ready for battle and exasperated by silence. The life in a city did not suit them: their weapons were covered in cobwebs and their daggers were getting rusty from a lack of throats to slit. They wanted some action, some fighting and carnage. They aspired to the rough life of campaigns and the glory of victory. Because of this, the Sibitti came to shake Erra and urged him to give his war cry.

The god of evil

At the sound of this cry, gods and men were panic-stricken and the mountains, sea and forests were distressed. Erra worked out a vast plan for death and bloodshed. He wanted to destabilize the world which was living in excess, overturn its customs, destroy its foundations, kill the majority and disturb the order the gods wanted.

The conquest of hell

'Inside the palace he seized Ereshkigal and dragged her by the hair from her throne to the ground, ready to cut off her head. Do not kill me, my brother, I have something to say to you. Nergal listened to her and let her go. She cried in all humility: be my husband, and I will be your wife. Let me make you king of the great earth and place the tablet of knowledge in your hands. You will be master, I will be mistress.' (Nergal and Ereshkigal)

None of this would be possible unless he could make Marduk, the protector of the city, 'rise up from his seat'. Erra acted with cunning. He made the god believe that he, Erra, alone could bring back lustre to Marduk's statue, which had been tarnished for a long time. (The god's statue in the temple was the symbol of royalty.) Marduk did not want anything to do with this; he remembered once before having risen from his seat and thus causing the flood. He saw the danger inherent in his departure and weighed the importance of his responsibilities. He hesitated.

Erra took advantage of this hesitation. He was insistent, answering all Marduk's objections and promising that he himself would soundly maintain the balance between heaven and earth, prevent demons coming up from hell and make sure that the temple was guarded by the gods Anu and Enlil. He swore that nothing would change and that all would live in peace and prosperity.

Little by little, Marduk was reassured, and eventually he accepted. He rose, left and went to the dwelling-place of the gods, leaving Erra in charge of the place. Erra kept his promises for some time. He kept quiet, and men and gods took advantage of the peace. Events continued to follow their natural course.

And then Erra broke out. The temples were profaned, inhabited places became deserts, rogues had access to the palaces of princes, sons hated their fathers and mothers hated their daughters, lame men ran faster than normal ones, young people were buried by the old and man ate man. All values were turned upside down and no one could escape death. Savagery reigned.

Eventually Erra got his temple back and order was returned. (*The Epic of Erra*).

The reign of Erra

'Whoever knows nothing of weapons will have his dagger unsheathed, whoever knows nothing of projectile weapons will have an arrow in his bow, he who knows not combat will engage in battle, he who cannot run will fly like a bird, the weak will overtake the swift, and the crippled will surpass the strong.' (*The Epic of Erra*, tablet IV, 1–3)

Ninurta

Sumerian god

War

A young warrior, Ninurta was made champion of the gods in the struggle for power.

Ninurta was the son of Mah, or Mami, 'the goddess of every shape', and Enlil, the sovereign god. He was big, strong, young, brave and heroic.

The fight against Anzu

When Anzu stole the tablets of destiny, the symbols of sovereignty, Enlil was naked and the world disrupted. The gods gathered together to find a champion who would fight Anzu. They were, however, filled with foreboding and declined to judge.

Mah brought her son, glorious Ninurta, and explained the plan which he was to follow. He should disguise his lovely features behind those of a demon and hide himself in a thick fog, so that when he shot his arrows his adversary would be taken by surprise.

Ninurta climbed the mountain, surrounded by the seven evil winds, and arrived in the presence of Anzu. The situation seemed to be reversed; the god was dark and enveloped in mists while the demon was full of the light which would give him the stolen destiny. Anzu roared like a lion and said to him, 'Who are you, young and presumptuous one? Show your face and make yourself known.'

Ninurta told him the names of those who had sent him, and Anzu gnashed his teeth. Darkness fell on the mountain and the champion of the gods shot his arrows. However, Anzu, the keeper of destiny, cried, 'Reed which comes towards me, return to your planting-ground' (*The Myth*

of Anzu, II, 60), and the arrow turned and went back.

Ninurta sent a messenger to tell Enlil what had happened. Enlil replied with some advice: 'Throw the seven evil winds against Anzu so that he is caught in the gale. Let his wings fall to his side, for then he is prevented from speaking. At that moment cut off his wings and shoot your arrows.'

Ninurta 'shuddered and shook but walked towards the mountain' (*The Myth of Anzu*, II, 145). He acted according to the instructions he had been given. 'The terror he inspired brought the bravest to the ground. He disturbed Anzu and cut his throat' (*ibid.*, III, 20). Once again the divine offices were performed by their rightful holders, and the tablets of destiny were returned to Enlil's keeping.

Lord of copper

Ninurta was the champion of order against chaos, of civilization against the savage life, of organization against crude and blind force. His adversary then was Kur, the cosmic, ill-shaped mountain. This latter made an array of stones rise up in order to invade the world.

Ninurta was also the *deus faber*, the craftsman god who made the instruments of civilization from the base matter and metal from minerals.

The champion of the gods

'I will praise Ninurta, the glorious, beloved of Mami, the strong one who was Enlil's firstborn, the progenitor of Ekur, first of the six hundred gods, the support of Eninnu, protector of the fold, watchman of house, street and town; an expert in fighting who twirls his sash; valiant, he is the conqueror of ferocious enemies. Tireless, his attack inspires fear. I want to sing the praises of his omnipotence.' (*The Myth of Anzu*, II)

Niobe

Greek heroine

The lady of stone

Niobe was a jealous mother, proud of her children who insulted Leto, the mother of Apollo and Artemis.

Niobe was the daughter of Tantalus and the wife of Amphion, the king of Thebes. Her marriage was a particularly happy one. Amphion, the son of Zeus, was an artist and drew such harmonious sounds from his lyre that the stones themselves moved, touched by the beauty of the melodies. In this way Amphion took part, by means of his musical instrument, in the building of the walls of Thebes.

Niobe, a fertile mother, brought seven sons into the world: Sipylus, Eupinytus, Ismenus, Damasichthon, Agenor, Phaedimus and Tantalus. She also had seven daughters: Ethodaea, Cleodoxa, Astyocha, Phthia, Pelopia, Astycratia and Ogygia. The children were 'blooming with youth', happy with life, strong and beautiful. What more could a mother hope for?

So proud of her offspring was Niobe 'with the lovely hair' that she ended up scorning mothers who had but a few children. She believed herself to be, and said that she was, superior to them. The arrogance of her father, Tantalus, still lived on in her. When

---

Niobe's torture

'I have been told of the end of the Phrygian woman, my blood relation, Niobe, the daughter of Tantalus, on the summit of Mount Sipylus. Just like the ivy which bound her, a covering of stone imprisoned her limbs; it is said that the rain and snow incessantly ravaged her exhausted flesh and that endless tears flow from her eyes down her neck. The destiny which will lay me in the tomb is like this.'
(Sophocles, *Antigone*, 822 ff.)

---

she was informed that homage was paid to Leto, she ordered that she, Niobe, should be worshipped also: 'Leto has had only two children, Apollo and Artemis, while I have had seven times as many. Leto was nothing but a wanderer, whereas I am a queen. Leto was poor whereas I am rich and powerful.'

Leto's revenge

Leto 'with the beautiful cheeks' heard these insolent words. As a goddess daughter of a Titan, beloved of Zeus and mother of two great Olympians, she could not bear such insults; she asked Apollo and Artemis to help her in her quest for revenge.

Leto's children came down from Olympus and went inside the palace where Niobe ruled. Apollo shot down the seven sons with his arrows. The seven daughters were killed by Artemis 'who shoots arrows'. In this way, 'although there were only two children of Leto, they killed all Niobe's children' (*Iliad*, XXIV, 604). The mother who was so sure of herself watched those children, of whom she was so proud, die.

As if this death was not enough, Zeus turned the hearts of the Thebans into stone so that the corpses of the children remained lying in their own blood, without any burial, for nine long days. Niobe wept for their disgrace and, as a sign of mourning and grief, refused all food.

At the dawn of the tenth day, the gods themselves, considering that vengeance had been exacted, started to bury the bodies. Niobe then broke her fast, but as she had lost all reason for living she withdrew to her father, on Mount Sipylus.

She was turned into stone and continued to suffer the torments inflicted on her by the gods. It is said that her eyes still weep for her children, and there is a stone, said to have been Niobe, from which an inexhaustible and abundant spring flows.

Njord

Norse god

The fertile shores

Njord was the first of the Vanir and dealt with fertility and fecundity.

As god of beginnings and of the earth, Njord was the father of Freyr and Freyja. His kingdom was the seashore where fishing took place, and thus he provided food and prosperity.

Njord married Skadi, whose realm was the mountains. Njord, however, could not bear the baying of the wolves, and Skadi could not bear the screeching of the gulls. Each of them felt very ill at ease in the other's territory and spent the greater part of the year in their own.

Tired of fighting each other, the Aesir and the Vanir each won in turn, made peace and exchanged hostages. The Vanir handed over the best of their men, Njord.

Njord succeeded Odin, and the Sviar called him their lord. Under his reign there was 'perfect peace and such good years that the Sviar believed that Njord was in command of the rich seasons and the wealth of men' (*Ynglinga Saga*, IX).

Njord was equated with Nerthus, a goddess whose name means 'earth-mother'. She was worshipped in an island's sacred wood.

> **The best of the gods**
> 'It is my consolation that I have been far from here, as a hostage sent to the gods. I have had a son who is hated by no one and who is considered the prince of the Aesir.'
> (*Lokasenna*, XXXV)

Norns

Norse goddesses

Fate

The Norns were virgins and decided the destiny of men at their birth.

There were three Norns: Urdr, who represented the past; Verdandi, the present; and Skuld, the future. They lived at the foot of Yggdrasil, the cosmic tree.

The Norns decided the fates of men and gods without reason or interest. 'You cannot outlive by a single evening the sentence of the Norns' (*Hamdismal*, verse 30). They dealt out as much good as evil. 'No one judges the decrees of Urdr, lest they be wrongly rendered' (*Fjölvinnsmal*, verse 47).

From birth the Norns appeared in the form of the Dies, or Disir. They determined the strength, intelligence and luck which would be given to each newborn child. Thus they forged the destiny of every individual, every clan and every nation.

On the field of battle they were associated with the Valkyries who chose warriors who were to be killed.

> **Fate**
> 'From there came three virgins, schooled in many things. All three came from the sea set under the tree, and they make laws and fix the lives of the sons of men and the destiny of mortals.' (*Volupsa*, verse 20)

Nymphs

Greek goddesses

The grace of nature

Nymphs were young women who symbolized the beauty and charm of springs, woods and the whole of nature.

Their cult did not lend itself to big public demonstrations, but they were still very popular. They were close to people and were worshipped without the intermediation of priests. Their shrines, nymphaeas, were no more than a place — spring, wood, rock, or fountain — which was linked with them and which peasants were able to decorate as they wished.

For the most part, the nymphs were daughters of Zeus and lived in caves. They spun and sang and were part of the entourage surrounding certain great deities, such as Artemis. They were not immortal, but their lives lasted several centuries.

The Melias were the oldest. They were born from the drops of blood which fell from the wound of the castrated Uranus. They lived in ash trees and, because of their bloody origins, ash wood was used for making spears. Naiads lived in springs and streams of water and were daughters of Zeus. They had the skills of healing but, since they were ambivalent, they could also transmit disease. The Nereids were the nymphs of calm seas, Oreads those of the mountains, Dryads those of woods and the Oceanids those of the sea.

As young, beautiful and seductive women, nymphs had many lovers: Pan, Priapus, satyrs and, generally speaking, all who dwelt in nature like them. Even the great gods were not impervious to their charms, with Zeus, Apollo, Hermes and Dionysus all succumbing to them. Sometimes they sought out young boys. Thus, moved by Hylas's beauty, they kidnapped him from Hercules and dragged him down to the bottom of their spring.

Nymphs, who were dark powers, were formidable. Their beauty could itself lead to madness. At midday they provoked sudden terror.

Nymphs were considered to be secondary divinities whose powers were limited.

The Nereids, *nymphs of the sea, personified the movement of the waves and the pleasant aspects of the sea.*

Metope from a shrine to Hera, discovered at the mouth of the Sele (near Paestum). 6th cent. BC. art.

142

Odin

Norse god

Fury

Master of wisdom and the occult sciences, Odin was the god of poets, sages, those who have trances, and warriors.

Odin, also called Odhinn, Wotan or Woden, was a grand old man, one-eyed and bearded. He wore an old threadbare robe of many colours and a wide-brimmed hat. He also wore a golden ring called *Draupnir*, and from it every ninth night a new ring came, which was just as beautiful as the first one. His weapon was a spear called *Gungnir*, which was made by the dwarves. His horse, *Sleipnir*, had eight legs and galloped through the air and on the ocean as well as on solid ground.

Three women were connected with Odin: Jord, the earth of origins; Frigg, the inhabited earth; and Rind, the earth which has again become uncultivated. Thus Odin incorporated the whole world. Of his three wives, Frigg was his favourite. She sat with Odin on the high seat, *Hlidskjalf*, from which the entire universe could be seen and heard.

Odin was called Rafnagaud, the 'god with the ravens' — two ravens, in fact, which sat on his shoulders. They were called Huginn and Munninn and flew across the world to see and listen to what was happening. They then came back to whisper in Odin's ear all they knew; thus, he was the keeper of all knowledge.

Odin was impetuous and wine was his only nourishment. He represented the frenetic and uncontrollable forces which take possession of the lover at the moment of orgasm, the poet in the middle of his composition, the priest in his trances and the savage warrior in the midst of battle. He was the power of instinct and the excess of rage which gives superhuman strength.

Sly and cynical, he inspired the deceit which fools enemies and the cunning which brings victory. He knew how to blind his adversary and paralyze him with fear. He loved intrepid warriors and, along with the Valkyries, chose those on the battlefield who would have a glorious death. He then took them with him to his Valhalla where they lived happily, feasting and fighting each other without doing any harm, while they waited for the battle of the last day. He was also Valfadir, the father of those who have been killed.

Mocking suffering, he accepted it for himself and caused others to suffer, without a trace of emotion. Odin loved power and influence. He was cruel and fond of human sacrifices, particularly those of kings, which reaffirmed his pre-eminence.

Odin was sovereign. 'He is the first and oldest of the Aesir; he reigns over all things and, although the other gods are powerful, they all serve him as children serve their father' (*Gylfaginning*, XIX). Odin's power knew no limits.

The murder of Ymir

'Ymir was very wicked, just like all his relations' (*Gylfaginning*, IV).

The sons of Bor—Odin, Vili, and Ve—killed Ymir. They took him away and from his flesh made the earth, from his blood the sea and lakes. From his bones they made the mountains, and from his teeth they made the piles of stones and pebbles. They

> **The unjust**
> 'Be quiet, Odin. You have never known how to share victory among men. You often gave victory to those to whom you should not have, to cowards. (*Lokasenna*, 22)

set the sea around the earth.

They also took Ymir's skull to make the sky and placed it above the earth, thereby making him the primordial being of creation. They provided a home for all firelight. 'It is said in the ancient poems of wisdom that it is since that time that night can be distinguished from day and time has been counted in years' (*Gylfaginning*, VII).

A frenzy of knowledge

Odin was a great traveller, ever up hill and down dale, and he wanted to know and understand everything. He stopped at the fountain of Mimir, about which it was said that anyone who drank from it would acquire absolute wisdom. Odin asked the guardian to give him a draught of this water to drink. 'What will you give me in exchange?', the woman asked him. Odin was prepared for anything to achieve his goal, but wisdom could not be bought with gold or silver. He therefore gave an eye so that he might truly see, and thus Odin remained blind in one eye (*Gylfaginning*, VIII).

His quest, however, did not stop there. The gods decapitated the giant, Mimir, who was famous for his knowledge, and sent his head to Odin. He carefully preserved it and, with the help of plants and magic processes, kept it in good condition. Thus he was able to consult it whenever he had some mystery to unravel.

The Ring
Richard Wagner, in *The Ring Cycle*, took certain liberties with the Norse myth. Odin, whom he calls Wotan, the powerful god of the ancients, experiences the anguish of man and hesitates constantly between love and egotism.

The quest for knowledge
'She alone sat outside when the Old One arrived, the fierce Aesir who looked into her eyes: 'What do you ask of me? Why are you putting me to the test? I know, Odin, where you have hidden your eye: in the glorious wells of Mimir. Mimir drinks mead every morning from (the eye) the pledge of Odin.'
(*Voluspa*, 28)

During the banquet which concluded the war between the Aesir and the Vanir, the gods spat in turn into a receptacle. From this ritual spittle came Kvasir a creature of astounding wisdom. He went all over the world to teach men wisdom. When he reached two dwarves called Fjalar and Galar, they killed him and spilled his blood. From a mixture of this and honey they made mead, a magical drink which gave whoever drank it the gifts of the poet and scholar.

After all sorts of incidents, the mead ended up in the hands of the giant Suttung, who gave it to his daughter Gunnlöd to look after. During this time, Odin was still travelling. He reached a place where nine of Suttung's slaves were reaping hay. He suggested that they sharpen their scythes, and the slaves were so astonished at the results that they tried to seize the grindstone. Odin threw it into the air and they went after it in such a way that they all beheaded each other with their scythes. Odin then offered to do the work of nine men and asked for a draught of the mead in payment.

Suttung refused, and Odin immediately bored a hole in the mountain. Then, transforming himself into a serpent in order to crawl into the hole, he came to the place where Gunnlöd was. He slept with her for three nights and she promised him three draughts of mead. In three draughts he emptied the three casks. Then he transformed himself into an eagle and flew away as fast as he could. When the Aesir saw the eagle arriving they set out basins. Odin spat out the mead but lost some of it behind him. No great importance was attached to it, however, as it was the portion for second-rate poets. (*Skaldskaparmal*, I)

The inventor of runes

Odin discovered runes, sacred writing which allowed thought to be set down and passed on. In order to do this, he hung from 'the tree which is battered by the winds, for nine whole nights' (*Havamal*, 138), pierced by a spear. Without having eaten or drunk, he picked up the runes, shouting.

Then he 'began to develop and know, to increase and prosper' (*Havamal*, 141). He carved wood and engraved runes.

Odysseus/Ulysses

Greek hero

The crafty one

A rare talent for knowing what to do and what to say enabled Odysseus to triumph during his travels.

Odysseus was the son of Anticleia and of Laertes, the king of Ithaca. It was said that, like Achilles, he was the pupil of the centaur Cheiron in his youth. During a hunt when he was young, he was wounded in the knee. Her was destined to keep the scar from this wound all his life.

On reaching adulthood, he received the throne of Ithaca and tried to marry Helen. But there was a considerable number of suitors, and Odysseus ended up marrying Penelope, the cousin of Helen and the daughter of Icarus. However, wishing to help Helen's father, he gave him the idea of demanding an oath from her suitors. By virtue of this oath, each of Helen's suitors had to defend the one she chose. This oath was to prove to be the cause of the Trojan War.

Telemachus, Odysseus's son, was still a child at the start of this war. Odysseus was hesitant about setting out for it. He went as far as feigning madness in order to avoid this trial, but his ruse was discovered by Palomedes. He therefore put all his enthusiasm into the battle and trapped Achilles, who had concealed himself among the daughters of Lycomedes. Odysseus turned out to be one of the most valiant fighters.

The Trojan War

Odysseus was among the leaders of the Achaeans. As he considered intelligence to be a warrior's most important quality, he often differed from Achilles, for whom courage was the prime quality. The ability of Odysseus was to prove as useful to the cause of the Greeks as the gallantry of Achilles.

Odysseus was the diplomat. He went on a mission with Achilles, who was in conflict with Agamemnon, concluded the armistice with the Trojans, gained acceptance for the single combat between Menelaus and Paris and convinced the Greeks to remain in Troy despite their difficulties. He was also a master of war strategies: he infiltrated the Trojan camp to steal the statue of Pallas, conceived the idea of the Trojan horse and urged Helen to commit treachery.

Odysseus was a worthy warrior and performed an ever-increasing number of courageous acts. Risking his life, he protected the retreat route of his companion Diomedes, commanded the detachment which was shut up in the wooden horse, and was the first man to emerge from it. In short, he had many victims among the enemy.

The Odyssey

At the time of the army's return to Greece, Odysseus was separated by a windstorm from his companions. A long period of roaming across the Mediterranean began. To start off with, he approached the shores of Thrace, but, being repelled, he massacred all the inhabitants of the region. He spared only Apollo's priest, Maro, who thanked Odysseus by giving him twelve jars of excellent wine—wine which was destined to be of service to him later on.

He reached the territory of the Lotophagi, who received him very amicably and offered him lotuses, the fruits of their country. These fruits were so tasty that Odysseus's companions no longer wanted to leave, and he had to force them to do so.

Having reached the territory of the Cyclopes, Odysseus was on his guard. Before entering their cave, he ensured that he took with him the jars of wine. When

Polyphemus, whose territory it was, arrived on the scene, promising to devour all the intruders, Odysseus offered him wine as a token of friendship. Because of this, Polyphemus told him that he would be the last to be eaten. But, when his host asked his name, Odysseus said 'nobody'. Soon the Cyclops was intoxicated and no longer knew what he was doing. Odysseus took advantage of this opportunity to plunge a pike into his one eye and fled. The other Cyclopes who came to the aid of their comrade burst out laughing on learning that he had been attacked by 'nobody'.

Following this adventure, Odysseus approached the island of Aeolus, the master of the winds. As a sign of hospitality, Aeolus offered Odysseus a goat skin containing all the winds except the favourable breeze. But, while Odysseus was sleeping, his companions opened the goat skin and the winds escaped from it. Aeolus refused to renew his gift, arguing that the gods clearly did not want Odysseus to get back home.

The journey to the land of the Lestrigons reduced the flotilla to a single boat; King Antiphates had devoured the remaining crews. At the home of the sorceress Circe, the men were changed into animals. Hermes then came to the aid of Odysseus.

Telemachus

Telemachus, the only son of Odysseus and Penelope, had been born before the Trojan War. When Odysseus feigned madness and ploughed a field, wild-eyed, someone placed the child Telemachus in front of the plough. Odysseus stopped and thus showed that he was not mad.

The words of Odysseus to Penelope on his return

'Wife, we have both had our full measure of trials. Here, you were awaiting my return in anguish and in tears, and, as for me, Zeus and the other gods were cruelly detaining me, far removed from my native soil which I longed to see again. Now that we have both met up again in this bed which is dear to our hearts, you will have to keep good watch over the possessions which I have in this home.'
(*Odyssesy*, XXIII, 242–250)

He gave him the magic plant called 'moly', blended with the drink offered by the sorceress. This plant prevented evil from being carried out. After her defeat, Circe became conciliatory and gentle.

Circe sent Odysseus to consult with the soothsayer, Teiresias. The latter told him that he would get back home alone aboard a foreign ship and that he would have to confront suitors who had come to ask for the hand of Penelope, his wife. He left Circe, defended himself from the seductive sirens by having himself tied to the mast of the ship, braved the passage between the Symplegades (clashing rocks) and reached the island of Thrinacia. There, herds of cattle belonging to the sun were wandering. The starving sailors killed several of them, but the sun complained to Zeus, who sent a terrible wind storm. Only Odysseus, who had not eaten any oxen, escaped.

The return of Ithaca

Odysseus came ashore on Calypso's island; she fell in love with her guest. The enforced stay with the goddess lasted for ten years. Finally Hermes ordered Calypso to release Odysseus, and he reached the island of the Phaeacians on a wreck. He was warmly received by King Alcinoüs, to whom he recounted his adventures and who took him back to a secluded coast near Ithaca.

For 20 years Penelope had waited for Odysseus. Enduring the entreaties of numerous suitors, she had made them wait by saying that she would choose her new husband when she had finished weaving the shroud for Laertes, the father of Odysseus, who had withdrawn to the country to await death. But each night Penelope gained time by undoing the work she had done in the daytime. When she decided to stop hesitating, she announced that she would choose the suitor who was best able to use Odysseus's bow. Then Odysseus himself arrived at the palace, disguised as a beggar. Though Odysseus was mocked by all the presumptuous aspirants for the hand of the queen, he nevertheless obtained permission to participate in the contest. He emerged victorious and was then recognized by the scar on his knee. All that remained for him to do was to massacre the crowd of suitors.

Oedipus

Greek hero

Family ties

Oedipus was an example of how nothing can be done to change the path of destiny decided at birth.

Oedipus was the son of Laius, king of Thebes, and Jocasta.

Destiny

From the moment of his birth, Oedipus was afflicted by a curse. An oracle had foretold that the child would kill his father, marry his mother and be at the root of an endless series of misfortunes which would lead to the ruin of his family.

To avoid this catastrophe, Laius decided to abandon the child. He bored a hole through his ankles so that he could tie them together with a strap. The swelling brought on by this injury gave the child his name Oedipus ('swollen foot'). In one version of the story, Laius had servants leave the child exposed on Mount Citheron near Thebes; in another, he put him in a basket and threw him into the sea. After being abandoned, Oedipus was found, taken in by shepherds and taken to King Polybus, who had no children of his own.

The murder of the father

As he had been brought up as Polybus's son, Oedipus believed himself to be so. When he became an adult, he went to consult the Delphic oracle. He learned there of the predictions which had been made at his birth and told to his real parents. Frightened, he decided to leave Polybus, believing him to be his father, and go into voluntary exile.

As he was heading through a narrow pass on the road to Thebes, he met the entourage of King Laius. The charioteer, Polyphontes, demanded that Oedipus let them pass and killed one of his horses. Oedipus then became angry and insulted the travellers. A fight ensued and Oedipus ended up killing both the king and Polyphontes. Thus, the first part of the oracle came to pass.

The Sphinx

In Thebes, Oedipus met the Sphinx, which was a monster half lion and half woman. The Sphinx asked passers-by questions and devoured those who could not answer them. Every day the Thebans were afraid of meeting it, and they racked their brains to find the answers which would satisfy the beast and prevent it from harming them.

'What being which walks sometimes has two feet, sometimes three, sometimes four, and is least strong when it walks on four feet?' the Sphinx asked first. 'Man', replied Oedipus, 'because he crawls on four feet when he is a baby, walks on two when he is adult and, finally, walks with a stick when he is an old man.'

The Sphinx then asked: 'Who are the two sisters who engender one another, with the second, in her turn, engendering the first?' 'Day and night', replied Oedipus.

The answers, so long the pretext for the monster's tyranny, had been found. Completely distraught, the Sphinx threw herself off the rock on which she was installed and killed herself.

The marriage with the mother

For the Thebans, the death of the monster was not only a personal feat for the hero, but a deliverance which deserved recompense. Recognizing the greatness of Oedipus, they crowned him and allowed him to marry Jocasta, who had become a widow since the murder of Laius.

However, the truth was eventually found out. Oedipus still had the scars of the wounds inflicted on his feet by Laius when he was a child, and this did not go unnoticed by Jocasta. She said nothing, though, perhaps putting it down to coincidence. However, an epidemic of plague started to spread throughout the region of Thebes, and soon the whole city was infected. It was a great catastrophe and the Delphic oracle was consulted. It replied that the reason for this misfortune was that the murder of Laius had not been avenged.

The 'time bomb'

Oedipus, as a good king should, pronounced a curse against the author of this crime, not knowing that it was he, himself, who was the guilty one. Teiresias, the seer, was consulted, but he dared not tell the truth and gave forgetfulness as an excuse. Oedipus threatened him and a quarrel broke out between them. Jocasta wanted to calm them down and, to do this, called into question the clairvoyance of Teiresias. The proof was that he had foretold the murder of Laius by his son, whereas he had been killed by brigands in a narrow pass near Thebes.

Oedipus pricked up his ears at these words, and he ordered that witnesses be looked for who could give an account of the circumstances of the killing. There is no doubt that he recognized the facts, but, troubled and confused, he said nothing. The mistake was not too serious, and there was no reason he should be recognized as the guilty party.

The discovery of the truth

At that moment, the death of Polybus was announced to Oedipus, and the crown that was his by right was brought to him. The oracle's threat was therefore partly averted, for Polybus, whom he believed to be his father, had died of natural causes. All that remained was the second part of the prophecy, which foretold his marriage to his mother. To reassure Oedipus the envoys from the kingdom of Polybus told him that he was not Polybus's natural son, but a child who had been found.

Then the truth dawned. Oedipus, the son, had killed his father and married his mother. Jocasta, aghast, killed herself, and Oedipus blinded himself by piercing his own eyes. As the victim of the curse which he had uttered against Laius's murderer, he was driven from the city and took to a wandering life. He was accompanied by his daughter, Antigone, who had taken pity on him.

After many long and painful journeys, Oedipus died at Colonus. The gods, recognizing his good faith, decided that the ground where his tomb was built should be holy. (Sophocles, *Oedipus rex* and *Oedipus at Colonus*)

The myth

There are numerous versions of the myth about Oedipus. They vary somewhat, but all of them tell of an Oedipus who goes from the status of hero, master of the city and pride and salvation of men to that of outcast and cause of everyone's misfortunes. Oedipus was both innocent *and* guilty; his mistake was to have become entangled with different generations. As his father's rival for his mother, Oedipus was the ultimate in disrupters, winning his place in the sun but with the cost being an essential violation: a destruction of the previous world.

An inexorable destiny

'If it is true, alas, that I have exchanged blows with my father and killed him, but without premeditation, without knowing whom I was taking on, by what right would you blame me for an involuntary crime? And then my miserable mother, without shame you force me to remember that I have married her! Well, I will not be silent, since you have not recoiled before this sacrilegious allusion. She brought me into the world, but she knew no more than I what she was doing when she conceived, to her shame, my children.' (Sophocles, *Oedipus at Colonus*, 981–986)

Ogmios

Celtic god

Eloquence

Due to a magical link, Ogmios could draw men by their ears.

Ogmios was an old wrinkled man. He wore a lion's skin and carried a club, a bow and a quiver. He could draw or tow a large number of men attached by their ears to a fine gold chain, the end of which passed through the god's pierced tongue.

Ogmios was the eloquence which is sure of its power, the god who attracted his followers by magic. He was also the symbol of the power of the ritual word which united the world of men with the world of the gods. It was his name that was offered in blessings for one's friends and curses against one's enemies.

In Ireland, he was called Ogma and was the inventor of *ogam*, a series of magic signs whose power was so great that it could paralyze an adversary. He was also the warrior who, by the encouragement he offered, played a useful role in the battle of Mag Tured.

Likened to Heracles, who possessed incredible strength, Ogmios was more the god of the feat and single combat than of war.

A Celtic Heracles

'In their mother tongue, the Celts call Heracles "Ogmios", and they portray him in a remarkable form. He is a very old man whose head is quite bald at the front and whose remaining hair is completely white. His skin is coarse, roughened almost as much as that of old mariners; he could be taken for a Charon of underground abodes'. (Lucian of Samosata)

Ogmios with a boar on his head and surrounded by threads of pearls to which heads are attached.

Gold stater (Gaullish coin).

Orpheus

Greek hero

Poet

Orpheus, prototype of the poet, possessed the extraordinary power of enchantment.

Orpheus was the son of Oeagrus, the king of Thrace, and Calliope, the most important of the Muses. He played the lyre and cithara, sang, and was a musician and poet. He bewitched gods, men, animals, and even inanimate objects such as stones and mountains. Enchanted, even wild beasts followed him. Trees leaned over as he passed, for nature was his company.

A strange power

Orpheus took part in the expedition of the Argonauts. He was not the intrepid hero, however, strong and brave, which could be expected in such an adventure. His role was more discreet, although just as effective. Since he was too weak to handle the oars, he beat out the rhythm for the others so that their efforts were more powerful.

His power came from magic, and he could act when warriors could do nothing.

Eurydice's gesture

At first light he stopped, overcome and forgetting all, alas! He gazed on Eurydice. And there all his efforts were for nothing; the cruel king broke his bargain and thunder filled the depths — 'Who has lost me, wretched me, and you too, my Orpheus? What terrible madness . . . And see, again I part. Cruel part! Torpor quite overcomes me. And so, goodbye! I am in immense darkness, holding out my hands, hands which, alas, are no longer yours.' (Virgil, *Georgics*, 490–500)

He sang when faced with unleashed torrents and calm was restored. Using his art, he overcame the melody of the sirens, destroyed their spells and returned his companions to the straight path. He was their intermediary with the gods of Samothrace into whose mysteries he was initiated.

In this way Orpheus's art showed itself to be very useful. In extraordinary circumstances, he acted with extraordinary means. The astonishing power of song and poetry, apparently feeble and capricious, overcame assaults from warriors, the forces of nature, and the wishes of the gods.

Orpheus and Eurydice

Orpheus married the nymph Eurydice. One day she was walking by the banks of a Thracian river and she met Aristaeus, the shepherd whom the Muses had made watch over their flocks. Aristaeus found Eurydice very beautiful and immediately fell in love with her. He pursued her so relentlessly that she had to flee through the countryside. In her haste, she stood on a serpent which reared up and bit her on the calf. Eurydice died of the bite.

Orpheus was inconsolable. He decided to go and look for his wife in hell. 'At the sound of his singing, from the inmost depths of Erebus, the ghosts of the dead, transparent shadows, rose as close together as the birds amongst the leaves. (Virgil, *Georgics*, IV, 471–473) He charmed the demons by playing his lyre. Even Persephone herself was moved and took pity on a man who demonstrated, with such art, the love he bore his wife. She promised that Eurydice would return to the light, but on certain conditions: Orpheus was to walk in front of the liberated captive and at no time was he to speak to her or turn to look at her.

Orpheus accepted and started the return

The power of poetry: **Orpheus,** *inspired, enchants nature and animals.*

Roman mosaic, 4th cent. AD (detail).

Orpheus's *lamentation at the tomb of Eurydice. The poet's extreme sensitivity has been celebrated in myths throughout history.*

Gustave Moreau: oil on canvas, 1890 (detail).

Orpheus *goes to search for Eurydice in hell. Cerberus, the three-headed dog, is spellbound and Hades, in the form of a demon, lets the beloved go free.*

Miniature on vellum, Bible of the Poets, 1493.

journey, followed by Eurydice. He was overjoyed to have found her and to have brought her back to life. However, the journey was long and doubts began to grow in his mind. Had Persephone deceived him? Was his loved one really behind him? Mindful of the conditions imposed by the queen of hell, Orpheus made an effort not to turn round; however, his disbelief grew little by little

Suddenly, he could not bear it no longer and, turning his head, saw Eurydice disappear and die once again. He retraced his steps and rushed to try and enter the underworld once more. Charon stood across the road, guarding the gate, and was intractable. The rescue could not be carried out a second time, and Orpheus had to return to the world of men, bearing his sorrow.

Orpheus did not know how to keep himself under control. Because he had allowed his love for Eurydice to blot out all consideration for others, he lost the love to which he clung.

The death of Orpheus

Orpheus was inconsolable. He cried out in his suffering and wept for his beloved. He never again looked at another woman and surrounded himself with boys. It is said that he therefore invented pederasty. The Thracian women were angry with him for staying faithful to Eurydice to this extent and saw in his behaviour an insult to their beauty and charms. One day they became so angry that they pursued Orpheus, seized him, and put him to death. They tore his corpse apart and threw the pieces into the river, which carried them down to the sea.

The poet's head and lyre were found and he was given funeral honours. His tomb was to be in Lesbos, in Thessaly. In the latter city a Dionysian oracle predicted that one day, if the ashes of Orpheus were exposed to daylight, a pig would ravage the city. The inhabitants made fun of the prediction because they had no fear at all of pigs.

However, during the siesta, a shepherd

fell asleep on the tomb of Orpheus. Dreaming, he began to sing the poet's hymns. Many workers in the nearby fields ran to him and jostled against each other so much that they managed to open the sarcophagus. Night came and a violent storm erupted. The rain poured down and the river flooded the whole town, knocking over the principal monuments. The river in question was called Sys, which means 'pig'.

Orphism

Orpheus brought back from his long stay in hell a wealth of knowledge about overcoming the barrier of death, avoiding eternal damnation and reaching the land of the blest. These revelations were circulated in a great deal of literature, hymns, epics, poems, and so on, and a great intellectual movement came into existence.

There were many Orphists in the 6th century BC. They were vagabonds who travelled from city to city, offering to obtain forgiveness for everybody's sins and to lead them to salvation. The discipline of their life had several characteristics: they dressed in white, ate no meat, and refused any contact with corpses. These features were in opposition to the life of the city, and particularly the official religion in which the sacrifice of animals was an essential part of worship. The Orphists taught the immortality of the soul and the impurity of the body. Death was considered by them to be a liberation. Their thiases (groups of initiates) were to multiply throughout Greece.

The death of Orpheus

'He went, remembering Eurydice and the hollow promises of those below. He became an object of hatred and, one night, as a victim offered to the gods, hysterical women tore him to pieces and sowed his body in the fields. His head, which had been pulled away from his most pure neck, rolled to the whirling Hebrus.'
(Virgil, *Georgics*, 519–524)

Osiris

Egyptian god

Vegetation

Osiris's destiny was marked by treachery and death, but also by the exceptional love of a woman.

Osiris was the son of Nut and Geb and the brother of Isis, Nephthys and Seth. He reigned over the 'beyond'. His death and resurrection symbolized the succession of the seasons and gave mankind hope of another life. He was also the sun in its nocturnal phase when it is preparing to return, while Re was the sun in its diurnal phase when it shines brightly.

The conspiracy

As the god of vegetation, Osiris gave the fruits of the earth. As a dominant god, he taught respect for the gods and the use of rites. As a sovereign god, he provided laws and customs. Osiris travelled the whole world, spreading civilisation everywhere. He was called *Wennefer*, which means 'the eternally good being'.

These privileges and the goodness towards mankind which characterized him brought him everyone's love. Seth, his brother, therefore took umbrage. He was jealous and gathered around him 72 accomplices to hatch a plot.

The death of the god

The conspirators thought up a strategy. They managed to take Osiris's exact measurements and made a chest of precious wood, just Osiris's size. It was a richly decorated 'objet d'art' whose sole function, it appeared, was to please the eye. Then they organized a great feast. Each of the conspirators admired the chest and praised the creator of such a treasure.

Seth, whom Plutarch called Typhon, presided over the party and created its atmosphere. By way of a game, he promised to make a gift of the chest to the person who could fill it exactly with his own body. Excitedly everyone tried, but there was not one among them whose size corresponded exactly with the object.

When it came to Osiris's turn, everyone feigned astonishment. The chest was made for him; he filled it entirely with no room to spare. As if they were going to check just how exact the measurements were, the conspirators rushed up to put the lid on the chest. They did not stop at that though. They nailed, bolted and sealed what had become a coffin. They carried it in a procession to the river and sank it in the water, which took the coffin out to sea.

The quest of Isis

Isis was inconsolable at the disappearance of her husband. Sad but resolute, she wanted to find him and set about travelling the world in search of his body. She finally discovered it in the Lebanese port of Byblos, caught in a tree. She took him back to Egypt, with many adventures on the way, and there, surrounding him with the very best care, she hid him very carefully.

Seth, who was just as vindictive as ever, learned of the schemes of Isis. He worried and could find no rest until he had discovered where the body of Osiris was hidden. When he did, he seized the cadaver, tore it to bits and scattered the pieces

---

The god who is both dead and resurrected

'Osiris, you have gone away, but you have returned; you were asleep, but you have been wakened. You died; but you live again.'
(*Pyramid Texts*, 1004 ff.)

Osiris, *wearing the* **Atef** *crown of Upper Egypt, flanked with two large feathers, carries his personal emblems: the flail and the crook.*

Fresco from the tomb of Horemheb, last pharaoh of the XVIIIth Dynasty (c. 1348–1320 BC). Thebes, the Valley of the Kings.

Osiris *presides over the tribunal of the dead. They present themselves with gifts, tokens of just and pious lives, appealing to the god who will give them a new life.*

Book of the Dead. Papyrus. New Empire.

throughout the whole of Egypt. Thirteen towns received a portion.

The resurrection

Despite this, Isis did not become discouraged. She took up her search again and, with the help of Nephtys, recovered all but one of the parts of her husband's body. She put him back together again, bound his wounds, anointed him with oil and perfumes, embalmed him and did so much for him that he almost took on the appearance of a living person again. (Perhaps he was actually brought back to life, thanks to Nut, Re, Thoth or Anubis.) Whatever happened, Isis the magician managed to make Osiris father a child called Horus. Isis then hid this posthumous son of hers in the marshes of the delta while she waited for him to reach adulthood, take his rightful place on the throne and take vengeance on her enemies.

The myth of Osiris has an important significance. Osiris guaranteed the survival of kings and the succession to the throne, and henceforth the dead king was called Osiris and the reigning king, Horus.

The cult

Osiris is usually depicted wearing the Atef, a crown with two great plumes. He is a green mummy, as green is the sign of fertility. His arms are crossed over his chest and he holds the insignia of his sovereignty: the king's sceptre, the judge's whip and the staff of long life. Isis and Nephtys are on either side of him and move their wings as if they are giving him the breath of life.

Little by little, Osiris took over all the prerogatives of the other Egyptian gods. He took their place, put the worship of the sun to sleep and became a god of the sky.

The town of Abydos was honoured by elaborate festivals during which the main events in the life of Osiris were represented: his death, his burial and the revenge wreaked on his enemies. However, alongside these public demonstrations were more intimate ceremonies, organized in the back rooms of the temples.

The 'growing Osirises'

These 'mysteries' evoked the god of vegetation. They took place at the time when the waters of the floods abated on the banks of the Nile and allowed farming to begin. Little statuettes of clay mixed with grain were made. Then, when the seed germinated in a few days, the statuette grew, but it still kept the shape it had been given. These were the 'growing Osirises'.

The 'growing Osirises' were the symbols of the renewal of nature in the spring, and they also signified the rebirth of men. At his death, every Egyptian became a new Osiris, had to appear before the underworld tribunal presided over by the god himself, and received a new life. Osiris was thus the ideal funeral god.

The cult of Isis and Osiris, always directed towards obtaining salvation, spread widely throughout the Middle East. It was found even on the shores of the Rhine and in certain regions of England. In Rome, under the Empire, the *Isia* were celebrated in November. They were great ceremonies which commemorated the death and resurrection of Osiris. The cult of Osiris is often thought to be like that of Dionysus.

Ever-living Osiris

'Whether I live or die, I am Osiris. I penetrated you and I reappear through you; I wither in you and I grow in you . . . The gods live in me because I live and grow in the corn which sustains them. I cover the earth; whether I live or die, I am barley, I cannot be destroyed. I have penetrated order . . . I have become the master of order, I come out of order.' (*Text of the Sarcophagi*, 330)

Pan

Greek god

A god for the inexplicable

God of shepherds and flocks, of nature and wild beasts, Pan was the god of animal instinct.

Half man and half goat, Pan had a long wrinkled face, eyes that shone with lust and two horns on his head. The lower part of his body was that of a goat, and his feet had cloven hooves. Bearded and hairy, there was something of the beast about him.

Pan was the son of Hermes and of the daughter of Dryops. As soon as she saw him, his mother was ashamed of having given birth to such a monster, but his father quickly wrapped him up in the skin of a hare, took him to Olympus and put him beside Zeus. When the gods saw this great blunder, they burst out laughing.

Pan was the god of pastoral regions and lived in the wilderness. He was swift, always on the move, and could jump with great agility from one place to another. He had his favourite places: steep hills which he could climb with ease, springs where he could quench his thirst, or little woods where he could rest in the coolness.

Dryops, whose name means 'tress', was a descendant of King Lycaon.

Ithyphallic means 'bearing an erect penis'.

Do not disturb

'At midday we are forbidden to play the syrinx. We are afraid of Pan. Tired from the hunt, that is when he rests. He is irritable and acrid bile flows from his nostrils.' (Theocritus, *Idylls*, 1, 15–18)

There he often met shepherds and their flocks, for whom he had a weakness. They were part of his family, and he was like them. He watched over them from afar, guided and protected them as he protected the wild animals in his domain. They were part of his world, his people. They were all, in some way, his subjects.

Pan held a staff or shepherd's crook, and he played the syrinx, also known as Pan-pipes. His melodies filled the countryside and, in an almost magical way, told where the good pastures were to be found. They had an aphrodisiac effect on those who heard them and induced mating.

God of panic

Pan was ithyphallic, lascivious and debauched. He was most comfortable in the processions of Dionysus, where he added his own form of madness. He was constantly pursuing nymphs who would flee in terror. Caves rang with the cries which escaped from their lips in the course of some furtive coupling with the god. However, Pan was no less interested in boys who often satisfied his needs.

He was short-tempered and could not bear being disturbed during his siesta. This is why we have to be silent near caves in the middle of the day. One of Pan's rages is particularly well known. He was in love with the nymph Echo, who had rejected him. He was also jealous of her musical talents. As a result, he attacked anyone who got in his way, which made the shepherds furious. They therefore caught the young woman, tore her to pieces and threw her limbs, still filled with music, all around.

Perhaps it was Pan's rages—like the singing, cries and noises which surrounded him and the caves where he took refuge, all slightly irrational things—which led him to be considered responsible for the uncon-

Pan pursues the nymph Syrinx. However, just as he is about to catch her, she turns herself into the reeds which tremble in the breeze. Pan then gathers them and uses them to make a musical instrument called a syrinx.

Jean Cousin the Son (c. 1522–1594). 'Pan and Syrinx' (detail). Pen and ink drawing with brown wash.

trollable 'panics' experienced by the Greeks of antiquity. He was the god of the inexplicable.

Pan was all the more dangerous when he took possession of a being. The possessed, the *panoleptic*, took on his bearing and would wander in the wild, laugh madly for no reason, throw themselves upon the opposite sex (if not their own) or be seized by epilepsy.

Although he was the god of nature, Pan had shrines in the city. At Megalopolis he was among the principal gods, and at Olympia three altars were dedicated to him. Also, in Athens he was honoured for having played a part in the victory of Marathon.

The Romans identified Pan sometimes with Faunus and sometimes with Sylvanus, the god of groves.

Pandora

Greek heroine

The first woman

*By seduction and entrapment,
Pandora led men to their downfall.*

Men lived without women. They grew from the earth like grain. They did not know fatigue, old age, or suffering. They disappeared while they were still young, looking completely at peace, as if asleep.

Zeus, from high up on Olympus, prepared a gift for them. He had Hephaestus use earth and water to make a figurine which would have the beautiful form of the immortal goddesses. All the great gods helped: Athena taught her manual dexterity, Aphrodite taught her grace and desire, and Hermes, probably as a joke, gave her the ability to lie and deceive. This was Pandora, divine in appearance but human in reality.

Zeus made a present of her to Epimetheus, the brother of Prometheus. Epimetheus was as absent-minded as his brother was provident, as clumsy as his brother was industrious, as foolish as his brother was clever. He had, however, been warned never to accept a present from Zeus. But Pandora was so beautiful, decked out in necklaces, pearls and flowers and dressed in the most sumptuous of gowns, that he received her as a gift from heaven.

However, this woman was a snare, a trap. Henceforth man was not alone: he had to compromise with her, with her needs, her whims and her sexual appetite. He had to charm and satisfy her, make her live and honour her in order to have children. He was seduced and fascinated and found himself to be possessive, jealous and sometimes even cruel. Solidarity, harmonious understanding and peace became things of the past.

The box

Among her luggage Pandora brought a mysterious jar ('Pandora's box'), which she was forbidden to open. But once she was settled in as a wife, she was consumed with curiosity and lifted the lid, letting out all the evils. They scattered throughout the world and mixed with the good so that one could not distinguish one from the other. Suffering and disease, old age and death, lies, theft and crime spread throughout nature, towns, houses and man.

Pandora, who was frightened by this eruption of evil, quickly replaced the lid. The jar was almost empty; everything that was cruel, violent or swift had left it. All that was left, right at the bottom, was a little thing which did not take up much space. It did not leap out like the others but was calm and assured. It was hope. It remained in the jar as if afraid, as if it had no right to spread.

Pandora was a beloved evil who could be neither ignored nor tolerated. She herself embodied all the contradictions of the human condition.

> **She through whom all evil came**
> 'And in her breast, the messenger, killer of Argos, created lies; deceiving words, a deceitful heart, just as Zeus with his angry mutterings had wished. Then the herald of the gods gave her the power of speech and the name of Pandora, because that name represented all the inhabitants of Olympus who, with this gift, made a present of misfortune to mankind.' (Hesiod, *Theogony*, 79–82)

Parasurama

Indian hero

The destroyer

*Uniting religious purity and
the impurity of the warrior,
Parasurama was a Brahman
warrior.*

Kartavirya was a powerful king. He had a thousand arms and a heavenly chariot. He imposed his power on the gods, the rsi, and all creatures. He believed that he was allowed everything, and even went so far as to interfere in the intimacy of Indra and his wife. Vishnu and Indra therefore took counsel to put an end to this situation and to create a champion who would destroy the ksatriya (warriors), who were just as insolent as Kartavirya.

King Gadhi had a daughter, Satyavati, the wife of the Brahman Rcika. Rcika prepared two bowls of boiled rice. One was intended to make his wife give birth to a Brahman, and the other was intended to make his mother-in-law give birth to a ksatriya. However, following some mishap, the bowls were exchanged so that the son of Satyavati, the Brahman's wife, would have the strength of a ksatriya, while the other, son of a ksatriya, would have something of the Brahman about him.

Satyavati was alarmed by this state of affairs and asked that the curse should fall instead on her grandson. Jamadagni, her son, therefore was pure Brahman. He married Renuka who gave him four pure Brahmans and a fifth son, Rama or Parasurama, who, although Brahman, possessed the talents of a ksatriya.

Renuka was the model wife of an ascetic Brahman. One day, however, she saw a prince down at the river dallying with his wives and slowed down in order to watch the spectacle. Jamadagni suspected what

had happened and was furious. He asked his sons to cut off their mother's head as punishment. The first four, pure Brahman, refused, and their father struck them down with his stare. Parasurama, with his particular nature, did not hesitate and beheaded his mother.

In gratitude, Jamadagni asked him what he would like to have. Parasurama became Brahman once again and asked that his mother and brothers be resurrected.

The destruction of Kartavirya

Jamadagni's house was splendid and sumptuous, thanks to a cow which provided everything one could desire. King Kartavirya was received there with every honour. However, such opulence made him jealous, and he asked his host to give him his cow. Parasurama flew into a violent rage, cut off Kartavirya's thousand arms and killed him. The latter's sons avenged their father by killing Jamadagni. Parasurama then decided to free the world of all the ksatriya and accomplished this task in 21 battles.

After this massacre, Parasurama poured the blood of his victims into five holes and performed ceremonies in honour of his ancestors. His grandfather appeared to him and reproached him for so much carnage, so he then offered a sacrifice to Indra and withdrew to Mount Mahendra (*Mahabharata*, III, 115–117).

A Brahman warrior

'I am a ksatriya; thus the strength, *bala*, is the characteristic, the proper rule, *svadharma*, of the warrior class, while it does not belong to the Brahmans, whose duty is the inner effort, the acquistion of calm and the resoluteness of the soul.' (*Mahabharata*, 6649 – 6695)

Pelops

Greek hero

Founder of the Olympic Games

Pelops, the legendary patron of the Peloponnesians, was the protégé of Poseidon.

Pelops was the son of Tantalus, king of Phyrgia, and Euryanassa. His adventures began as soon as he was born. Tantalus, to test the gods' keeness, killed his son, carved him up, made him into a stew and offered it to the immortals. They all noticed the treachery except for Demeter, who was too preoccupied with her search for her daughter, Persephone. As Demeter was starving, she ate Pelops's shoulder from the stew.

The gods, furious at having had doubt cast upon them, resurrected little Pelops and made him a shoulder of ivory to replace the one Demeter had eaten.

Pelops grew into a handsome young man. He was loved and protected by Poseidon who raised him to heaven and made him his cup-bearer. Tantalus, thought, took advantage of his son's new position, making him steal the nectar and ambrosia of the gods so that he could give it to mere mortals. The theft was soon discovered, however, and Pelops was driven from Olympus and forced to return to earth. Tantalus was sent to hell, where he was put under an enormous stone that was balanced above him and threatened constantly to fall on him (the torture of Tantalus).

Pelops's prayer to Poseidon

'Close to the foaming waves, all alone in the darkness, he called out to the power of the deep, the master of the great trident, and the god rose immediately at his side.' (Pindar, *Olympian Odes*, I)

Later, Pelops fell in love with Hippodameia, the daughter of Oenomaus, and wanted to marry her. Unfortunately, this could not be accomplished without difficulty; Oenomaus had been warned by an oracle that he would be killed by his son-in-law. Therefore, he did all he possibly could to prevent Hippodameia from getting married.

The test

Whenever a suitor presented himself to Hippodameia, he had to submit to a test. This test consisted of taking part in a series of chariot races, in which the ultimate winner would have Hippodameia's hand. Oenomaus, of course, was anxious that there should not be a winner and took part in the competition himself, driving the divine chariot given to him by Ares. With this advantage, Oenomaus won each successive two-man competition. After each race, he hurried to kill the presumptuous young man who had had the audacity to try and take his daughter away from him.

Twelve young men had already lost their lives in this way when Pelops arrived. The situation in his case was different, though, for Hippodameia had fallen in love with him. She therefore bribed Myrtilus, the king's charioteer, to replace the chariot's wooden linchpins with linchpins made of wax. When the race began, Oenomaus was sure of victory, but soon the heat from the turning wheels melted the wax. Oenomaus's chariot disintegrated, and he was thrown down onto the race track and killed.

Meanwhile, Pelops drove his chariot, drawn by the winged horses given to him by his protector, Poseidon, to victory. He was then able to marry Hippodameia. He founded the Olympic Games in memory of his victory (Pindar, *Olympian Odes*, I, 40).

Pelops had many children, including Atreus, Thyestes, and Pleisthenes.

Perseus

Greek hero

Slayer of the Gorgon

Thanks to the protection of the gods, Perseus magically accomplished the greatest of deeds.

Acrisius had been warned by an oracle that his grandson would kill him, and so he imprisoned Danaë, his daughter, in an underground room made of bronze. Zeus, who had fallen in love with her, turned himself into shower of gold (which opens all doors) so that he could enter Danaë's prison through a crack in the roof. Thus, he obtained the favours of the young woman. Acrisius's precautions, therefore, were in vain and Danaë gave birth to Perseus, whom she nursed secretly for several months.

As the child was growing up, he began to play noisily and was heard by Acrisius. He was furious at having been deceived and, suspecting the nurse of complicity, killed her. He then shut Danaë and her son up in a chest and threw it into the sea.

Polydectes

The chest ended up on the shores of Seriphos, as Zeus had commanded. Dictys,

the brother of Polydectes, the island's tyrant, took in the castaways, gave the mother hospitality and brought up the son. After several years, Perseus grew into a handsome young man who was proud and courageous.

Danaë's beauty attracted attention, and Polydectes pestered her relentlessly. Perseus, however, barred his way, stopping the tyrant from achieving his ends. A fierce hatred grew up between the two men, a hatred hidden beneath the superficial civility imposed by their situation—for one was the king and the other, the son of Danaë.

The murder of Medusa

During a feast at which Perseus was present, Polydectes asked the guests what would be the best present for a king. All but Perseus agreed that a horse would be the most suitable gift. Perseus, however, said that it would be the head of a Gorgon. The next day, each of the guests brought a horse, but Perseus had nothing to give. Polydectes therefore claimed the Gorgon's head and threatened Danaë with violence if Perseus did not obtain it.

So Perseus had to achieve this feat. He received the help of Hermes and Athena and went to find the three Graeae, guardians of the land of the Gorgons. Amongst them they had only one eye and one tooth, which they passed from one to the other. Perseus managed to put the Graea who was guarding the eye into a deep sleep, whereupon he stole the eye and was able to continue on his way.

Nymphs gave him winged sandals, a pouch and Hades's helmet, which made whoever wore it invisible. Hermes also armed Perseus with a very sharp, unbreakable sickle. Thus equipped, Perseus reached the lair of the Gorgons, whom he found asleep.

The Gorgons were monsters with bronze hands and wings made of gold. Anyone

> **The winged horse**
> 'And when Perseus had cut off her head, Chrysaor and Pegasus, the horse, sprang forth. Pegasus received his name because he had been born at the edge of the ocean waves, and Chrysaor received his name because he held a golden sword in his hands. Pegasus flew away from the earth, the mother of sheep, and went to the immortals. Now he lives in the palace of Zeus and carries the thunder and lightning for wise Zeus.' (Hesiod, *Theogony*, 280 ff.)

Perseus beheading Medusa.

Metope from the Temple of Selinus (Sicily). Beginning of the 6th cent. BC

who met their gaze was turned instantly to stone. Of the three Gorgons, two were immortal. Medusa was the only one who could die, and so it was her head which Perseus had to get.

Thanks to his winged sandals, Perseus was able to fly above Medusa while Athene held a mirror in front of the monster's gaze, Perseus beheaded her with Hermes's sickle. Pegasus, the winged horse, was born from the blood which spurted out. Perseus put the head into the pouch and fled. The two other Gorgons could not follow him because he had been made invisible by Hades's helmet.

Perseus and Andromeda

On his way home, Perseus saw Andromeda. She had been tied to a rock by Poseidon and promised to a ravenous sea-monster as punishment for the imprudent words of her mother, Cassiopeia, who had claimed to be more beautiful than Hera. Perseus immediately fell hopelessly in love with the young captive and promised her father, Cepheus, that he would free Andromeda if he were allowed to marry her afterwards.

The bargain was signed on the spot, and Perseus, thanks to his magic weapons, killed the monster and asked for his reward. Andromeda, however, had been promised to one of her uncles who now plotted

against Perseus. The hero defended himself by showing the head of Medusa, which still retained its power, and all the accomplices were turned into stone.

The return home

When he arrived home with Andromeda, Perseus found his mother, Danaë, and Dictys, taking refuge in a temple to protect themselves from the violence of Polydectes. Perseus made his way to the palace, brandished the head of Medusa, and turned the tyrant and his courtiers to stone. He then gave the power to Dictys and returned the sandals, pouch and helmet to their rightful owners. Athene, who received the head of Medusa as a token of Perseus's gratitude, set it on her shield.

After these adventures, Perseus went to see his grandfather, Acrisius. Fearing that the oracle which had predicted his death by his grandson would come true, Acrisius, however, fled to the land of the Pelasgians. By chance, Perseus went there too and took part in the public games. During the games he threw a discus, which was blown off course by the wind, hit a spectator and killed him.

The victim was Acrisius. Despairing, Perseus gave his grandfather funeral honours. Then, not wishing to succeed him, he exchanged his kingdom for that of Tiryns.

Perun

Slavic god

Storm and thunder

As the god of rain and of fertility, Perun controlled the seasons.

A supreme god, Perun was represented as a human being with a silver head and a golden moustache.

A warrior god, he took part in the battle of heaven, with thunder and lightning, and of the earth with soldiers: in effect, he was right in the middle of the fighting troops. The treaties were signed in his name.

As a beneficent god he came in the springtime to bring rain, fertilize the earth, chase away the clouds and make the sun shine. However, it was also said that he destroyed the countries of wicked men with hail.

Perun was believed to be the Slavic version of the Germanic god, Thor, and the Jupiter of ancient civilization. His name, like Thor's, means thunder. He was also likened to Perkunas, the Lithuanian god of thunder and Parjanyah, the ancient Indian god of storms. All of these seem to have had a cult which made sacrifices, immersed victims, gave libations and held banquets.

The cult of Perun spread throughout the Slavic countries, from Czechoslovakia to northern Italy. When Christianity appeared, he was assimilated to the prophet Elijah, master of the elements.

Phaethon

Greek hero

The rash and imprudent driver

Phaethon claimed that he was the equal of Helius, but he did not have his skills.

Phaethon was the son of Helius and Clymene, daughter of Oceanus. When his mother revealed to him the identity of his father, he boasted of it to his friends. They then challenged him to prove his ancestry. The young man, therefore, went to his father, who was happy to see him and granted whatever he wished for. Since he wanted to dazzle his comrades, Phaethon asked to be allowed to drive his father's chariot for a day. Helios regretted his promise, but, could not evade it.

Phaethon took up the reins and sprang forward. However, because of his awkwardness and the difficulty of the task, the chariot was tossed high and low, the horses bolted, the chariot veered off its appointed route and everything in their path was set afire. The earth complained to the king of Olympus, and Zeus struck down the imprudent charioteer.

> **Icarus shows the same rashness**
> Icarus, son of Daedalus, escaped from the labyrinth by fixing wings to his shoulders with wax. He was foolhardy, however, and went too close to the sun, which melted the wax.
> The foolish young man fell from the sky and drowned in the sea.

Poseidon/Neptune

Greek and Roman god

The power of the sea

Just as his brother Zeus possessed the sky, so Poseidon possessed the sea and everything in it.

Poseidon was the son of Cronos (Saturn) and Rhea. He was represented wielding a trident and being pulled by monsters in a chariot. Poseidon was brought up by the Telchines, women who were half land creatures and half sea creatures with the power to cause rain and hail. When he grew up, Poseidon fell in love with one of them, Halia, and had many children with her.

After Zeus's victory over Cronos, the young gods (deities who preferred life on earth) decided to claim various domains for themselves. Zeus got the sky, Poseidon the Sea, and Hades the underworld. To exercise his power, Poseidon was surrounded by other deities such as Nereus. Poseidon's wife, Amphitrite (daughter of Nereus), shared his underwater empire.

Poseidon was a chthonic god, like Zeus, Hades, Demeter and many others. Chthonic gods represented the hidden forces of germination and death. They had powerful links with the earth, who was called Gaea, the mother of the Titans. As subterranean gods, they reigned in hell and shook the world from inside. Poseidon caused earthquakes when he made love to his wife.

A certain misfortune

When men started to organize themselves in cities, each god chose one town in which he would be particularly honoured. It so happened that several of the gods wanted to claim the same place, and as this was not possible, some sort of arbitration was necessary. Poseidon was never successful in disputes, and thus he lost Corinth to

Helius, Aegina to Zeus, Naxos to Dionysus, Delphi to Apollo and Athens to Athena. However, he did manage to keep the mysterious island of Atlanta for himself.

Poseidon's power was great. With his trident, the weapon of tuna-fishers, he could provoke storms, set fire to the rocks on the shore and cause springs to gush up.

He was not always in agreement with Zeus and took part in a conspiracy with Hera and Athene to put the king of Olympia in chains. But Briareus, the hundred-handed giant called by Thetis, intervened, and the fear which his power inspired put an end to the plot.

Poseidon's pride

Poseidon took part in the construction of the walls of Troy with Apollo and Aeacus, a mortal. But when he failed to receive payment, Poseidon called up a monster which devastated the area; also, during the Trojan War, he sided with the Achaean camp. However, as he was proud of the wall he had helped to build, he protested against the decision to construct another wall around their ships and, infuriated, vowed to destroy it.

Poseidon had many lovers, but his children were mostly wicked and violent. He had Polyphemus the Cyclops by Thoosa, Chrysaor the giant by Medusa, Nauplius by Amymone, the bandit Sciron by Cercyon, and the Aloeidae by Iphimedeia. He even had to bury some of his children in

---

Polyphemus's prayer to Poseidon

'Answer me, Poseidon, god of the dark hair who carries the earth. If I am really your son and if you claim to be my father, grant that Odysseus will never return; Odysseus, that pillager of towns, son of Laertes, who has his home on Ithaca.' (*Odyssey*, IX)

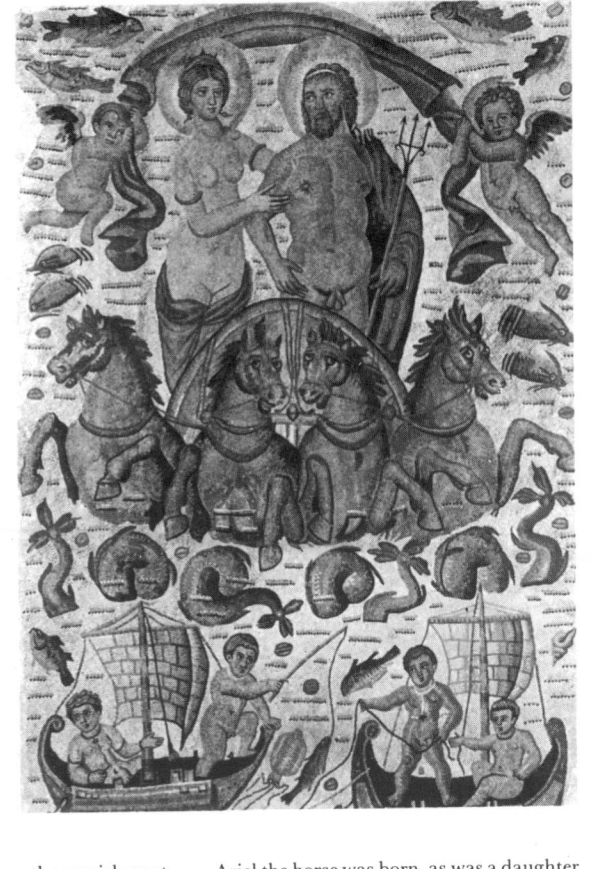

The triumph of **Poseidon** *and his wife, Amphitrite. The god wields a trident, which is his symbol. He stands on a chariot pulled by four horses and rules the sea where men are fishing.*

Detail. Roman mosaic, 3rd cent. AD (discovered at Constantine, Algeria).

order to shield them from the punishment they deserved.

Poseidon appeared in the guise of a horse in the Peloponnesus, a guise he had adopted to mate with Demeter, herself transformed into a mare. From their union

Ariel the horse was born, as was a daughter whose name was known only to the initiated.

Neptune was a Roman water god who was later associated with Poseidon. A feast day, the *Neptunalia*, was held for him every year, and he had a temple on the banks of the Tiber. He was associated with humidity and fresh water.

Nereus

was another ancient sea-god, one of the gods of the earthly elemental forces. The son of Pontus (Sea) and Ge (Earth), he was older than Poseidon. He had the power to transform himself into all kinds of animals. Amphitrite was one of the daughters and led her sisters' chorus.

The spiteful one

'The gods all took pity on him, all except Poseidon, whose implacable bitterness pursued the divine Odysseus until his return home.' (*Odyssey*, I)

Prajapati

Indian god

The primordial being

Everything was contained in Prajapati. He was the universe, time and the sacrificial altar.

Prajapati played the role of the demiurge who put order into the unseen unity. He was the thirty-fourth god alongside the thirty-three others, bringing them together and uniting them.

Creation

In the beginning there was only water. The water created an egg by increasing its intense inner activity. From this egg, Prajapati was born, master of creatures and posterity. After breaking the egg, Prajapati found himself in its shell, floating here and there for an entire year.

During the course of this year he uttered the word 'Bhur', and the earth appeared; he said 'Bhuvar', and the air appeared; he said 'Suvar' and the sky appeared. From these five syllables, he created the seasons. Prajapati then stood up. He was born aged a thousand years. 'Just as one can see the far shore across a river, so could he contemplate the far shore across his age.' (*Catapatha-Brahmana*, XI, I, 6, 6).

From his mouth Prajapati conceived the gods who, as soon as they were created, took possession of the sky. With his inner breath he created evil spirits, the Asurs, who took possession of earth as soon as they were created. They were darkness. Prajapati also created man, melodies, and the sun. His creative acts were done by 'emanation'; which could mean perspiration or even ejaculation.

Sacrifice

When he created, Prajapati wasted away, exhausted. 'After Prajapati had issued the living beings, his joints started to dislocate. Prajapati represented the year, and his joints were the junctions of day and night, the full moon and the new moon, and the beginning of each season. He was unable to get up because of his slack joints, and the gods cured him by the ritual of agnihotra, which tightened his joints again' (*Satapatha-brahmana*, I, 6, 3, 35–36).

The disjointed body of Prajapati was reconstituted by sacrifice, which maintained the living god – that is, the unified and fertile world. The ceremony was necessary for the cycle of day and night, which had to be rhythmic. 'The sun would not rise if the priest did not make offerings of fire at dawn' (*Satapatha-brahmana*, II, 3, 1–5).

The celebration of the ritual was the counterpart of the act of creation. It reunited what had been scattered, restored original unity and gave coherence and structure to the world. The sacrifice, constantly repeated, allowed Prajapati to 'pursue his creative work' (*Satapatha-brahmana*, I, 1, 5, 1).

The sacrifice

'Prajapati said to his son Indra: "I must sacrifice to you, to help this sacrifice which is the culmination of desire." "So be it," was the reply. The sacrifice completed, Indra expressed this desire: "May I be everything!" And he became the word, because the word is everything. That is why it is said that Indra is the word.' (*Catapatha-Brahmana*, IX, 18)

Priapus

Greek god

The impotent chauvinist

The story of Priapus illustrates how excess breeds failure.

Priapus, the last of the gods, is represented as being a small, bearded man who raises his apron loaded with fruit to reveal a fully erect penis of immense size.

According to some traditions, Priapus was the son of Zeus and Aphrodite. His mother's beauty fascinated all the gods, but it was Zeus who seduced and dominated her. But Hera, Zeus's jealous wife, was afraid that this adulterous liaison would be as beautiful as his mother and as powerful as his father. She therefore saw to it that the child was born ugly and deformed. When Aphrodite saw him, she was ashamed of the son to whom she had given birth. Fearing that she would become an object of ridicule, she abandoned the child in the mountains where Priapus was taken in and brought up by shepherds.

Diminishing virility

The whole legend is based on Priapus's large penis. He guarded the orchard, scaring off any thieves who came near, especially female ones, with his huge penis. He also threatened them with sexual violence. However, since Priapus was impotent, his threats of sexual violence were purely verbal. The crop he was supposed to be watching over was paltry; the symbol of fertility he represented was of no use and thieves stayed away. Sometimes he despaired and begged his potential aggressors to break into the enclosure so that he could relieve himself by punishing them.

As usually Priapus failed miserably in his attempts, to woo the nymph Lotis. One day, he found her asleep and, delighted by his stroke of luck, prepared to do her harm. Just at that moment, however, a nearby donkey started to bray and woke up the young woman. Priapus had no choice but to flee, exposing himself to the ridicule of all and sundry. There was, after all, something rather ridiculous about a god who was constantly failing.

Invalid

Priapus was compared with the ass, considered to be a lecherous animal, and he took part with it in Dionysus's procession. Each of them was lewd, and they gave the impression that they were competing in obscenity. It is said that they once held a contest to find out which of them had the longer penis. It turned out to be the donkey and Priapus, not willing to admit it, wanted to kill him.

Priapus lent his name to priapism, an incurable illness where the penis remains painfully erect but incapable of ejaculation. This condition has nothing to do with satyriasis, which does not include ejaculation or pleasure. Satyriasis occurred in satyrs which were half human and half animal, whereas Priapus was wholly human in appearance.

Up until Roman times, crude statuettes of Priapus were fashioned from fig wood. They would be daubed with rouge and placed in orchards. From being a symbol of fertility, Priapus gradually developed into an obscure gnome.

> **Priapus the guardian**
> 'There was no reason whatsoever for Eustochides putting me here — me, Priapus — to look after his vines enclosed by this sloping embankment. Whoever climbs up . . . will find nothing to steal — except me, the guardian.' (Lucian)

Prometheus

Greek hero

The revolt against Zeus

Prometheus had a passionate ambition to be the equal of the gods.

Prometheus was the son of Iapetus, the Titan, and *Clymene* (or Asia). He was Zeus's cousin and had several brothers: Atlas, Moneotius, and Epimetheus, who was the best known because he was the exact opposite of Prometheus. Indeed, Prometheus was as intelligent, cunning, and provident as Epimetheus was loud, naive and irresponsible.

Prometheus symbolizes the revolt of man against the gods. In his hands, ingenuity and treachery were powerful weapons. He managed to deceive Zeus himself and to bring humanity (it is claimed that he was its very creator) all the good things refused it by the gods. All this was not achieved, however, without a price.

Sacrifice

The gods were living in harmony with men and shared the same table. It was the Golden Age. Prometheus brought in a large ox, killed it and cut it into two parts. One of these parts was the flesh; covered with skin it looked repulsive, but was actually the best part of the beast. The other part consisted of the bones, hidden under a layer of white fat. Although this part looked very appetizing, it was actually completely inedible.

Zeus chose between the two portions, naturally picking the one which was most tempting to him — the fat-covered bones. Thereafter, whenever a sacrifice was made, men burned the bones; the gods savoured the aromas and flavours of the meat, while the men ate their fill of the dead animal's flesh. Their hunger kept on renewing itself, however, and they experienced weakness, fatigue, illness and death.

Zeus took great exception to his young cousin's trick and decided to punish Prometheus. He hid the fire used to cook the meat, and forced man to work hard at growing the seed which, until then, had grown in abundance without so much as a glance. So the Golden Age ended.

The abduction of fire

Prometheus came once again to the aid of mankind. He stole a piece of fire from the 'wheel of the sun' (or perhaps from Hephaestus's forge) and hid it in a stem of fennel, thus bringing it down to man. Since then, fire has always burned in earthly homes.

However, this fire had lost its permanence. It was precarious and had to be carefully guarded, protected and sustained. It was as mortal, in fact, as man. Yet it underlined the difference between man and beast, linking man to some extent with the gods by the fact that through it, sacrifices could be made.

Punishment

The punishment for this theft was great. Zeus sent mankind the 'wicked beauty', Pandora. Epimetheus, ever gullible, accepted her as a wonderful gift, a godsend. However, she lifted the lid off an earthenware jar and allowed a whole manner of

---

Prometheus' torture

'As for Prometheus with his skilful ploys, Zeus bound him inextricably to a column with painful shackles which he wound to waist height. Then he let loose an eagle and the eagle ate of his immortal liver.' (Hesiod, *Theogony*, 521 — 524)

***Prometheus**, with his gift of fire, was to be the inventor of men. He is seen here sculpting his own body out of stone with the stick he used to bring the fire secretly down to earth.*
Piero di Cosimo (1462–1521): 'The Story of Prometheus', oil on wood, ca. 1515 (detail).

evils — such as fatigue, disease, suffering and death — to spread all over the world.

Prometheus was punished by being chained to a mountain. All day, every day, an eagle tore out his liver, which grew again. Passing the spot where he was chained up, Heracles killed the eagle with an arrow and freed Prometheus. Proud of his son's feat, Zeus eased the punishment, insisting only that Prometheus wear a ring made from his chain and a little piece of the rock as a symbol of his punishment.

Immortality

The ever-cunning Prometheus heard the cries of the centaur Cheiron who, although born immortal, had been wounded by one of Heracles's arrows. He was in constant suffering and begged for death to release him from his misery. Prometheus offered to exchange death for immortality and Cheiron, unable to endure any more, accepted. Thus Prometheus became immortal in Cheiron's place.

Ptah

Egyptian god

The earth which rises up

By the combined activity of his intellect, will and effective word, Ptah was the creator of the earth.

Ptah was portrayed in human guise, swathed like a mummy, and with his head covered in a tight-fitting cap. He wore the beard of the gods on his chin and carried a sceptre. He was the principal god of the city of Memphis. His wife was Sekhmet and his son was Nefertum. Ptah became a god single-handedly: 'Body which created its own body, when heaven did not exist, when earth did not exist' (Papyrus no. 3048, Berlin Museum).

Ptah was the creator; he preceded even the sun. He created by an act of his heart (intellect and will) and the power of his word, 'the one conceiving, the other decreeing the wish of the former' (theological document at Memphis, 22, III). He was the 'father of both man and woman' (tenure of Ptah as demiurge, 24c). He was the master of craftsmen and the patron of metallurgy, construction and sculpture. Subsequently, he was regarded as a healing god in the form of a flat-headed dwarf, and as a protective spirit.

> **The creator**
> 'You have built up the earth, you have summoned your flesh, you have counted your limbs, and you have found yourself to be the unique being who has created his own resting place; God who has formed the two earths.'
> (Papyrus no. 3048, Berlin Museum)

Purusha

Primordial being of India

The master of immortality

Purusha was the entire world—the world past, the world present and the world to come.

Purusha was thought to be a gigantic man who completely covered the earth and went beyond it. He was immortal in heaven which made up three-quarters of his being; the fourth quarter consisted of all mortal creatures.

Individual creation was born of Purusha. Man and the natural elements were part of his body: his mouth became the Brahmans, his arm the noblemen, his thighs craftsmen and his eye the sun.

Purusha's own energy—and thus the strength of the ascetic, the plant's sap, the warrior's courage and the violence of the storm—was represented by his consort, Prakriti. Purusha was the universe. He penetrated and sustained all beings and was unique, immutable and immeasurable. He was the beginning and the end. He was being and non-being.

Pwyll

Celtic hero

The wise one

Pywll always emerged victorious from a thousand trials and acquired both courtesy and power.

Pwyll was prince of Dyfed. He hunted deer and one day captured one which had already been brought down by dogs. These dogs belonged to Arawn, king of Annwn. Consequently, the stag rightfully belonged to the king and Pwyll was reproached for his lack of courtesy.

To redeem himself, Pwyll offered his services for the killing of Hafgan, Arawn's permanent enemy. Arawn accepted and it was decided that Arawn and Pwyll would exchange roles for a year, Pwyll going to reign over Annwyvn and Arawn taking charge of the principality of Dyfed.

Pwyll's apprenticeship in courtesy

Pwyll had to learn the good manners which were the norm at the court of Annwn. He killed Hafgan with a single lance thrust (the condition for killing him being that there be only a single blow) and restored the kingdom to its legitimate owner.

When he returned to his domain, he found that his subjects were accustomed to a courteous, likeable and generous sovereign, and they did not want this to change. Pwyll became what was expected of him, and the two kings kept up their friendship by exchanging a great number of presents.

Rhiannon

Pwyll, during a ride, spied a beautiful young woman mounted on a white steed. He speeded up in order to catch her, but she slipped away without any apparent haste. Then Pwyll stopped pursuing her and called to her. She approached and revealed that she was Rhiannon, the daughter of Heveidd Hen, and that she had spurned the suitor chosen for her out of love for Pwyll. As a result, Pwyll married her.

After a feast, Pwyll carelessly promised a supplicant that he would grant him any request. The supplicant was Gwawl, Rhiannon's former suitor, and his request was for Rhiannon. Before being escorted away, Rhiannon handed over to Pwyll a bag of magic provisions which enabled him to hold up to ridicule Gwawl and take back his wife.

Rhiannon gave birth to a son, but the child disappeared one night without anyone knowing how. The child's nurses suggested that a crime had been committed by his mother, and she was punished. She had to remain seated near the entrance to the palace, recount her crime to passers-by and carry them on her back.

Meanwhile, there was a similar event taking place in the home of Teyrnon, a vassal of Pwyll. Every year his mare had a foal, of which no trace could be found. So Teyrnon kept watch, cut off the thief's arm and pursued him, but then lost the thief in the darkness. When he returned he found Pryderi, Rhiannon's missing son, at the door of his stable. Safeguarding the foal had led to the return of the child (*The Mabinogi of Pwyll*).

The chieftain of Annwn

'From that moment, they dedicated themselves to consolidating their friendship. They sent one another horses, hunting dogs, falcons, and all the precious objects which each of them considered appropriate to please the other. Following his stay in Annwn, since he had governed there so successfully and had reunited the two kingdoms on the same day, Pwyll's title of prince of Dyfed was dispensed with. Henceforth, he was named merely Pwyll, chieftain of Annwn.' (*The Mabinogion, Welsh Bardic Tales*)

Qat

Hero of Oceania

The civilizer

Originally a man, Qat was the organizer of both life and death.

Qat, or Ambat, was born from a rock which had been hollowed out in the centre to allow his birth. He had eleven brothers, called the Tagaros; among them were Tagaro Gilagilala, who understood all things and could teach others, and Tagaro Loloqong, who knew nothing and behaved like a madman.

Qat created things, beginning from a pre-existent world. He delighted in fulfilling creation and, being a genius, was successful in all his undertakings. He carved out the bodies of men and women from a tree and hid them for three days. Then, for three more days, he exposed them to the light and, by dancing to the beat of a drum, gave them life. Marawa, who was more his rival than his enemy, found Qat's creation interesting and wished to do likewise. He began, therefore, to carve out men from another tree and buried the figurines he had made in the earth. But when he tried to retrieve them six days later, he found they had completely decomposed. It was thought that this, perhaps, was the way in which Marawa invented death, but there is another version of this invention.

The invention of death

In those days men did not die; instead, their bodies just renewed themselves. This did not occur, however, without causing problems. Because the lands always had the same owners, the same farming methods were always used and there was no progress or change.

Qat summoned a man by the name of Mate, promising that he would do him no harm. Mate was stretched out on a stone and a slaughtered pig was placed on top of him. Then a funeral meal was organized. Five days later, Qat lifted up what was on top of Mate and only bones remained. Mate had to go away, either to the subterranean world or to the world above. Tagaro Loloqong positioned himself on this latter road, blocking the way; Mate, therefore, headed for the lower world. This was the origin of human death.

It was said that Qat had to go to the foot of heaven to find Night. In exchange for a pig, Night taught Qat how to sleep when she was present and how to cut her at dawn with an obsidian blade to allow daylight to appear. Qat taught all these things to his brothers.

Qat had a very pretty wife, and his brothers were jealous; therefore, they were determined to capture and kill her. This legend has several versions: either Qat is always saved, thanks to his rival Marawa who was still his friend, or else he dies and his wife commits suicide out of despair at the sight of blood on her comb.

Qat is supposed to have canoed away to a far country, doubtless to the land of the dead, taking with him all the hopes of mankind. But we are assured that he will return.

> **The dead**
> For the inhabitants of Oceania in general, the existence of the dead depends on the memory of the living. But there is always a moment when the dead leave this existence (which is almost like life) in order to descend into the lower regions, the regions of oblivion, hell.

172

Quetzalcoatl

Aztec god

The plumed serpent

Quetzalcoatl was the god of vegetation and therefore, the god of earth and water.

Quetzalcoatl was depicted as a bearded man, wearing a mask with two forward-protruding tubes, two earrings with pendants, a pectoral ornament called 'the wind's jewel' and a conical hat. He was the son of the sun god and of Coatlicue, one of the five goddesses of the moon. He was regarded as the god of vegetation as well as the god of wind.

Quetzalcoatl was the life-force, and together with his twin, Xolotl, he entered the subterranean world. There he found the bones of the ancient dead and brought them back with him, ground them to a pulp and sprinkled them with his blood. These remains came back to life and gave birth to mankind.

A kindly god, he reigned in Tula and refused human sacrifices. He gave to his faithful worshippers the growing of maize, the arts, technology, sculpture and writing. He taught them how to measure time by

A monolith in reddish-purple porphyry, representing the beneficent **Quetzalcoatl**, *the plumed serpent.*

Mexico, Aztec civilisation, early 16th cent.

The Aztec calendar

The Aztec calendar had two different years, occurring simultaneously:

—One was a solar year, made up of 18 months of 20 days each and five additional ill-fated days called *nemontemi*, for a total of 365 days. The year bore the name of the first day, and because of the discrepancy caused by the shifting of the nemontemi backwards or forwards, only four days could start it off. These were *acatl, tecpatl, calli,* and *tochtli*.

—The other one was a divinatory year, composed of 260 days denoted by 20 names and bracketed with a number ranging from 1 to 13: 1 cipactli, 2 cipactli, . . . 13 cipactli; 1 ehecatl, 2 ehecatl, and so on.

Thus the days bore simultaneously the names of the solar year and those of the divinatory year. It was only after the passage of 52 solar years, called the 'Mexican century' or *xiuhmolpilli*, that the same two signs indicating the same day were found.

means of the calendar and how to discover the movement of the stars. He was present at the start of civilisation. Students were put under his tutelage.

The king of Tula

Quetzalcoatl, the king of Tula, was the bearer of peace and prosperity. One day, Tezcatlipocan appeared and told the king about the intoxication one could experience by drinking pulque. He used a mirror to show Quetzalcoatl his crumpled face and attempted to seduce his daughter. He did all of this so well that Quetzalcoatl refused to leave his palace and finally decided to go into exile. The wickedness and evil spells of the intruder made the king lose power and the country its prosperity.

Quetzalcoatl headed westward. Having reached the ocean's edge, he fasted for four days, attired himself in his finest garments and had a funeral pyre prepared. Then he hurled himself into the fire. Birds flew out of the flames, and in the midst of them, the king's heart could be seen heading heavenward and changing into the planet Venus. 'The ancients maintained that he became the star which appears at dawn, and for this reason they used to call him "the lord of the dawn"' (*Annals of Cuauhtitlan*).

Quetzalcoatl was regarded as one of the chief gods of the Aztecs. Sacrifices of flowers, incense and tobacco were made to him. However, none of the great annual festivals was dedicated to him. He owned a circular temple in the sacred heart of Mexico and was particularly honoured in Cholula, where his sanctuary was situated on top of the world's largest pyramid.

> 'It is said that in the year "ce-acatl", having reached the edge of the celestial, divine water, Quetzalcoatl began to weep. He donned his plumed adornments, put on his mask of green stones, mounted the funeral pyre, and was burned to death'. (*Annals of Cuauhtitlan*)

Quirinus
Roman god

The citizen

A former Roman god, Quirinus was the last of the supreme triad made up of himself, Jupiter and Mars.

Quirinus, the god of the Roman hill of the Quirinal was probably, because of his Sabine origin, a warrior god. The Greeks were to compare him with Ares, the god of war. But Servius, in *Scholia in Virgilium*, made him a Mars of peace. He was initially, therefore, a god of the city; the citizens were the Quirites. He watched over the material well-being of the community, saw that it was fed and protected the peace. He was, therefore, the absolute opposite of a god of war.

He was also likened to Romulus. Proculus was supposed to have had an apparition of Romulus, the founder of Rome, in which he was alleged to have told Proculus that he wished to be honoured under the name of Quirinus (Cicero, *De legibus*, I, 1, 3; Virgil, *Aeneid*, I, 292). Like the two other great gods, Jupiter and Mars, he had a chief priest (or flamen) and was invoked in the city's solemn prayers. The salii collini were his priests.

His son Modius Fabidius founded a town called Cures, which means 'spear' in the Sabine language.

> **Mars Quirinus**
> 'Mars, when he runs wild, is called Gradiuus. When he is calm, he is called Quirinus'.
> (Servius, *Scholia in Virgilium*, 1, 292)

Rama

Indian hero

The incarnation of the god Vishnu on earth

The model of a perfect prince, Rama was the essential point of reference for good government.

King Dasaratha of Ayodhya had three wives but no children, and so he offered a sacrifice to the gods so that he might have an offspring. In the course of the ceremony, an extraordinary being appeared on the scene, offering Dasaratha a bowl of magic gruel which his wife had to eat in order to give birth to a son.

This king offered half the gruel to Kausaalya, his first wife, and she gave birth to Rama. He offered three-quarters of the remainder to Sumitra, his second wife, and she gave birth to the twins Laksmana and Satrughna. Finally, he offered the remainder to his third wife, Kaikeyi, who gave birth to Bharata.

Bharata was wholly devoted to Rama, and the twins were destined to be of service to both of them. These children formed a united team of ksatriya (princes) under Rama's orders. All of them were, to a greater or lesser extent, incarnations of Vishnu, depending upon the quantity of gruel taken by their mothers before their birth.

Rama and Visvamitra

They had become young adults when Visvamitra arrived on the scene, requesting help from the king. He wanted Rama to get rid of the raksasa (demons) which were preventing him from completing his sacrifice. Visvamitra claimed that Rama alone was capable of killing the raksasa, and Rama was given permission to go. During the journey, Visvamitra taught him magic spells which were intended to make him invincible.

Provided with incredible weapons, Rama had no difficulty in rendering harmless the raksasa oppressing Visvamitra and killing Tataka, the mother of one of the demons.

Rama and his brother Laksmana continued their journey to Mithila. There, King Janaka had in his possession the bow of Shiva. No one was capable of drawing the bow because so much strength was required, and Janaka had promised his daughter, Sita, in marriage to anyone who managed this feat. Thanks to the magical powers given to him by Visvamitra, Rama had no difficulty in stretching the bow to breaking point. Consequently, he received Sita as his wife and his brothers also received wives from the family of Janaka.

On the way back, Rama encountered Parasurama, the destroyer of ksatriya, who challenged him to draw a bow. This time, the bow in question was Vishnu's. Rama drew it without difficulty. Parasurama conceded defeat and greeted, in Rama, an earthly manifestation of Vishnu himself.

The exile

Rama returned to the country and prepared to become the heir apparent. But Queen Kaikeya, the mother of Bharata, wanted the crown for her son. She reminded Dasaratha that she had saved his life and that he had then promised her the reward of her choice. She therefore asked that Rama be exiled and that Bharata he declared heir presumptive. The king, bound by his oath, had to agree to her demand.

Rama gave in with good grace and set off for the forest. Sita, like a faithful wife, followed him. Faced with this heart-rending situation, Dasaratha died of grief and Bharata ascended the throne. But at the same time, Bharata discovered his mother's schemes and refused to rule. He then went in search of Rama to persuade him to return but Rama refused because the binding power of the oath had not been broken by the death of the person who swore it. Bharata therefore contented himself with administering the country in the name of Rama in his absence.

The abduction of Sita

Rama set up his retreat at Pancavati, and all the rsi (sages) living in the vicinity sought his protection. Surpanakha, the sister of the demon Ravana, fell in love with Rama and appeared before him, dressed in all her finery and promising all sorts of pleasures. But Rama remained faithful to Sita, just as Sita was faithful to Rama. Laksmana then released Rama from these temptations by cutting off the nose and ears of the demoness, and Rama exterminated the raksasa who were determined to avenge her.

Surpanakha did not let the matter rest, however. She went off and found her brother Ravana and extolled so forcefully to him the charms of Sita that Ravana had the most violent craving to possess her. He went to Pancavati, aroused the passions of a golden stag which attracted Sita's gaze and incited Rama to pursue him. During

Rama's absence, Ravana abducted Sita by pulling her away by her hair.

He carried her off to Lanka and tried daily to seduce her. He had decided not to take her forcibly. Sita's virtue was a match for any trial, so Ravana was not likely to succeed in his aims.

Rama and Laksmana set off in search of Sita. They came across Hanuman, counsellor to King Sugriva, who had been dispossessed by his brother Valin of both his kingdom and his wife. Rama and Hanuman sealed an agreement and resolved to provide one another with help. Hanuman had found the jewels dropped by Sita during her abduction.

Hanuman was the first to reach Lanka. He did not free Sita, though, as this honour belonged by rights to Rama. But Hanman did warn Ravana of his approaching doom. The combat began when Rama arrived, and Lanka was totally destroyed. Vibhisana, Ravana's brother, had taken sides with Rama; thus, he was established on the throne and Sita was set free.

Rama then said to Sita, 'There is lingering doubt about your conduct. What man of honour and good family would allow himself to be so carried away by passion as to take back a woman who has sojourned in another man's house?' (Ramayana, VI, 115, 17–20), and he sent her off into exile in the forest. But there was constant talk about Sita's virtue, and his sons daily beseeched him to take her back, declaring her innocence: 'Neither in her words, nor in her heart, nor in her mind, nor in her glances, has your virtuous, beautiful wife shown herself to be unworthy of your noble feelings' (Ramayana, VI, 118, 6). Rama allowed himself to be convinced and went in search of her. But Sita, returning to her native soil, had begged it to take her back. The earth had then opened up and swallowed her.

Rama could not bear the loss of his beloved wife and so decided to give up his royal status. He went to the banks of the river Sarayu and uttered one last prayer for the glorious heroes who had accompanied him out of love (Ramayana, VII, 110, 17). Then he entered the water along with his entire retinue and was received by Brahma, who carried him off into heaven. There Rama regained all the glory of his divine nature.

A perfect being

'Rama shows sincere sorrow for the misfortunes of others, and in every festival he rejoices like a father in the bosom of his family. Candid in his speech, a skilful archer, full of respect for old age, master of his senses, accompanying his words with a smile, cleaving to duty with all his soul, a faithful guide in doing good, taking no delight in slanderous tales, discoursing with an eloquence equal to that of Vacaspati; with his handsome eyebrows, his large, copper-coloured eyes, he is like Vishnu personified.' (Ramayana, II, 2, 40–43)

The Ramayana is one of India's greatest epic poems. Composed over a period of centuries, it tells of the adventures of Rama.

Rhiannon

Celtic heroine

The great queen

Often identified with the goddess Epona, Rhiannon was mistress of horses and horsemen.

Rhiannon was the pretty girl whom Pwyll met. She rode a white steed and, despite her calm, serene charm, the horsemen were unable to catch her. When Pwyll called to her, however, she approached, showing that she had decided to speak to him. She then confessed to him that she had refused all her suitors out of love for him.

Rhiannon's punishment

Pwyll took Rhiannon away with him and prepared to marry her. However, in the course of the nuptials, a tall, dark, princely young man appeared, saying to Pwyll, 'I have come to make a request of you,' and Pwyll replied, 'Whatever you desire, if I am able to grant it, you will have it'. The visitor, who turned out to be Gwawl, Rhiannon's previous suitor, claimed her. She was therefore compelled to follow him, but as she departed she left with Pwyll a magic bag of provisions.

A year later Pwyll went to Gwawl's court. He was disguised as a beggar and carried the magic bag. He succeeded, through trickery, in shutting Gwawl up in the bag until he promised to set Rhiannon free.

Rhiannon finally became Pwyll's wife and quickly bore him a son. The latter mysteriously disappeared, and Rhiannon was accused of infanticide. She was condemned to stand at the gates of the palace, tell her story to all the visitors coming in and carry them on her back. When the matter was cleared up and the child found again, just as mysteriously, her penance ended.

Rhiannon and Pryderi

After Pwyll's death, Pryderi, Rhiannon's son, gave her in marriage to his friend Manawyden. One day, when they were all together, the palace and the whole country-side magically disappeared. They found themselves in the middle of a desert.

In order to survive, they had to do all sorts of jobs, facing both 'villians and rogues' and experiencing dreadful misfortunes. Pryderi, attracted by a magic fortress, became its prisoner, as did his mother. Then everything disappeared again. Pryderi, Rhiannon and the palace no longer existed. During this time. Manawyden set about growing grain, but only straw emerged from the soil.

Unable to endure this situation, Manawyden kept watch and surprised one of the mice eating the grain. He carried it off with him as his prisoner. He was on the point of hanging it when Gwawl's avenger appeared, asking him to spare the mouse's life. When Manawyden refused, the visitor explained that mice were members of his retinue, and that it was he who had cast a spell over the country.

Before setting his prisoner free, Manawyden demanded that life be restored to the land and that his friends be set free.

Rhiannon's love for Pwyll
'Oh, Prince, I am Rhiannon, the daughter of Heveidd Hen. Contrary to my own wishes, they want to give me in marriage to someone. I have never desired any man because of love for you, unless, of course, you reject me. I have come so that I might have your reply on this matter.' (*The Mabinogion, Welsh Bardic Tales*)

Rod

Slavic god

The master of husbandmen

Rod personified the identity and life of the Slavic people.

Rod was initially the god of husbandmen, as working the soil was essential for survival. His attributes, however, went far beyond this. Rod was a universal god, the god of heaven, the thunderbolt and rain. Originally, he was the god who created both the world and life; he created man, established the family and gathered the nation together. He was represented as being 'seated in the air', throwing down little pieces of an unidentified substance which created children. He was responsible, therefore, for the nation's increase. He was also closely linked with the worship of ancestors.

Rod had a wife called Rozanica; but since this word is always plural and polygamy was common among the Slavic people, it actually implies that he had several wives.

Later, Rod was dethroned by Perun. Perun's qualities were more exclusively bound up with fertility and fruitfulness and seemed better able to meet the needs of the people.

> **The religious practices of the Slavs**
> 'They also pay homage to rivers, nymphs and other spirits, and make offerings to all of them.' (Procopius of Caesarea, *The History of the Wars of the Emperor Justinian*)

Rosmerta

Gallo-Roman goddess

The great provider

Rosmerta represented foresight and providence and necessities of life.

In the rare instances when Rosmerta is indicated to have been the subject of a cult, she is represented as being an adult woman, standing draped in a long robe and holding a cornucopia and a patera.

Often associated under Roman occupation with Mercury, the god of exchanges, voyages and trade, she is sometimes seen bearing, like him, the caduceus. In many representations of Mercury she is shown alongside him. Rosmerta was invoked to obtain fertility, fruitfulness and everything essential for a better life. She was entrusted with the distribution of wealth and was the procurer of material benefit, well-being and prosperity.

Rosmerta was sometimes described as a queen (an inscription recently discovered at Lezoux, Puy-de-Dôme). This means either that she became a sovereign goddess or that she became associated with worship of the emperor

> **The Celtic name** Rosmerta originates from 'smert', which means 'supply', and from the initial 'ro', which means 'great'. 'Rosmerta' therefore means 'the great supplier'.

Rudra

Indian god

The red one

Rudra was the terrible one, the destroyer. He cast his evil spells over both men and beasts.

Prajapati desired to have a child. He therefore practised the strictest asceticism, became inflamed and as a result, five beings were produced: Agni (Fire), Vayu (Wind), Aditya (Sun), Candramus (Moon) and Usas (Dawn). Usas changed into a nymph and appeared before her brothers who, greatly aroused, scattered their seed. Prajapati collected this seed and a being with a thousand eyes and a thousand feet was born from it. This was Rudra, the product of an incestuous act between Usas and her brothers (*Sadvimca–brahmana*, 6, 1, 3, 7–8).

Other traditions say that he was born of the Fury, Manyu (*Sadvimca-brahmana*, 9, 1, 1, 6), or again that, following an incestuous act between Prajapati and his daughter, the gods sought to punish him. To do this, they combined the most terrible characteristics of each and produced Rudra, who pierced Prajapati with an arrow (*Maitrayani-samhita*, 4, 2, 12).

Rudra married Rudrani, and they were united in a long embrace. The gods were apprehensive about the child this union might produce, and they asked Rudra not to reproduce. He agreed and henceforth maintained total sexual abstinence. The godess was furious and condemned the gods to having no offspring either. Only Agni, who was not present, was spared from this curse (*Mahabharata* XIII, 84–86).

Rudra had his abode on earth. His hideout was in the mountains. He came down from these, crossed forests and the fields and entered inhabited places. He did enter villages but preferred isolated localities where men were seized with fear at the prospect of meeting him.

The god of strangeness

With plaited hair, a blackbelly and a red back, Rudra was clad in animal skins and armed with a bow and arrows. He was a hunter and the master of the beasts of the forest. The 'Rudras', Bhava and Carva, ran in the wilds like untamed wolves. Rudra had no contact with civilized life. He was uncouth and unrefined. Brigands and thieves were his friends. He was the patron of all those who killed, either from necessity or for pleasure.

Rudra was the great destroyer. Under his control were the 'Noisy, the Destructive, the Hissing and the Flesh-eating,' (*Rig*

The all-powerful one

'In truth, Rudra is unique; no one can act as his second-in-command. Through his powers, he has control over all the worlds. He stands facing every creature and is guardian of every being. Even though he created them, at the end of time he becomes irritated with them. His eyes, face, arms and feet turn in every direction, and, he, the only creative god, welds together both heaven and earth with his two arms and his wings.' (*Svetasvatara Upanishad*, III, 2 – 3)

Rudra-Shiva

Rudra was a Vedic god. Destructive and irritable, he found himself amid kindly powers such as Mitra, Varuna and Indra. He often played the role of a demon. At a later stage of Hinduism he almost totally disappeared. Shiva a newcomer, absorbed Rudra's destructive and subversive features, though also preserving his own benevolent character. Rudra and Shiva were one and the same god.

Veda, 4, 19, 8). He spread both illness and death and attacked beasts and men. He used poison and wielded lightning, spreading terror all around him. It was to him that the gods appeared if they wanted evil works to be carried out.

Rudra existed on the fringes of society. He loved whatever was abnormal, all those who did not live as other men or even those who fought them. He was in sympathy with strangers, outcasts, reprobates and those who lived alone, withdrawn from the world. He was a divine, wild, untamed, and dangerous power.

He was therefore a god who was feared. People begged for his favour, protection and friendship. From being a destructive god, he then became Shiva, a benevolent god to whom sacrifices were offered. He bore the name of Cambhu, 'the Kindly One', or Cankara, 'the Beneficent One'. 'Shiva is your name. You are a remedy, a medicine for cows, horses and men, the symbol of happiness for both rams and ewes' (*Vajasaneyi-samhita*, 3, 63).

When divine rites made the gods ascend into heaven, Rudra, as always, found himself isolated. He saw that he was an outcast and began to follow the others. The gods, fearing he would rain down blows on them,

promised him another sacrifice. Everything had already been offered up, however, and only a few scanty offerings remained. Nevertheless, these were dedicated to him. For this reason he was called Vastavya, the 'god of remnants' (*Sadvimca-brahmana*).

The Rudras

The name Rudra is frequently found in the plural. These Rudras were his 'sons' or representatives. They were often likened to the Maruts. There were thousands of them in towns, on roads, in the sea and in rivers. They caused a reign of terror.

The Rudras were manifestations of Rudra. Disease, catastrophes, poisonings and crimes were attributed to him, and his multiplication under the name 'Rudras' simply revealed his ubiquity.

Prayer to Rudra prior to sacrifice

'Oh, Bhagavan, Rudra, o thou who art adored by all the worlds, if, o sovereign god among gods, I have obtained your favour, help me, you yourself, supreme master of the gods, to celebrate my sacrifice.' (*Mahabharata*, VIII, 120 – 122)

Rudra *and Shiva are two aspects of the same god. Here they are both represented. Rudra and his wife are seated on the body of Shiva, who himself is placed on a funeral pyre. Spirits are dancing and crawling around as they look at the master.*

A sketch on paper from the Pahari school, late 17th cent.

Sarasvati

Indian goddess

The word

Sarasvati was the personification of the actual word of the Veda and of the feminine energy of the god.

Sarasvati was a beautiful young white woman who carried the book of the Veda, a musical instrument and a rosary composed of the letters of the alphabet. She was the mother of the scriptures, the sciences and the arts.

Also called Savitri, Gayatri, Brahmani, or Satarupa, she was born of Brahma. He, wanting to create beings, had divided himself into two parts. One was Sarasvati and the other remained Brahma.

The five-headed god

Brahma fell in love with Sarasvati as soon as he saw her, and he determined to make her his wife. Sarasvati, delighted at being in the company of the one who gave her life and wishing to honour him, danced around him. Brahma, overcome with sexual desire, followed her with his eyes in such a way that one head grew out of him on the right, another on the left, one in front, one behind and finally a fifth on top of him (*Matsyapurana*, III, 30–41).

Sarasvati was associated with water; she was the goddess of the sacred river. She was present in the holiest place in India, the confluence of the Ganges (the white river) and the Yamuna (the black river). There she could be seen only by the initiated.

> **The essence of truth**
> 'Divine Sarasvati, who is the very essence of truth, who is the daughter of Brahma and who is also called Rita, represents my words and is forever on my tongue.' (The words of Krishna, as contained in *Mahabharata*, 243)

Sarasvati, the goddess of poetry and music. Marble relief form the Vimla Vashi Temple in Dilwana (Mount Abu), the cent.

Saturn

Roman god

The master of agriculture

A very ancient Italian god, Saturn was associated with the Golden Age, which was synonymous with religious festivals and bacchanalian feasts.

Very little is known about Saturn. It is unclear whether he originated with Greek settlers, the Etruscans or the Sabines. It is certain, though, that he was firmly established in Rome from the time of the Republic, and that his temple was there, close to

the forum. He has been likened to Cronos, the father of Jupiter (Zeus). He was supposed to have ousted his father from the throne and to have been likewise ousted by his own son.

Saturn was welcomed to Rome by Janus, and his reign corresponded with a time of happiness and exceptional prosperity. He invented the dressing of the vine, taught man to husband the soil and provided men with their first laws. He is always depicted as being armed with a sickle or scythe.

Emancipation festivals?

The saturnalia, or festivals of Saturn, were occasions for peasant merry-making. For several days on end, there were constant sacrifices, banquets, dances and outdoor events. Society was completely turned upside down: presents and invitations were exchanged; schools, law courts and offices were shut; and crowds ran through the streets, shouting, '*Io saturnalia! Bona saturnalia!*'

These festivals were supposed to put an end to the social distance between men. Everything was permitted, even to slaves.

*The awful **Saturn** devouring his children to safeguard his power.*

Francisco Goya Lucientes (1746–1820): oil on canvas, 1819–1823.

> **The Golden Age**
> 'You see these two places in the ruined walls? They are traces and monuments of men from former times. The august Janus built this stronghold. Saturn built the other one. This one here is Janiculum, that one there is Saturnia, as they were called in the past.'
> (Virgil, *Aeneid*, VIII, 355–360)

The freemen no longer wore their togas, and all men, both masters and slaves, donned the pileus, the symbol of emancipation and freedom. One could even witness masters serving their slaves, who showed no hesitation in giving vent to their pent-up feelings either in words or in action. They were entitled to drink wine and tended to overdo it on this occasion.

The festivals began on the seventeenth of December and lasted for several days. Caesar, however, extended their duration. They signified the passage of time from one year to the next. Among the presents offered were wax candles, *sigillaria*, symbolizing the sun whose light would become brighter every day. The saturnalia would seem to be at the origin of the present-day festivals and customs which occur around Christmas and New Year's Day.

Strangely, the *planet* Saturn, in contrast to the *god* Saturn, represented evil for astrologers. But perhaps this seeming contradiction points in actual fact to a similarity. If Saturn symbolized uprootings and partings, the trials of life and its necessary

sacrifices, it was because he was entrusted with the task of freeing man from the limitations of his animal nature, from his instincts and his passions, and also from the constraints of his social life. Saturn symbolized freedom.

Cronos

Cronos was the son of Uranus (Heaven) and of Gaea (Earth), and the brother of the Uranian Cyclopes and of the Hecatonchires. Gaea, exhausted by the numerous pregnancies inflicted on her by her husband, requested her children to free her from this burden. All of them declined to accept responsibility, except her youngest, Cronos. He took the sickle given to him by his mother, caught his father unawares and cut off his testicles. He then threw them into the sea, deposed Uranus and ascended the throne.

He had as his wife his sister, Rhea, and was the father of Hestia, Demeter, Hera, Hades, Poseidon and Zeus. He, in turn, was to be dethroned by Zeus.

Sekhmet

Egyptian goddess

The mighty one

As the eye of the frenzied Re, Sekhmet destroyed the sun's enemies.

Sekhmet (the exact meaning of her name is 'the mighty one') lived at Memphis. She was the wife of the god Ptah and mother of Nefertem. Her marriage to the creator god did not make her quite his equal, but her own power was known and feared. Effigies of her were very common (nearly four hundred of them have been discovered), showing the importance of the cult dedicated to her both at Memphis and in other

regions of Egypt.

In Ptah's temple at Karnak, a statue in grey diorite, two metres high, depicts her with the head of a lioness and the body of a woman. Sekhmet was a terrible, bloodthirsty goddess, responsible for epidemics, death, carnage and war. All misfortunes were supposed to originate from her, and she inspired great fear.

But although she caused death, she also had the power of healing. A special ritual called 'the appeasement of Sekhmet' was performed in order to win her favours and be healed by her. Her priests formed an association of doctors and veterinarians. She thus became the protector of both the king and his subjects.

Seth

Egyptian god

Evil

Seth was the very embodiment of fury, violence, storm, crime and dishonesty.

Seth, called 'Typhon' by Plutarch, was associated with the 'abominable' animals: the pig, the donkey and the hippopotamus. He himself was depicted as a strange being with a stiff, forked tail, a long gaunt body, a tapering snout, huge erect ears and protruding eyes.

Seth was the incarnation of the forces opposing Maat, the goddess of order, equilibrium and justice. He was as brutal as she was gentle, as ugly as she was beautiful, as hated as she was loved.

Seth and Apopis

The world needed Seth's brute force. Seth 'was the prow of the vessel of Re (the sun)'. He fought the demon Apopis, who threatened him every morning and evening. On each occasion Seth was victorious, but Apopis always revived to commence battle again. As a result of this permanent conflict, the equilibrium of forces and universal harmony were born.

But the use of violence is always ambiguous, and in time the two enemies tended to become identified with one another. Seth

---

The god of confusion

'Behold, I am Seth, the creator of confusion, who creates both the tempest and the storm throughout the length and breadth of the heavens'. (Edouard Naville, *The Egyptian Book of the Dead of the XVIIIth to XXth Dynasties*, p. 39. Berlin, 1886)

---

became the personification of hostile forces and the symbol of revolt against man and the gods.

Seth signified disorder and violence. He was said to be a ravisher, a pederast and fractricidal. He took possession of certain men in order to make them irresponsible, and they became like him: menaces to society. A god of destruction, he destroyed crops with fire and hail. All disasters were caused by him. He was the enemy god and the god of enemies. People feared his power, but they also envied it. They tried to tame him and make him change sides. Certain pharaohs even adopted his name, as if to deny his hostility.

Seth and Osiris

Seth was the brother of Osiris and his total opposite. The universe could function only as a result of their contrasting natures. Seth killed his brother (who was later revived by Isis); then he went on to fight Horus, the son of his enemy. He was emasculated in the fight but managed to tear out one of his adversary's eyes. The victory remained undecided, as is the victory of light over darkness.

The Egyptians alternated between a sort of fascination, tinged with fear, for the violence represented by Seth and a rejection of the cult dedicated to him. Some people began to celebrate his castration and destroyed effigies of him. Others cut off his ears and replaced them with horns, turning him into representations of Amon. Eventually, those towns which worshipped him were forbidden to do so.

The Greek Typhon

He was a monstrous creature, capable of touching both east and west with his outstretched arms. Zeus crushed him by hurling Mount Etna on top of him.

Shamash

Babylonian god

The sun

The light of Shamash shone brightly in the sky, over the earth and in hell. He also presided over justice.

On a tablet discovered at Sippar, the seated god Shamash is shown bearing a head-dress with four rows of horns. He has a large beard, his hair is coiled up, and he wears a long robe. He holds a staff and a hoop. He is symbolized by a solar disc rising between two mountains or alternatively, by a simple spoked wheel.

The god of light

Shamash, the son of the moon-god Sin and Ningal, was the brother of Ishtar, the goddess of love and war. His wife was Aya, who was described as 'the young wife'. He gave light to the world. By day he travelled the heavens, seeing, inspecting and discovering everything, revealing secrets, giving assistance to anyone in need of it, punishing anyone deserving punishment and rewarding anyone worthy.

The first known written laws, the code of Hammurabi, were drawn up under Shamash's authority. As the god of justice, he dictated his wishes to the king of Babylonia and oaths were sworn in his name. Shamash forbade lying. Two minor gods assisted him in his task: Girru, the god of fire, and Nusku, the god of light. Requests addressed to him were halfway between magic and religion. Ever-present, he was sure to answer on condition that precise rituals were respected.

His cult was concentrated in the towns of Larsa in the south and Sippar in the middle of the country. In these two towns his temple was called the Efabbar (the shining house).

The sun-god Shamash, was flaming shoulders, brandishes his knife with its serrated edge and ascends the mountain.
Cylinder seal. Serpentine. Agade era (c. 2200 BC).

Shango

African god

The thunder

Every African tribe had its god. He was called Obatala by some and Yansan, Ogun or Shango by others. Shango was the god of thunder and the ancestor of the kings of Oyo.

Shango was virile and virulent. He dispensed justice, punishing wicked people such as liars, thieves and criminals. His favourite weapon was the thunderbolt which was regarded as the god's punishment: a house, tree or forest stricken by it became taboo. Because he was guilty, the owner was compelled to pay heavy fines and to appease the divinity by means of sacrifices.

Flint stones were important in the worship of this god. They were regarded as sacred objects or amulets and placed on his altars. The blood of sacrificial animals was poured over them in order to restore their vigour and their efficacy.

As well as sacrifices, the ritual consisted of dances and trances to the sound of a kind of rattle made from a lengthened gourd. During this ceremony, the two-headed axe, Shango's emblem, was waved about. The ceremony also included licentious acts.

Shango had three wives: Oya, who was the river Niger, and Oshun and Oba, two other rivers. It was said that Shango was the ancestor, the fourth king of the Yorubas and the master of thunder. He was supposed to have had the power to make jets of fire shoot from his body.

The apotheosis of Shango

Shango was a cruel king. His subjects were originally said to have been very divided in their opinions of him. Some wanted to chase him away, while others trusted him entirely. After many changes of heart, it was the first group who won the day; Shango quit the country and hanged himself from a tree. His supporters, on learning of his death, went in search of his body. They couldn't find it, but at the foot of the tree from which he had hanged himself, they spotted a hole from which emerged an iron chain. They concluded from this that Shango had become a god.

They built a temple on the site and, together with priests, they devised a form of worship to celebrate him. However, though he was a god for some, he was merely the deceased king for others. For a time, some shouted, 'The king has hanged himself!'; others shouted, 'The king is not dead!' There was terrible confusion until Shango made himself heard. He sent a terrible thunderstorm which destroyed the houses of those who disparaged him. Then everyone recognized that Shango had become a god.

Shango-worship, which originated in the region of the river Niger, was introduced into Brazil by the black population deported there as slaves. It has become rather confused with worship of Saint Jerome, but the parallelism is probably due merely to the presence alongside the saint of a lion, also an emblem of the kings of Oyo.

The assistance of the god

'Shango can help us, Shango, Oya's husband. We have only to follow him. Let him come and do with us whatever we are incapable of doing without his help. Unlike him, we are incapable of uttering imprecations. All we have to is to greet Shango.' (P. Verger. *Notes on the Worship of Orisa and Vodun*, p. 317. Dakar, 1957)

Shiva

Indian god

The favourable one

Shiva and Rudra were undoubtedly aspects of the same divinity. Rudra was a destructive force while Shiva was a beneficent one.

Shiva was called Mahâdeva ('the Great God'). He was a sovereign god, the organizer of the world. He was also known by the names of Bhairava ('the Terror'), Hara ('the Ravisher'), or Kala ('Death').

Representing darkness, his eyes were filled with snakes and he had a girdle made of skulls. He was surrounded by spectres and vampires and wore the crescent moon as a diadem. He had four arms: the first held a gazelle, the second wielded an axe, the third made a gesture of appeasement and the fourth made a sacrificial gesture. Shiva had a third eye in the middle of his forehead, with which he could strike down anything he looked at.

He danced amid devils on cremation sites, accompanying his dancing with a small drum. The dance was supposed to represent the world's constructive and destructive periods (*Mahabharata*, 13, 17, 50). This was his Rudra aspect.

Shiva defended his rights. It was said that because of his undesireable aspect, he was not invited to the sacrifice of Daksa, the father of Sati, his wife. Shiva was furious and prevented the rituals until such time as he received reparation (*Mahabharata*, 12, 283 ff.)

Shiva was Yogesvara, 'the prince of the ascetics'. He was represented in a meditative posture, covered in ashes, with his plait of hair coiling over his skull. Asceticism is associated with the reinforcement of energy and therefore with the mastery of vital forces.

The marriage of Shiva

Shiva was a dirty, hirsute, roving individual; yet Parvati, who was also called Sati or Uma, was in love with him.

Shiva gave her only one child in the normal way, a child called Kumara, and Ganesha and Skanda were obtained by artifice. He lost interest in sexual intercourse but still had mistresses, including Manasa, Ganga (*Mahabharata*, 3, 109), and many others, preferably from the unclean castes.

Compared with this boorish churl, Parvati was a perfect wife, a woman madly in love who allowed Shiva all his whims. She represented the energy of the god, the power which creates, maintains and destroys. Parvati was also the prototype for the fanatic devotee.

The Hindu phallic image

Shiva is represented by a cylindrical vertical stone emerging from an almost flat wash-basin with a spout, and the entire

---

An individual without honour

'By what mad whim did you manage to become infatuated with this boy who has neither lineage, social distinction, honour, nor caste, and who is of unknown parentage? He lives from begging, sleeps on cremation sites; he dances naked like demons and devils. He takes marijuana and hallucinogenic drugs and coats his body with ashes. He is a belligerent yogi who plaits his hair in a bun and detests sexual pleasures . . . Reasonable women would listen to your advice. As for myself. I am but a besotted woman, in love with a madman!' (*Parvatimangal of Tulsi-Das*, 49 ff.)

figure rests on a base. This is normally viewed as a phallic symbol emerging from a woman's genitals. Supposedly, Shiva's penis had fallen off as a result of the curse uttered by the sages of the forest of Daruka. They had made the curse because the god, disguised as a young, handsome, naked ascetic, had made their wives lose their heads.

Above all, the linga (the Hindu phallus) represented mastery of the world. Vishnu and Brahma disputed this with one another; while they were exchanging arguments, a luminous penis emerged, of which neither the bottom nor top could be seen. Brahma changed himself into a bird to search for its point, and Vishnu changed himself into a wild boar to grub around in the earth and find its base. They returned without finding anything. At that point Shiva made his appearance through the linga, which was cleft into a lozenge shape. The two other gods then recognized his supremacy (*Shiva-purana*, 2, 5).

Another version says that Brahma claimed to have reached the top of the shaft of the penis and began to insult Shiva as he appeared. Shiva, in a fury, cut off one of Brahma's five heads, but then found himself burdened with a great sin. As a result, he had to take a vow that he would be a beggar for 12 years.

The linga was a cult object. During ceremonies, it was sprinkled with water, milk or oil, liquids which were collected in the basin. The penis represented the god inside the temples, effigies of him remaining outside.

The protector of the world

'When one knows Shiva, who is more subtle than subtlety itself, who, from the centre of vagueness, emits all the diversities of the world, and who, in his variety of shapes, clutches the whole universe to himself alone, one experiences peace forevermore. He is the protector of the world within the bounds of time, sovereign of the universe, who is hidden in every being, and to whom the seers and prophets of the Brahman caste and the divinities are all subject. When he has been recognized as such, one is severing the bonds of death.' (*Svetasvatara Upanishad*, 1, 14)

The death of Kama

Shiva was despised by his father-in-law, Daksa, which led to the suicide of his wife, Sati. After mourning for her, Shiva decided to withdraw into the mountains and meditate deeply. Sati, having been reincarnated, took up her place alongside him and adopted the same lifestyle.

But the world needed Shiva. It was threatened by a terrible demon called Taraka, to whom Brahma had granted invulnerability and who could be destroyed only by a son of Shiva. Kama, the god of love, was called upon for help. He approached Shiva, waited for sixty million years and then sent his first arrow.

Shiva, furious at having been disturbed, reduced Kama to ashes with his third eye. Then he spotted Sati and saw the ascetic life she was leading. He was filled with lust for her. They came together and produced Kumara, who put the demon Taraka to death (*Kumarasambhava*).

Ganapati

Shiva was still in love with Sati. She sometimes wished to go into retreat on her own, and so created, from the impurities of her skin, a guard for her door called Ganapati (Ganesha). Shiva came and looked at his wife while she was bathing, and Ganapati loosed his fury on him. Vishnu came to Shiva's aid, sending his maya, a magic illusion which spread confusion all around. Shiva took advantage of this to cut off Ganapati's head.

Sati aroused a thousand goddesses to harass the gods and requested that Ganapati be restored to her. Shiva submitted and requested that he be brought the head of the first thing to be encountered. This turned out to be an elephant, and henceforth Ganapati had the head of an elephant (*Shiva-purana*).

The heroic deeds

Shiva was recognized as the one who, in order to save the world, swallowed the venom spat out by the serpent Vasuki (*Mahabharata*, 1, 18). He was the one who destroyed an elephant in which a demon had concealed itself; the one who emerged from the linga to thrust aside death which was seeking to lay hold of one of his devotees; and the one who destroyed three fortresses which were in the hands of demons (*Mahabharata*, 7, 202, 64).

Shiva defended his devotees. When a young cowherd sprinkled his cows' milk on a linga he had shaped from sand, his father arrived, flew into a rage and kicked over the linga. Shiva then arrived on the scene and gave the boy the post of watchman of his house.

Shiva also knew how to appreciate each individual's value. During a hunt, Shiva and Arjuna killed the same prey, and naturally the god and the hero both claimed ownership of the beast. After exchanging insults they came to blows, and a battle ensued. The god won the day, but, recognizing his adversary's worth, gave him what he wanted.

The bull

Shiva's mount was a black bull called Nandin. Shiva himself was sometimes invoked as a bull, the symbol of fertility. The bull is usually shown in front of the temple, lying down facing the sanctuary.

The cult

Together with Brahma and Vishnu, Shiva formed part of the great triad of Hindu gods. But for many sects he was the supreme being, the absolute: the sole reality to become manifest in the world. It was he who acted, created, maintained and destroyed in the world. The ambivalence inherent in the god—who was both creator and destroyer, who was the symbol of both fertility and sexual abstinence—formed the basis of his personality.

The worship given him consisted mainly of appeasing him with gifts of flowers and libations. But the observances involved were numerous. For example, Shiva's worshippers had to cover their bodies with ashes, pronounce magic formulae, participate in processions, laugh, sing and dance.

Yoga

The objective of these rituals was to make man unaware of his surroundings. Yoga is

193

Shiva *Vinadhara Dakshinâmurti, a player of the vina, master of sciences and the arts, and protector of the forests and the wild beasts. The emblem of this last function is the doe, which he carries in one of his four hands.*

Made from bronze with a green patina, approximate 11th century A.D.

one of the practices which liberates man from the world's constraints with the aim of attaining perfect realization of the self. Shiva was the ultimate yogi, and his devotees took him as their model. However, Shivaism also inspired popular licentious practices.

Sin

Sumerian god

The moon

Sin sailed over the waters in celestial space, wearing a head-dress of the crescent moon with its two points raised like a small boat.

Sin was also called Zu-en or Nannar by the Sumerians and Nannar by the Akkadians. He was represented as being seated on a throne, with a long beard tumbling down his chest, holding an axe, a sceptre and a staff.

Sin was the moon and the father of Shamash, the sun. Sin's light was benevolent and guided the caravans. The sun's light, however, was pitiless, burning things and drying them up. The crescent of the moon was like a pair of horns, and Sin was likened to a young bull whose strength grows as the months proceed.

Sin was as oracle. His predictions were binding upon the gods just as they were on man. An eclipse was the most formidable sign given by Sin, since he was then concealing himself and thus announcing catastrophe.

The worship of Sin spread from Ur in Babylonia and Haran in Assyria. The highest authorities were involved in it: the daughter of Sargon, king of Akkadia, became the god's wife; one of the sisters of the kings of Larsa was its high priestess; and one of Assurbanipal's brothers was high priest of the temple of Haran.

Homage to sin

'Proud bull calf with thick horns and perfect proportions, with a lapis beard, full of virility and abundance [. . .]. merciful, indulgent father, who holds the whole country's life in his hands [. . .]' (St. Langdon, *Oxford Editions of Cuneiform Texts*, t. IV, p.6)

Sirens

Greek demonesses

The enchantresses

The Sirens' songs were irresistible.

The Sirens were daughters of the Muse Melpomene and the god Achelous and were also the companions of Persephone. When Persephone was carried off by Hades, they asked the gods if they could have wings so that they could go and look for her. That is why the Sirens were half woman, half bird (Ovid, *Metamorphoses*, v. 512–562). There were three Sirens: Pisinoe, Aglaope and Thelxiope, also called Parthenope, Leucosia and Ligia. One held a lyre, the second sang and the third played the flute. Their singing was very harmonious.

They lived on an island, using their voices to enchant sailors to the point of shipwreck. They then devoured them. The Argonauts sailed past that way, but the singing of Orpheus triumphed over that of the Sirens. Ulysses asked his sailors to stop their ears with wax. As for himself, not wanting to miss such a beautiful melody, he had himself tied firmly to the ship's mast.

Sita

Indian heroine

The woman born of the furrow

Sita was an earthly manifestation of Lakhsmi, just as Rama was of Vishnu.

Sita's birth was extraordinary. She emerged from a furrow under King Janaka's ploughshare as he was ploughing his field in preparation for sacrifices. She was therefore born of holy ground, and the king immediately made her his adopted daughter (*Ramayana*, I, 66, 13).

In time, Sita became a very beautiful girl who attracted the attention of many men. Janaka promised to give her in marriage to the man who succeeded in drawing Shiva's bow, which was in his possession. He was convinced that no man would be successful in doing this and that he would thus keep his daughter to himself.

Rama

He had not reckoned, however, with Rama. Rama managed to draw the bow and to break it. Janaka, bound by his oath, was compelled to give up his daughter and to give her hand in marriage to Rama. The couple vowed that they would love each other absolutely.

Sita was a faithful wife. When Rama lost his royal status and was forced to go into exile in the forest for 14 years, Sita, who was not herself bound by this obligation, refused to remain in the royal palace. She followed her husband into disgrace and endured with more fortitude than Rama the ascetic life.

The misfortunes of Sita

Sita was faithful to Rama under the worst circumstances. She was carried off by Ravana, who had been seduced by her beauty, but she never succumbed to his cleverest attempts at seduction. Ravana, aspiring to genuine love, was unwilling to take her by force. Ultimately, his seduction attempts failed; meanwhile, despite their separation, Sita and Rama composed the most beautiful love songs for one another.

The reunion, however, was not what these songs might have led them to hope for. Sita remained faithful even when her husband, convinced that she must have succumbed during her long abduction, punished her unjustly and subjected her to the test of fire. She said to him, 'if, O proud prince, despite the proofs of my love for you during the time we lived together, I am still a stranger in your eyes, my loss is irremediable' (*Ramayana*, VI, 116, 10). Without flinching, she ascended the funeral pyre, but since the fire refused to burn her, she emerged from the situation victorious. The lovers were once again in a state of absolute euphoria.

Rama, however, was again seized with doubts and forced Sita into exile in the forest. There she gave birth to her twin sons, Kusa and Lava. This separation was a long one, and the intervention of the children was required before Rama finally recognized Sita's innocence.

Sita returned, but no sooner was she in the kingdom than she requested that the earth which had given birth to her should take her back. The earth opened up and swallowed her forever (*Ramayana*).

Skanda

Indian hero

The young man

Skanda was chief of the divine armies.

Skanda was the son of Shiva. Shiva trying to father a child, had remained a long time in union with the goddess. Already the gods were afraid of the product of this union, who could not fail to be tremendously strong. They requested that Shiva abstain from procreating and he agreed, henceforth practising complete sexual abstinence. He was warned too late, however, and a little of his sperm fell to earth and landed in the fire.

Agni, the god of fire, deposited the embryo created from Shiva's sperm within Ganga. The pregnant Ganga could not stand the heat created within her by Agni and Shiva and abandoned the embryo on mount Meru. There the Pleiades came and suckled it.

As soon as Skanda was born, the gods, terrified by the prospect of his power, hastened to see him. They even thought of killing him because he filled them with such fear. In his presence, however, they could not help but be impressed, and they therefore subjected themselves to him and requested his protection. Shiva himself came to meet him and recognized his son. Skanda

---

Skanda honoured under the name of Subrahmanya

'His statue is worshipped throughout all the pagodas. He also has pagodas which are dedicated to him, to him alone, and which bear his name . . . He is alleged to have had two wives, one of whom is called Dewanei, the other Walliamei — the latter is supposed to hail from the race of basket-makers.' (B. Ziegenbalg, *Detailed Description of Malabar Heathenism*, 1711, p.45. Edited by W. Caland, Amsterdam, 1926)

---

placed himself under his orders.

Skanda was a handsome young man, filled with ardour and strength. His brother Ganesha however, was ugly, fat and crafty. What the first obtained by his courage and willpower, the second obtained by means of guile. To the first fell war, liberation and violence; to the second fell peace, the smooth running of affairs and government. Skanda was the perfect commander of the armies of the gods.

Skanda had two wives: Valli, the daughter of the mountain and a huntress, and Devasena, whose name means 'army of the gods'. Devasena was a young girl whom Indra met while out walking. She was grappling with an asura, an enemy of the gods. Indra rescued her and she asked him, as a favour, to give her a husband. Indra gave her Skanda as a spouse.

As soon as he was old enough to begin his duties, the gods informed Skanda that they had already been defeated in combat with the asuras and that Taraka, the leader of their enemies, was wreaking havoc throughout the world. Skanda didn't need to be asked twice and set off for battle immediately. He killed Taraka with his infallible weapon, a magical device which made him invincible.

The misogynist

Skanda was honoured across the whole of India. By virtue of his birth, which was entirely due to his father, he was very opposed to women. Women were forbidden entry to his temples. He didn't like them and pursued them angrily, threatening them with puerperal fever up to the sixth day of their confinement. He was also a child abductor, although people prayed to him in order to have children. The Pleiades, his adoptive mothers, helped him in this evil work. Provision was made for rituals to appease them and to ward off their curses.

Soma

Indian god

The drink of the gods

Soma, divine drink, was essential to the gods' immortality and to the sacrifices made by man.

Soma was the moon god. He brought nocturnal coolness and marked the rhythm of the days and months. In particular, he was the nectar of immortality, 'a god and a heavenly beverage'. This juxtaposition emphasizes 'the value of a sacred liquor, an essential element in sacrifice.

The sacrificial beverage

Soma was a beverage extracted from a plant of heavenly origin which grew on remote mountains. The rituals which had to be observed during the manufacture of the soma were stipulated down to the very last detail. They made up the main ceremony of the religion.

The plant from which soma was made was undoubtedly a mushroom. The first, preparatory stage consisted of watering the stems until they became swollen with water. This was followed by a pressing process and another washing in water. Then the stems were placed on top of millstones and beaten with stones. Finally, the juice was extracted and filtered through sheep's wool to rid it of impurities.

Throughout this entire process, poets sang. The poetry encouraged the priests, speeded up the decantation process and made the soma more potent. To compensate, the soma gave inspiration and fervour to the poets. Soma rituals and words were intimately linked with one another to make the sacrifice effective.

Soma was drunk either pure or blended with milk. Its effects were potent, acting on both the mind and body. It stimulated ideas, intellectual vigour, and physical strength and courage. It cured illnesses and strengthened sexual potency. It was an elixir of life.

Soma was the drink of the gods. It gave them strength, splendour, security and finally immortality. Drunk by both gods and men, it created bonds of friendship between them and was at the very heart of the sacrifice.

The state of intoxication created by soma was not unrelated to the effects of hallucinogens, but the objective was quite different. It was an intimate union with the gods and also communion with the universe. Soma was not an ordinary drink—it was the very heart of the universe.

The origin of soma

The myth concerning soma's origin link ideas which, at first, seem unconnected. It offers an explanation of those elements which were essential sacrifice—the drink, the word, the excitement and the sacrifice—as well as of the different stages of the ceremony. It caused the most marvellous things to happen, showing that the drink was a god. Even the poets' lines were transformed into birds.

In primordial times Soma dwelt in the sky, and the gods had their abode on earth. They wanted to make him come into their midst, and in order to do this they decided to create two female beings: Kadru, the Earth, and Suparni, the Word.

Kadru and Suparni were complete opposites. They began to have a sort of contest to determine who could see the furthest. Suparni could see a white steed tethered to a pole, but Kadru could see the wind which blew its tail about. Kadru was thus the winner and, according to the rules they had

---

'**Soma** is stallion's sperm with the vigour of a male'. (*Taittirya samhita*, VII, 18, 2).

193

imposed upon one another, she took possession of her companion's soul.

Suparni, however, managed to redeem herself by going up into the sky in search of Soma on behalf of the gods. Suparni entrusted this task to her children, who were the metrical forms of the Veda called *jagati*, *tristubh* and *gayatri*.

The metrical forms, to accomplish their mission, changed into birds. To begin with, the lines all had four syllables. The jagati was the first to leave and flew off. At the half-way stage, she was exhausted and incapable of holding on to three of the syllables, which fell. Having only one syllable left, she was unable to go as far as Soma and returned home, bringing back only ascetic fervour.

In turn, the tristubh set out. She experienced the same difficulties; but, forewarned by her companion's experience, she made great efforts to retain her syllables, and lost only one. Unfortunately, she had nonetheless become so impoverished that she could not reach Soma. She returned home, bringing back only the *daksina*, the money offered to priests for the sacrifice.

The third one to set out was the gayatri. More gifted and noble, she managed to reach the sky complete with all her syllables. She terrified its guardians and seized Soma between her talons and beak. On the way back, she retrieved the syllables lost by the jagati and the tristubh and thus assumed the form which she has today, the octosyllabic. This is the most perfect form of versification, the one used in the most important moments of the ritual. The gayatri had carried in her right claw the morning pressings, in her left claw the midday pressings, and in her beak the evening pressings. But, since this latter had been sucked during the journey, it was not pure and had to be blended with milk, butter and sacrificial victims so as to be worthy of the sacrifice.

The gayatri alone took charge of the morning pressings. Then she joined up with the two others, weakened by their adventures, for the midday and the evening pressings.

The flight of the soma

The soma's adventures were not at an end, however. Having been made a drink again, the soma was stolen by the Gandharva, a demon. The gods, knowing that the Gandharva was madly in love with women, undertook to tempt him by sending Suparni to him. Suparni had been changed into a one-year-old woman and was entrusted with retrieving the soma. She succeeded in her mission, but the Gandharva was not pleased. He wanted at least to get back Suparni, for withour her (the Word), he was unable to perform the sacrifice. It was decided that Suparni would choose her own fate, and the Gandharva and the gods undertook to seduce her. The Gandharva recited the Veda's sacred word to her and the gods, who were more cunning, played her the lyre. Suparni, the Word, made her choice and rejoined the gods, remaining eternally with them (*Taittiriya-samhita*, VI, 1, 6, 1 ff.).

Henceforth gods and man had at their disposal both the word and soma. Men prepared it and the gods drank it and, transformed by the ritual into ambrosia, it made them immortal.

The sacrificial beverage

'We have partaken of the soma,
We have become immortal.
Having reached light,
We have found the gods [. . .].
Enflame me like the fire
Which is born from friction.
Illuminate us, and make us more
fortunate [. . .].
Nectar which has penetrated our souls,
Immortal in us mortals, this soma [. . .].'
(*Rig Veda.*)

Sucellus

Gallic god

The sure striker

The god with the mallet, Sucellus was rich, powerful, sovereign and majestic. He was compared with Jupiter.

A bearded figure in his prime, Sucellus was shown with his tunic, cowl and boots. He wore a wolfskin over his head and held a club/sceptre in his left hand and a pot-bellied vase in his right.

The mallet he held, comparable with that of the Irish god Dagda, appeared to be the mark of sovereignty. The pot-bellied vase indicated that he was the dispenser of food. Sucellus was a benefactor associated with bountiful nature. Caesar made him into a national god, the father of the Gallic race (Caesar, *De Bello Gallico* VI, 17–18).

The wife of Sucellus was Nantosuelta, the river goddess. Representing fertility, she held a cornucopia in her hand. She can also be seen bearing in her hand a tiny round house. This was intended to show that the wife was the very core of the home.

Sucellus was often likened to Sylvanus, the god of forests, who was also a dispenser of gifts and good things.

The god with the mallet

The name Sucellus can be split into two parts: 'su', meaning 'well', and 'cellus', meaning 'to strike'. Sucellus was the god who was a sure striker, and therefore the god of a merciful death.

Svarog

Slavic god

Fire

Svarog, the god of heavenly light, illuminated both earth and mankind.

Svarog was the Pan-Slavic god of fire. He was called Svarizic as national god of the Veletes (Thietmar de Merseburg, *Chronicles*). Dazbog, his son, was god of the sun.

The Slavs believed in one god, but a god so terrible and so distant that even to pronounce his name was forbidden. Svarog was the last earthly manifestation of this 'idle god', who was made more 'present' by the insignificance of the intermediary gods.

He was the dispenser of all wealth: a legislator, judge and protector of monogamy. His name means 'to weld'. As the god of fire, he had the skill of the blacksmith, who used fire to weld metals. He was also both a magician and soothsayer.

Svarog (or Svarizic) was honoured in numerous towns. Temples were dedicated to him in Rethra, Stettin (Szczecin). Wolin, Wolgast, Gützkow, Kiel and many other places. Following military campaigns the standards of the armies were laid down in his temples, and the priests would perform sacrifices of domestic animals and sometimes of men.

Sventovit

Slavic god

The lord

By virtue of his strength and ardour, Sventovit, or Svantovit, was regarded as the god of war.

The multiplicity of names for the gods, all of which were constructed on the same model, doubtless concealed different aspects of one and the same divinity. Sventovit means 'energy'; Iarovit, 'wrath'; Porevit, 'power'; and Rujevit, 'rutting time'. But the appearance of the gods represented by these names also differed. Porevit had four or five faces, Rujevit had seven, and Triglav, the Pomeranian god, had three.

Sventovit's statue in Rügen is eight metres high. It has four necks and four heads, two of which look to the front and two to the back. When one is directly in front of it, however, it seems to be looking both right and left. In his right hand he holds a trumpet, and in his left, a bow, and both his arms are held close to his body. He is clad in a tunic (Saxo Grammaticus, *Gesta Danorum*).

Sventovit was the god of fertility, fruitfulness and destiny. He owned a horse which was kept in his temple. It was alleged that he mounted it at night, while by day only his high priest had the privilege of mounting it. This horse had the gift of divination: it was forced to pass between two lances fixed in the ground and, depending on its position, the meaning of the oracle it was intended to signify could be determined.

> **A multi-form god**
> Slavic religion never managed to decide once and for all between monotheism and the multiple energies of which they believed the world to be made up. The four faces of the idols corresponded more or less to the four elements: air, fire, earth and water.

*Worship of the god **Sventovit** who, with his four faces, protected the world from four sides. The column illustrated here was found in Husiatyn in Polish Galicia. It is 9½ft high.*

An engraving by Ivan Bilibin, 1934.

Tane

Divinity from the Pacific Islands

The Illuminator of the heavens

As a demiurge, Tane kept heaven and earth apart, thus permitting the world to exist.

Tane was the son of Rangi (Heaven) and of Papa (Earth). The sun, which was established on top of heaven, was at risk of destroying Papa's children. Tane lay down on top of his mother; then, lifting his feet and placing them on top of Rangi, he separated heaven and earth and thus kept them at a safe distance from one another.

At the time of this separation, certain of Rangi's and Papa's children remained clinging to their father. They were not destined to die but would live forever. Those who remained on top of the mother were mankind, and they would experience death.

Tane was the god of forests: the branches of the trees were his legs; the trunk was his head; and the wood of the canoes and houses was his flesh. Tane was thus man's protection against the wrath of Rangi, who had been separated from his wife.

Finding a wife

Tane wished to have offspring and began to search for the female element. He produced the birds, trees, creepers, rata tree, insects and reptiles.

Then Tane found a wife, but he was so unskilled that he had difficulty in begetting children. First of all he claimed that he was using the 'house of life' (?), but without success. Then he tried using his wife's eyes, which made her weep; then her nostrils, which made her produce mucus; then her mouth, which made her produce saliva; then her ears, and all he got was wax; then her armpits, which produced sweat.

Finally, he found the right opening and begat a daughter, Hine ahu one, whom he immediately claimed as his wife. Then he begat Hine ahua rangi, whom he also took as his wife.

When the latter asked who her father was, Tane said that it was he and she rushed away in terror. He set out to look for her, discovered her hiding place, and asked her to return. She refused, however, and became the goddess of death.

The origin of evil

The god Tangaroa, who had transformed himself into a fish, was the enemy of Tane. Certain of Tangaroa's children decided not to follow him into the ocean and took up their abode on dry land. Tane asked the descendants of Tu-matanenga, his brother who was the god of fierce men, to make nets and fight with their lances and fishhooks and kill Tangaroa's children. From that time, men have been eating fish. Tangaroa, in order to avenge himself, flooded the earth and destroyed the whole shoreline.

From this war were born misfortune and death, for Tane and Tangaroa wished for their mutual destruction, and their quarrels led them to devour their enemies.

Often, Tane was regarded as the god of good and Tangaroa as the god of evil.

Tane, the organizer of the world

'May the sacred sky, the cloudless, clear sky, never become overcast. Know the contents of the basket of Tane, which was taken there to adorn his father, the sky, beautifully balanced, with the stars Canopus, Rigel and Sirius up aloft. The basket has been empited to shape the fish in the sky (the Milky Way), extending into the distance in a most beautiful arrangement.' (E. Best, *The Maori*, Wellington, 1924)

Taranis

Gallic god

The thunder

Like Jupiter, Taranis was the omnipotent master of the universe. His weapons were the thunderbolt and rain.

Taranis, terrifying and sublime at the same time, inspired fear with rumblings of thunder and sudden lightning flashes. Without any warning he ravaged the earth with thunderbolts and floods; at the same time, though, he brought forth the gentle rain which fed the earth and made crops grow.

Taranis was depicted as a bearded man in his prime, holding a large wheel (the basin of Gundestrup in Denmark). The wheel symbolized the thunderbolt and the rumblings of the thunder. He was also represented on horseback, overcoming a giant with a serpent's tail, as if to show his domination. But his comparison to Jupiter and the latter's victory over the giants is perhaps the explanation for this iconography.

Taranis was a cruel creature who demanded human sacrifices. His victims were shut up in wooden cages which were then set alight. Severed heads were also offered to him.

Traces of his cult are found in Gaul as well as in Germany, Hungary, Yugoslavia and Great Britain.

A Gallic Dagda

Just like the Irish Dagda, Taranis was reputed to be the master of the elements. The thunderbolt, his weapon, was said to blind anyone who saw it, deafen anyone who heard it, and kill anyone struck by it.

***Taranis** the Gallic god of the thunderbolt, hurling the wheel of fire with his arms raised.*

Detail from one of the tablets decorating the interior of Gundestrup's cauldron. Embossed silver (c. 50 BC).

Tengri

Mongol god

The supreme being

Tengri, Od or Odlek was the great god of heaven.

As an eternal god, Tengri showed his power in the order imposed by him on the world. The order of the natural world, the organization and movements of the stars and the government of the Mongol empire were attributed to him. He was said to be great and merciful. He showed his anger by sending thunderstorms.

Tengri acted from the very inmost being of man. He procured the energy which was essential to them and the course of action which was best for them and the universe. He distributed good luck and wealth. Creation was not openly attributed to him, but he ensured that the world was maintained and functioning properly. He delegated his power to the emperor, who was entrusted with the promulgation of Tengri's decrees.

Tengri was demanding, punishing mercilessly those who disobeyed him. For man, punishment was death; for a people, it was genocide. No retribution was conceivable in the next life either for good or evil actions.

Tengri had a favourite animal, the horse. It was said that he mounted it and rode through the world, repairing what had been broken and encouraging peace. On certain occasions the emperor, who was his high priest, organized together with the people the sacrifice of a horse.

Associated deities

The lower deities were also called tengri. They were Tengri's children or envoys. Earth, the mountains, water, fire and trees were tengri, and they were very closely associated with the supreme being because they had a power which Tengri controlled completely.

The sun and moon were more independent. Venus was called 'the one with masculine strength'. She was a warrior who chased away the other stars at the end of the night. A form of worship was therefore reserved for the stars, consisting mainly of walking about to emulate their apparent movements in the sky.

Some peoples also honoured a great goddess, although her connection to Tengri was not actually stated. She was called Umai and was the goddess of maternity, 'the pure mother with the seventy cradles'. She had abundant golden hair, which was the symbol of wealth.

Origin of the shaman

The tengri of the west created man who, at the beginning of time, lived happily, experiencing neither illness nor sorrow. But later man incurred the displeasure of the tengri of the east and started to fall ill and die. The tengri of the west became terrified by the fate of man and deliberated about how to come to their aid. A decision was taken: to help human beings fight against evil spirits, they would give them a shaman, and for this purpose the eagle was chosen.' (Régis Boyer, *The Religions of Northern Europe*, 1974)

The shamans

The shamans formed the bond between the lower and upper worlds. Their practices, which were a mixture of magic, trances and ecstasy, allowed them to enter into communication with the spirits without being dependent on them. The ecstasies were ascents towards the god of heaven to present the offerings of the community, or descents to subterranean regions in search of the soul of a sick person who had been carried off by demons, or else to accompany the soul of a dead person to his last abode.

Teshub

Hurrian god

The thunderstorm

With Teshub came the end of the reign of the ancient gods and the start of the reign of modern gods.

Teshub, the god of the thunderstorm, had the bull and the cudgel as his symbols. He was represented as being mounted on a bovid, riding over mountains. He had an axe in his right hand and thunderclouds in his left. Ishtar was his sister, Hebat his spouse and Saruma his son.

Hebat had a whole courtly retinue. Among its members were Ishtar, Kubaba of Karkemish and Ishara (the goddess of Medicine). It also contained other goddesses: those of erotic pleasure, war, fertility and fruitfulness. Hebat was a queen and Teshub was the embodiment of a sovereign.

The three terrible gods

Teshub was the son of Kumarbi or Anu. During the course of a battle to determine who should be the king of heaven, Kumarbi swallowed Anu's virility. From this virility were born three gods: Teshub, Aranzah and Tashmishu. Teshub was entrusted the task of dethroning Kumarbi. He succeeded in doing this and thus became the supreme god (*The Heavenly Royalty*).

After his fall from power, Kumarbi pondered his revenge. He intended to make war on his rebellious sons. In order to do this, he impregnated a huge stone. A son was born, called Ullikummi, whose body was made of diorite (greenstone). Ullikummi grew and kept on growing. Gradually he occupied the whole of space, crushing anything that surrounded him and reaching both the sea and the tops of the temples.

Tranquil strength

The young gods were then panic-stricken. Teshub and Tashmishu 'took one another by the hand' and emerged from the temple. Ishtar descended from heaven. Teshub looked at the terrible man of stone. Dumbfounded, he prepared for battle. He summoned a thunderstorm, rains and winds and sent forth shafts of lightning. Battle took place, but Ullikummi's tranquil strength prevailed over both the cries of rage and the gesticulations of the god of the thunderstorm.

Ullikummi continued to grow; he caused both heaven and earth to quake; he forced Hebat to leave her ruined temple and seek refuge in heaven. He threatened to destroy the whole of humanity, which would have deprived the gods of sacrifices. The attempts made by Ishtar to seduce him and by Ashtabi to annihilate him were fruitless.

So, Teshub returned to battle. Éa, his devoted friend and protector, caught Ullikummi unawares and 'cut off his feet.' Teshub descended towards the sea, brandishing thunder, and became locked in a battle whose outcome seemed uncertain. However, he hung on courageously and won the victory.

Teshub worship spread at the start of the second millenium into countries where the Hurrian language was spoken. His sanctuaries could be found in the Hittite empire, in Babylonia, in Sumer, and down the Syrian coast as far as Anatolia.

He was compared with other gods of the thunderstorm, such as Baal of Canaan and Adad of Assyria.

Teutates

Gallic god

The father of the people

*The protective god of the tribe,
Teutates, or Toutatis, was a god
cruel beyond all others.*

Teutates was a warrior god, sometimes compared to Mars and Mercury. It is perhaps he who is depicted on a bas-relief on the Mavilly pillar on the Côte d'Or. He is armed in Roman style, and a serpent with a ram's head towers beside him. A warrior goddess whose left breast is bare also stands next to him.

There is evidence of Teutates worship in Latin inscriptions found in Great Britain, Germany and Rome. He was often likened to Ogmios, the god of eloquence, because Ogmios carries a cudgel, bow and quiver. He was also thus identified because in Celtic thinking the leader of the army was, above all, the man who knew how to use words to train his troops and who wrote history in such a way that war played a predominant role.

Like all tribal gods, Teutates was a protector of oaths. An oath was taken with these words: 'To the god by whom my tribe swears'. Also, the name Teutates (or Toutatis) means 'people', 'tribe' or 'nation'.

The bath of death or of immortality

Teutates was a cruel god. It is known from Lucian's *Bernese Scholia* that he demanded human sacrifices. The victims were plunged into a vat of water until they drowned. This scene is also portrayed on the Gundestrup basin (Denmark). It is possible, however, to interpret this as a bath of immortality given by the god of war to his warriors.

It is also reminiscent of the three vats of cold water into which the hero was plunged to cure him of his murderous mania. It might possibly, then, be a curative bath.

The bloody gods

'And among these cruel gods, Tuetates is appeased by sacrificial blood, the hideous Esus is appeased by savage altars, and Taranis is no more gentle than Diana of the Scythians'. (Lucian, *The Pharsalia*, I, 444 – 447)

The Gallic gods

Teutates, Taranis and Esus were the three great, cruel gods of Gaul. There were, however, other peace-loving gods. Smertrios, for example, was the god who supplied wealth. He was revered as a protector, one who kept his foes at bay and made an impression on them by virtue of his strength — a strength comparable to that of Hercules. Cernunnos, the old man, was the god of plenty; Belenus, the brilliant one, was the god of medicine; and Ogmios was the god of eloquence.

Esus

Esus appears on a relief of the pillar of the boatmen of Lutetia (in the Cluny Museum), dressed as a woodcutter. He is busy pruning a tree in the forest where the bull with the three cranes is hiding. On a Gallo-Roman stela in Trier, he is felling a large tree with an axe. He was particularly well known because of the bloody sacrifices with which he was honoured. The wounded victim was hanged from a tree until he was completely drained of blood.

Tezcatlipoca

Aztec god

The smoking mirror

The god Tezcatlipoca, a malevolent sorcerer, brought the custom of human sacrifice to Mexico.

Tezcatlipoca was represented in human form with a stripe of black paint across his face and an obsidian mirror replacing one of his feet. Legend has it that he was mutilated by the mythical crocodile on which the earth was supposed to rest. He was also called Yoalli Ehecatl, ('nocturnal wind'). Yaotl ('the warrior') or Telpochtli ('the young man'). As creator god, he reigned over the first of the four worlds which were destroyed prior to the creation of the present one. He had the animal form of a jaguar.

The omnipresent god

He was the god of the great bear and the night sky. He was also honoured as the god of the thunderbolt. With his mirror he was able to see everything and was aware of both human actions and thoughts. He had the gift of being able to be everywhere at once, but normally he remained invisible. He was associated with Tlazolteotl, the goddess of luxury and illicit love, who used to receive the confession of sinners once in the course of their lives.

Tezcatlipoca was the protector of young men and the patron of military academies. He was also the protector of slaves and severely punished masters who ill-treated them. Finally, he rewarded good people by making them both rich and happy and punished the wicked by making them poor and ill. It was he who provided the name for any new emperor.

Tezcatlipoca was a malevolent wizard. He attacked the kindly Quetzalcoatl, the plumed serpent, who was opposed to human sacrifice. When he entered Quetzalcoatl's, kingdom, he taught him to drink pulque and to thus become intoxicated. He then showed him his face, that of an old man, and the good king was terrified by it. Next, disguised as a naked, handsome young man, Tezcatlipoca attempted to seduce Quetzalcoatl's daughter and sowed the seeds of dissension throughout his kingdom. He did all this so well that Quetzalcoatl no longer wished to reign over this country of woes. He abandoned his capital in Tula, thus bringing to an end the golden age.

Human sacrifices

Tezcatlipoca then assumed power and introduced human sacrifice. During the great feast celebrated in honour of him, a handsome young man who was supposed to represent the god was chosen. Along with four of the most beautiful young girls in the town, the young man lived for a year in princely luxury. He was served and honoured like some great personage.

Then the day of the celebration came round again, and the young man mounted the steps of the temple, trampling down everything which had been of service to him during his triumph. Having reached the top, he lay down with his back on a stone called the 'techcatl'. Four men kept him in position, holding him by the arms and legs, while a priest, armed with a flint knife, cut open his chest. The priest then tore out the young man's heart and placed it in an earthenware jar.

A god of Toltecan origin

Tezcatlipoca was honoured from the 10th century in Aztec lands. He was brought there by the warrior Toltecs, who had come from the north.

Theseus

Greek hero

The slayer of monsters

Heracles was a champion among the gods and Theseus was a champion among men.

Theseus was the son of Aegeus. His Aegues had had no children by his various wives. He was upset about this and went to consult the Delphic oracle, who gave him only a very obscure clue. On his return he went to Pittheus, the king of Troezen, and explained his position to him.

Pittheus did not like to see Aegeus in such despair and made him drink until he became unconscious. Then he put his daughter, Aethra, into Aegeus's bed. She made love to Aegeus and conceived a child, who was to be Theseus. But the father's identity was never certain, for Aethra, before going to Aegeus's bed, had gone to an island to make a sacrifice to Poseidon and the god had raped her. It was unclear, therefore, whether Theseus was the son of Aegeus or of Poseidon.

His childhood

Theseus was brought up by Pittheus, his grandfather. Aegeus, whose hold on power was not very secure, had not wanted to take Theseus with him to Athens. Before his departure, he hid his sword and a pair of sandals under a rock, saying that he did not want to see the child until the latter was able to move the rock and retrieve these objects.

When he was 16, Aethra considered Theseus to be strong enough to undergo the test prescribed by Aegeus. She took him to the appointed spot and, without difficulty, Theseus moved the rock which concealed the sword and the sandals. He then discovered his origins and decided to set out for Athens.

The trials

The road to Athens was ridden with danger. Heracles, a slave in the home of Omphale, was no longer there to frighten off the monsters infesting the region. Theseus therefore determined to equal Heracles and make his way through all these dangers.

He killed the lame Periphetes, who used to slay travellers with his club, and the giant Sinis, who used a tree to hurl his victims into the distance like arrows. With one thrust of his sword, he ran threw Crommion's sow, which was ravaging the country, and the robber Sciron, who threw travellers into the sea. He defeated Cercyon in battle and crushed him into the ground. Finally, he killed Procrustes.

Procrustes was a highwayman. He used to intercept travellers who passed his way and carry them off to his home. There he forced them to lie down, the short ones in a huge bed and the tall ones in a tiny bed. Then he would stretch the former so that they would fit the size of the bed and cut off the feet of the latter for the same purpose.

The death of Ariadne

'I saw Phaedra, Procris and the fair Ariadne, the daughter of the evil Minos, who had been previously abducted from Crete by Theseus. He took her to the hill of the holy Athene, but he did not enjoy the fruits of his abduction. Having been previously denounced by Dionysius, she perished, struck down by Artemis on the wave-encircled island of Dia.'
(Odyssey, XI, 320 – 322)

These victories did not fail to bring him glory, and when he arrived in Athens, he received a triumphant welcome. Medea, however, the sorceress who had seized King Aegeus in her claws, took exception to this. She urged Aegeus, who did not yet know the identity of Theseus, to invite the young man to a banquet. There, with the weak king's agreement, she prepared a poison which would liberate the palace from this troublesome, perceptive intruder.

But during the meal, Theseus drew his sword with the intention of carving the meat. At the sight of this weapon, Aegeus acknowledged his son before the presence of the assembled citizens. Medea was forced into exile. Other traditions claimed that the acknowledgement of Theseus by his father took place during the sacrifice of the bull of Marathon, which Medea had asked him to hunt.

As a result of being acknowledged, Theseus became an obstacle to the claims of his cousins, the 50 sons of Pallas, who coveted the royal status of Aegeus. Thus, no longer having any rightful claim to defend, they decided to seize power by force.

The Pallantides divided into two troops: one attacked openly, the other set an ambush. But there was among them a spy who revealed their battle plan to Theseus. He then attacked the members of the second troop, who were not expecting this, and massacred them. The others fled in terror.

Theseus and the Minotaur

Since the murder of Androgeus and the victory of Minos over the Athenians, Athens had been compelled to send a

Theseus seizes the Minotaur by the neck and kills him with his sword, while Ariadne passes him the length of wool which will enable him to find the way back to the exit from the labyrinth. Attic amphora, first half of the 6th cent. BC.

tribute of seven young men and seven young women every nine years as fodder for the Minotaur. Protests arose in the city against Aegeus, who had made no attempt to end this horror.

Theseus appointed himself as one of the victims, knowing that the one who killed the monster would be spared. He was the leader of the expedition, and, as he was about to set out, he was presented with two sets of sails. One of the sets was to be used on his return: the white ones were to announce victory, the black ones, defeat. The boat also carried off Periboea, a girl of whom Theseus was fond, and Minos fell in love with her as soon as she arrived in Crete. Theseus, the son of Poseidon, claimed to be just as worthy of her hand as Minos, the son of Zeus. Minos, to demonstrate his might, begged his father to send forth a flash of lightning. Then, throwing a ring into the sea, he asked Theseus to bring it back to him. Theseus dived in immediately and fetched the ring. He then married Periboea, the first of his wives.

On Crete, Theseus was seen by Ariadne, one of the daughters of Minos. After being seduced by the hero, Ariadne gave him a ball of wool that would enable him to find his way back out of the labyrinth. She imposed only one condition: namely, that he must marry her. After Theseus was shut up in the labyrinth with his companions, he killed the Minotaur and, with the help of the wool given to him by Ariadne, found the way out and was saved.

Theseus, the master of Athens

On the way back to Athens, Theseus wished to rid himself of Ariadne and left her asleep on Naxos. Dionysus was alleged to have fallen in love with her and to have asked Theseus to leave her for him. But Theseus forgot to change the ship's sails, and Aegeus, seeing from afar the black sails that meant defeat, hurled himself into the sea in despair. Theseus then assumed power in Attica.

Theseus was reputed to be a good administrator of the city. He introduced democracy, gave the town its principal monuments, had coinage struck and introduced the Panathenaea—a festival celebrating the political unity of Attica. He also introduced the Isthmian games to honour Poseidon.

As a great war leader, he had the task of defending the city against the Amazons. They had come to recapture Antiope, one of their number whom Theseus was holding prisoner. (He had either received her as a captive or abducted and seduced her.) The Amazons almost won the day, but finally they were compelled to sign a peace treaty.

According to certain traditions, Theseus is supposed to have participated with Jason in the expedition of the Argonauts.

Theseus and Phaedra

Theseus is also thought to have married Phaedra, Ariadne's sister. But Phaedra fell in love with Hippolytus, a son of Theseus by the Amazon Hippolyta. The young man did not like women, however, and warded off the advances of his step-mother. In order to avenge herself, therefore, Phaedra accused her step-son of having raped her. Hippolytus was put to death and Phaedra, full of remorse and despair, hanged herself.

Destroyed by ambition

Peirithoüs and Theseus were great friends. Together, they decided henceforth to marry only daughters of Zeus. So they abducted Helen for Theseus and then travelled to hell to seize Persephone for Pirithous. Helen was freed by Castor and Pollux, who installed another king in Athens; Pirithous found himself a prisoner in hell, unable to get off the chair of oblivion on which Hades had compelled him to sit. Theseus alone was allowed to go back up to earth.

On his return to Athens, Theseus found that his situation had completely changed and that he was now powerless. He was therefore forced into exile. He made his way to Lycomedes, a relative of his in Scyros, who received him amicably. However, while taking Theseus to see a mountain, Lycomedes threw him down into a ravine and killed him.

The remains of Theseus were gathered up with loving care. His tomb was a sanctuary for slaves in flight and for miserable wretches who had been maltreated.

Thetis

Greek goddess

The woman with the silver feet

Thetis was the mother of Achilles. Married to a mortal, she was an unhappy goddess.

Thetis was the daughter of Nereus, the old man of the sea, and of Doris, the daughter of Oceanus. Thus Thetis was an immortal sea deity. She was a very mighty goddess whose power was comparable to that of the Olympians. She saved Zeus himself from a fall from power: she sent Briareus, the being with the hundred arms, to frighten off the conspirators Hera, Poseidon and Athene, who were attempting to capture Zeus (*Iliad*, I, 348 ff.).

Thetis was so beautiful that she was desired by the greatest gods. Zeus and Poseidon, however, shunned her because an oracle had predicted that the son she would bear would be mightier than his father. Zeus was unwilling to suffer what he had made his father Cronos suffer. It would therefore be necessary to force Thetis to marry a mortal man.

The bad match

The centaur Cheiron suggested to his protégé, Peleus, the king of Phthia, that he take advantage of this opportunity to marry a goddess. But Thetis fled from Peleus. To escape this bad match, she changed, in succession, into a bird, a serpent, a lion, a fish, a cuttlefish, and even into water and fire. Peleus refused to let this chance elude him, though, and he persevered. Gradually, he succeeded in subjugating Thetis and making her produce children.

As an immortal being married to a mortal, Thetis was determined to use every means at her disposal to make her children immortal. All of them were destined to perish in the attempt. Achilles alone escaped with his life, thanks to his father Peleus. But in the end, Thetis could no longer stand her aging husband. She 'went back to the home of her father, the eternal old man of the sea, to the brilliant grotto, where she was surrounded by the Nereids, her sisters' (*Iliad*, XVIII, 35).

The mother of Achilles

Thetis ensured that her son would be protected. She hid him among the daughters of Lycomedes so that he would not set out for the Trojan War. She prevented him from being the first to arrive on Trojan shores and gave him weapons specially forged by Hephaestus. She also tried to dissuade him from killing Hector. But all of this was to no avail: destiny had decreed that Achilles was to die, and he did die. The 'most unhappy of goddesses' had been able to give her son nothing but glory.

Because her destiny decreed that she could not aspire to Zeus's love, Thetis was the ally of Hera. She received Hephaestus, the son of Hera, and granted him her protection. By order of the queen of the gods, she took over the piloting of the ship Argos during the difficult crossing between the Symplegades (the clashing rocks).

Alcman, in the 7th century BC, made Thetis a demiurge associated with metallurgy. Knowledge of metallurgy was brought to men by Hephaestus.

A goddess married to a mortal

'Alone, among all the other goddesses of the sea, he made me submit to a man, to Eacides Peleus, and very reluctantly I gave birth to a mortal. This man, exhausted by dismal old age, lies at present in the bowels of his palace. But now I have many other worries. Peleus has caused me to bear and to bring up a son superior to the heroes . . .' (*Iliad*, XVI, 11, 22)

Thor

Nordic god

The god with the hammer

Endowed with unimaginable strength, Thor was a well-known god, always ready to play tricks.

Thor, or Donar, was the son of Odin, and Jord, the wild earth. A god of mature years, red-bearded and broad-shouldered, with knotted muscles and a flat stomach, he was a warrior, the enemy of giants and the protector of men. He was armed with the hammer Mjöllnir, which was like thunder and possessed the special quality of returning automatically to the hand of the one who hurled it. He also had a magic belt, which doubled the strength of its wearer, and a pair of iron gloves. Through his possession of these weapons, he guaranteed the sovereignty of the Aesir and the gods and protected them.

Thor was the god beloved by the Vikings, for, like them, he was free. He always made sure that his domain was prosperous, although he was occasionally tempted on military expeditions to bring back booty. Again like the Vikings, he was fond of playing tricks and was partial to jokes that tended to be vulgar.

Thor and the giants

Loki was constantly playing practical jokes on Thor. One day, he cut off the golden hair of Thor's wife, Sif. Thor grew angry and 'would have crushed all Loki's bones if he had not sworn an oath that the black Alfes would provide Sif with golden hair which would grow like any other head of hair' (*Skaldskaparmal*, 33).

Thor's relations with giants were ambiguous. He fought them, but in spite of this he also found accomplices among them. Thus, another day, Loki convinced him to

take up arms to confront the giant Geirröd. But Thor has been forwarned by the giantess Grid, to whom he had paid a visit, and she had lent him the belt and gloves and also a staff called Gridstav.

When Thor arrived at Geirröd's he was asked to sit down, but he immediately sensed that his chair was rising up. He had just enough time to seize his staff to prevent his head from bumping against the farmhouse beam. Then he slumped heavily in his seat and came back down quickly, breaking the backs of Geirröd's daughters, who had come to witness the combat.

Then Geirröd took a white-hot coal and threw it at Thor. Thor, however, caught it in his iron gloves and hurled it back at the giant. The coal passed clean through 'the pillar, Geirröd and the wall and plunged deep into the earth' (*Skaldskaparmal*, 18).

'Thor did not remain long at his house' (*Gylfaginning*, 47). Disguised as a young man, he arrived in the evening at the home of the giant Hymir. He spent the night there at his host's invitation, setting out with him next morning to go fishing in the sea.

Once at sea, they fell into disagreement. Thor wanted to go far offshore, but Hymir did not want to stray far from land. Without daring to say so, Hymir was afraid of Midgard's serpent, the sea creature Thor wanted to catch. To this end, Thor had brought as bait the head of the biggest ox he

---

Thor's threats to Loki

'Be silent, you abject being, or my powerful hammer, Mjöllnir, will reduce you to silence. With my right hand I shall slay you, I, the murderer of Hrungnir, and all your bones will break [. . .] I have sung before the Aesir, I have sung before the sons of the Aesir what my spirit incited me to sing. But, when confronted by you alone, I will go out, for I know that you will strike.' (*Lokasenna*)

had ever encountered. The serpent was quickly caught and pulled very hard onto the fish-hook. 'Thor assumed the strength of As, and braced himself so hard that his feet went through the bottom of the boat.'

Hymir changed colour, and just as Thor seized his hammer, the giant got hold of the knife and with one stroke severed Thor's line. The serpent sank into the sea. Then Thor became angry and struck the gaint on the ear (*Hymiskvida*).

Thor disguised as a woman

Thor was disorderly. One day his hammer was stolen and the sovereignty of the Aesir was threatened. The crafty Loki quickly discovered who had committed the theft. He chanced upon Thrym, the thief, who said to him, 'I have hidden Thor's hammer eight miles below the surface of the earth; no one will succeed in recovering it unless he gives me Freyja as a wife' (*Thrymskvida*, 8).

Freyja was already married and refused to be exchanged like a prostitute: 'Do you know that I would be the best runner among women?' (*Thrymskvida*, 13). Then Heimdallr had this brilliant idea: 'Let's attach the bride's veil to Thor's head' (*Thrymskvida*, 15), and he proposed that Thor go thus disguised to see Thrym.

This was no sooner said than done. Thor found himself being shown into Thrym's house disguised as Freyja. Thrym was very astonished to see his intended stuffing herself with an ox, eight salmon and three measures of mead; but Loki explained that she had not eaten for a week. Thrym was terrified of the wild flame in her eyes, but

---

Thor disguised in female clothing

'Then Thor, the powerful As, said these words: "The Aesir will treat me as a confounded idiot if I allow the bride's veil to be attached to my head." Then Loki, the son of Laufey, replied as follows: "Be silent, Thor, do not utter these words! Unless you get your hammer back, the giants will immediately take up their abode in Asgard."' (*Thrymskvida*, 17 – 18)

Loki explained that she had not slept for a week in preparation for their meeting. Then came the moment for exchanging presents. The hammer was brought to the betrothed girl and Freyja, who had become Thor again, got to his feet, reassumed his aggressive behaviour and slayed Thrym, his entire family and all his retinue.

Thor and Hrungnir

In Thor's absence, Odin invited the giant Hrungnir to come and have a drink with him. Freyja was on the point of serving him when Thor arrived. He asked who had allowed evil giants to sit down and drink in the hall of the Aesir and was told that it was Odin who had done so. 'You will regret this invitation', Thor said to Hrungnir, and they arranged to fight a duel at Jötunheim.

Thor appeared in all his As fury. He hurled his hammer at Hrungnir. The latter seized his flint club in both hands and threw it at Thor. The hammer and the club met in mid-air. The club shattered: 'One piece fell to the ground and left a mountain of flint' (*Skaldskaparmal*, 17). The other piece rebounded off the head of Thor, who fell flat on his face. The hammer struck Hrungnir's skull and broke it into pieces.

Hrungnir, however, fell on Thor in such a way that Thor was caught beneath the giant's leg. All the Aesir tried unsuccessfully to free Thor. Then Magni, Thor's son, appeared and succeeded in doing so without difficulty. Thor realized that his son 'would surely be a brave man' (*Skaldskaparmal*, 17).

On the day of Ragna rök (the end of the world), Thor was destined to fight his last battle against the serpent of Midgard, which had become so big that by biting its own tail it could embrace the whole world in a monstrous ring. The other Aesir fought against other monsters—the wolf Fenrir, Surt, the dog Garm, and many others. The fight was hard and unrelenting; it was the last in the world's history. 'Thor slew Midgard's dragon, walked nine paces, then fell to the ground dead, killed by the venom spat upon him by the snake.' Then 'Surt hurled fire upon the earth and consumed all the worlds' (*Gylfaginning*, 50).

Thoth

Egyptian god

The scribe

Thoth, secretary to the gods, was the master of effective speech.

Thoth was the god with the head of an ibis. Highly skilled at calculation, he was the moon whose complex route in the sky was dependent on exceptional dexterity with numbers. Thoth was also the divider of time and the inaugurator of the calendar, and it was he who controlled the writing of history.

Thoth authenticated decisions and legalized the name chosen for the pharaoh by writing it on the tree of history in the temple of Heliopolis. He studied places intended as sites for temples and made sure that the work on them was carried out according to the rules. He checked the balance of the scales on the day of judgment of the dead. Thoth was the judge.

He was the supreme scribe and the patron of human scribes. The special offering made to him was a writing desk, and his town of Hermopolis had the finest library in the empire. He wrote the laws, the accounts, the histories and the book of life. He was the master of language and speech.

Thoth was a demiurge. He was knowledgeable about hieroglyphics, the words used to create things. He was called 'the tongue of Ptah', the tongue of the one who brought the universe into existence, or 'the heart of Re', creative thought. He created what he desired simply by desiring it.

The magician

Thoth knew magic spells. It was known that he possessed spells such as this one, which was cast to ensure that one's love was returned: 'Should she drink, eat or sleep with anyone else, I shall cast a spell upon her heart, I shall cast a spell upon her breath, I shall cast a spell upon her three physical apertures; but in particular I shall cast a spell upon her vulva, which I wish to penetrate, until she comes to me and until I know what is in her heart, what she has been doing, what she is thinking of, now, now, immediately, immediately' (National Library, Paris, *Greek Manuscript IV*, 147–153).

Thoth knew the formulae which were capable of providing cures. He helped Isis when she was attempting to resurrect her spouse, Osiris. He also cured Horus, who as a child had been stung by a scorpion. He restored life to the eye Seth had torn from Horus. Prayers were offered to him for the sick

---

Thoth, the scribe

'He who revealed himself as the heart, he who revealed himself as the tongue, in the guise of Aten, he is Ptah the very ancient one who gave life to all the gods and to their genii. It is through this heart from which the god Horus stemmed, through this tongue of which the god Thoth was the issue, in the form of Ptah.' (Hermann Junker, *The Mythology of Memphis*, Berlin, 1940)

Hermes Trismegistus

Likened to Hermes (the Rosetta stone), Thoth had a great reputation in hermetic literature under the name of Hermes Trismegistus (the thrice great). He was the inventor of the arts and sciences and also the initiator of practices whose aim was to restrain the divinity and to give to the initiate some sort of omnipotence by comparing him to god: 'You are I, and I am you.' The Hermetic Body was regarded as having been written by him. He gathered together many dissimilar beliefs, with different origins and was involved in magic, astrology and alchemy.

Tiamat

Akkadian goddess

The original sea

Tiamat was a primordial divinity who represented salt water. Her husband, Apsu, represented fresh water.

Tiamat was the sea. She had her whimsical moods: sometimes calm and sometimes furious. She was a primordial and indifferent character, having within her all the force and power of what was wild. Her husband was Apsu, the fresh water on which the world depended. From Tiamat and Apsu were born the first great gods: Lakhmu and Lakhamu, then Anshar and Kishar, and finally Anu and the rest. Each generation outshone the previous one in understanding and in vigour.

But the young, energy-filled gods were noisy. Apsu, who could not sleep, flew into a rage: 'Their behaviour is intolerable to me. I cannot rest by day; I cannot sleep by night. I am determined to annihilate them so that I can put an end to what they are doing and so that silence may reign' (*Enuma elish*, tablet I, 37–39).

Tiamat was patient. She was unwilling to destroy those to whom she had given life. But Apsu's words were reported to the young gods. One of them, Ea, caught Apsu

off guard, 'snatched his brilliance from him' and put him to death. Then Ea fathered Marduk, the most capable and wisest of the gods.

War with the young gods

Then Tiamat, urged on by the old gods, changed her attitude and became angry: 'Let us create monsters'—monstrous snakes with cruel jaws, furious dragons charged with supernatural brilliance, enraged dogs. She created all these wild beasts and made them like gods. She elevated Kingu and put him at the head of the troop; she then made him her husband, thus giving him supreme dignity; and she handed over to him the tablet of destiny.

The young gods searched among them for a champion to confront Tiamat, and Marduk was chosen. He was vested with powers by the assembly of the gods and received supreme authority. Then, armed with the four main winds which determined both space and time, he mounted his chariot and moved forward to do battle.

Marduk released the evil wind at the very moment when Tiamat opened her mouth, and she was no longer able to close it. He shot an arrow at her which pierced her stomach and stabbed her heart. The remaining members of the troop of monsters disbanded. Kingu was ranked with the dead gods.

Marduk took Tiamat's corpse and 'cut it in two like a dried fish' (*Enuma elish*, tablet IV, 137). From one half, he made the vault of heaven, telling it not to let the waters escape. From the other half, he formed dry land: 'He positioned the head and a mountain piled up on it, springs flared out from it and living water ran from it. From her eyes he opened up the Euphrates and the Tigris; her nostrils were blocked up and he made reservoirs from them. On her breast, he piled up the distant mountains' (*Enuma elish*, tablet V).

The defeat of Tiamat

'He made certain of his hold over the captive gods and returned to Tiamat, whom he had conquered. The lord then placed his foot on Tiamat's rear-quarters, and with his unrelenting harpé (a sickle-shaped sword) he split open her skull, and cut her veins. The north wind carried her blood far away. At the sight of this, his forefathers (the new gods), exulted with joy and gave him gifts and contributions.' (*Enuma elish*, IV, 127–133).

Tlaloc

Aztec god

The god of mountains, rain and springs

Tlaloc, the god of peasants, was 'the one who made things stream with water'. He had control over fertility.

Tlaloc was represented as a man painted black. He had huge, round eyes with circles or serpents around them and long fangs which made him resemble Chac, the Mayan god of rain. He wore a hat which looked like a fan. Near him was a ploughing tool and an axe that symbolized a bolt of lightning. He was said to be present at the four cardinal points of the compass.

Tlaloc had two companions: Uixtocijuatl, the goddess of salt water and the sea, and Chalchiutlicue, 'the one with a skirt of precious stones', the goddess of fresh water. She represented the beauty and ardour of youth.

Thaloc, the god of rain, was regarded as being equal in rank to Huitzilopochtli, the god of the sun, and he was as essential as the sun for the fertility of the soil. They both had their sanctuaries at the top of the great temple of Mexico at Tenochtitlan; the sun's was painted white and red, and the rain's was white and blue. Their high priests were equal to one another in both rank and honour.

Tlaloc lived at the summit of the mountains. There he was surrounded by numerous minor gods, called the Tlaloques. Under his orders, the Tlaloques distributed either the rain which fertilized the plants or the hurricanes which flattened the crops.

Worship of Tlaloc

The prayers addressed to Tlaloc were full of hope. The god's decisions, could not be changed, but they were submitted to, or even better, welcomed as benefits: 'O my lord, O sorcerer prince, it is really to you that the maize crop belongs' (B. de Sahagun, *The General History of Things in New Spain*.

Tlaloc's importance can be measured by the number of ceremonies dedicated to him throughout the year. On certain days his priests would bathe in the lake, making noises like water animals and waving foghorns about. On other days they would make little idols out of amarantine paste, symbolically kill the idols and eat them. Finally, they sometimes performed sacrifices by drowning children, the most precious possession that a people devoted to its offspring could have.

Tlaloc was an ambivalent god, thanked for the benefits he provided and feared for his fits of rage.

Sometimes he killed by means of a thunderbolt, by drowning, or by water-related ailments. But his victims were not cremated like other deceased persons. They were buried with a piece of dried wood, and Tlaloc received them into his paradise, called Tlalocan. This was a land full of verdant pastures and orchards, where the dead experienced a blessed eternity. The dry wood that they had taken with them came back to life and became covered with leaves and flowers.

The paradise of Tlalocan

'It was said that Tlaloc sent the soul of a drowned man to an earthly paradise. To facilitate this, the corpse was carried, with great veneration, on a litter so that the man could be buried in one of the oratories called *ayauhcales*. The litter was adorned with reeds and the flute was played in front of the body.' (B. de Sahagun, *The General History of Things in New Spain*)

Tlazolteotl

Aztec goddess

Carnal love

Tlazolteotl, the goddess of lust, was also Tlaelquarni, which means 'the cleansing one'.

Tlazolteotl was a young girl who wore a rubber mask and a crescent-shaped ornament in her nose. She had spindles entwined in her hair to show that she was the patron of spinners.

She was responsible for conjugal infidelities, and at the same time she was the granter of pardon. The Aztecs made their confessions to Tlazolteotl in the person of a priest, but this ritual was preceded by many penances. The letter of confession enabled the ritual which had been performed to be authenticated. It also enabled the person confessing to be released from accountability for the legal consequences of his misdemeanours. It was a pity that one could perform this ritual only once in the course of a lifetime!

Tlazolteotl was also the patron of steam baths, called *Temazcalli*, and the goddess of renewal. In this capacity a young man was sacrificed to her annually. He was killed, his skin was stripped off and the statue of the goddess was covered with his skin.

The sin of the flesh

Extramarital affairs were reputed to spread a stench around those who indulged in them, a special smell, called *tlazolmiquiztli*, which can be translated as 'death produced by love'.

Triglav

Slavic god

The soothsayer

A three-headed god, Triglav had three functions: he was a priest, a warrior and a nourisher.

Triglav had three silver heads and a golden veil which covered his eyes and mouth. The significance of this veil was supposed to be his desire to disregard human faults. The three heads indicated that Triglav could see everything. This multi-headedness in a god was found in many Slavic regions.

His temple at Stettin (Szczecin) contained a golden statue of him and magnificent sculptures depicting creation. Both men and animals were skilfully portrayed. A tenth of all the booty from war was placed in the sanctuary. Consequently, a large amount of treasure was to be found there. Triglav was also honoured in the form of a sacred oak tree situated above a stream.

Triglav was a soothsayer. One of the methods of divination used by him consisted of observing the posture of a black steed in a particular situation: the steed had to walk between lances which had been stuck in the ground; if it succeeded in doing so without touching any of the lances, it was a good omen. Triglav's priests were held in high esteem.

Tristan and Isolde

Celtic heroes

Invincible love

Tristan and Isolde were united in an indestructible love, although it was a love both blameworthy and illicit.

Tristan was the son of King Léonois and Blanchefleur, sister of King Mark. His father died shortly before his birth, and his mother died while bringing him into the world. He was brought up by Gorvenal, who taught him to handle both the lance and sword. He also taught him to help the weak and detest treachery. Gradually, Tristan became a master harp-player and a master huntsman.

Isolde was the daughter of the king of Ireland. She was fair-haired, young and beautiful. Cornwall, where Tristan's uncle, King Mark, had his kingdom, was bound by treaty to Ireland. By virtue of this treaty, Cornwall had to offer up to Ireland 300 youths and 300 maidens. The king of Ireland agreed, however, that this obligation did not have fulfilled to be if a champion beat his brother-in-law, the giant Morholt, in single combat.

The wound

Tristan accepted the challenge and conquered Morholt, but he was wounded. He was struck by a poisoned hunting spear and declared to be incurable. He was therefore abandoned on a ship to await death.

The ship approached the shores of Ireland, and Tristan, who did not reveal his identity, was brought to the palace. There he was cured by one of the sorceress queen's speeches. He admitted his identity to Isolde, whom he met there for the first time. She then swore fierce hatred against him because he had murdered her uncle, Morholt. Shortly afterwards, Tristan returned to the court of King Mark in Cornwall.

The love potion

Mark decided to marry the golden-haired Isolde and sent Tristan to Ireland to fetch her. The contract was quickly concluded, and the queen allowed her daughter to leave. However, the sorceress entrusted to the maid-servant Brangien, who was to accompany the young girl, a love potion which she had to give to the betrothed couple on the evening of their wedding night. Brangien hid the lidded goblet containing the love potion in the boat.

The sun shone warmly during the return voyage, and Tristan and Isolde, who had met on deck, needed a drink. They discovered the goblet and together quenched their thirst with its contents. 'It was not wine, it was passion, it was bitter joy, endless

---

The love potion

'Beware, daughter, that only those in love can partake of this beverage. For such is its quality that those who drink of it together will love one another with all their senses and with all their thoughts, forever, in both life and in death.' (*Tristan and Isolde*, Ch. 4)

Tristan calls Isolde

'Tell her that she alone can bring me comfort; tell her that if she does not come I shall die; tell her to remember her past pleasures and the great anguish, and the great sadnesses, and the joys and sorrows of our loyal, tender love; to remember the potion we drank together aboard ship; oh! it was our death which we drank. Tell her to remember the oath I swore to her to love only her; I have kept this promise.' (*Tristan and Isolde*, Ch. 19)

anguish and death. Isolde took long quaffs of it then handed it to Tristan, who finished it off (*Tristan and Isolde*, Ch. 4). The unhappy deed had taken place and henceforth they would be bound to one another by an indissoluble love.

They arrived in Cornwall and the nuptials were celebrated. But when evening had come, Brangien, to make good her error, took the place of Isolde in Mark's bed while the queen went off in search of Tristan. The lovers' treachery was not immediately discovered by Mark, who regarded Tristan as a faithful knight and Isolde as a queen honouring his court.

This state of affairs could not continue. Baron knights were jealous of Tristan's prominant position. They came to see Mark and spoke to him as follows: 'Be aware, therefore, that Tristan is in love with the queen; this is a proven truth and already many a word has been spoken about it' (*Tristan and Isolde*, Ch. 6).

The separation

The king wanted proof and so kept watch on both Tristan and the queen. But Brangien noticed this and forewarned the lovers. Then Mark, unable to dispel his suspicions, asked Tristan to leave the castle. Tristan, who was still in love, could not go very far away and went to live in the house of a burgher. He 'languished, tormented by fever, more wounded than on the day Morholt's pike had poisoned his body'.

The lovers' wiles were endless. Despite the watch kept by the king's aides, they

---

Isolde during the storm, in the course of the last journey, said these words: '[. . .] Tristan, if I had spoken to you one last time, I would grieve little about dying afterwards. Oh my love, if I fail to reach you, it is because God does not wish it, and this is my worst grief.' (*Tristan and Isolde*, Ch. 19)

---

succeeded in meeting again in the orchard behind the castle. Having been denounced once more by the wicked dwarf Frocin, they were both condemned to be burned alive; but once more fate smiled upon them. Tristan succeeded in escaping and came in search of Isolde at the very moment she was being taken away to the funeral pyre. Both of them fled.

Tristan and Isolde found themselves in the forest, where they led a wretched existence. 'They wandered around, seldom daring to return at night to their previous evening's shelter. They ate nothing but the flesh of wild animals and missed the taste of salt', but 'they loved one another and did not suffer' (*Tristan and Isolde*, Ch. 9).

The king searched for them and one evening discovered them. They were lying alongside one another, asleep. He drew his sword, but noticed 'that their mouths were not touching and that their bodies were separated by a naked sword' (*Tristan and Isolde*, Ch. 9). Then, seized with pity, he put his own sword in place of that of Tristan, replaced a ring on Isolde's finger and went off, full of sadness.

The lovers, moved by his great generosity, returned to the court. Mark agreed to take Isolde back, but not to keep Tristan there. The latter went off into exile in Brittany, where he tried to forget Isolde of the golden locks in the arms of Isolde of the white hands, the daughter of the duke Hoël, whom he married.

Death

Love mocked the separations it had to endure. Tristan could not have intercourse with his wife and remained faithful to his first love. During a battle, he was wounded by a thrust from a poisoned lance. Many doctors arrived on the scene, but none knew the antidote for the poison and Tristan's condition worsened. He felt that life was draining away from him and realized that he was on the point of death.

Then, pulling himself erect, he said to his faithful companion Kaherdin, 'I would like to see the fair-haired Isolde once more'. Kaherdin decided to set out in search of his master's beloved. It was agreed that should he succeed in fetching her, he would hoist a white sail; should he fail, he would hoist a black sail. Unfortunately for the lovers, Isolde of the white hands—the abandoned spouse—overheard the conversation. With the appearance of the first breath of wind, Kaherdin put to sea.

The fair-haired Isolde was informed of her lover's state of health, and she left immediately on her journey to bring Tristan the comfort of her presence. Each day Tristan asked that a watch for her be kept on the sea. When Isolde of the white hands announced the arrival of Kaherdin's boat, she lied and said that the sail was a black one. Tristan said 'I cannot remain alive' and gave up the ghost. The fair-haired Isolde arrived and learned of the calamity. She then went up to the palace, lay down beside Tristan, their bodies and their mouths touching, and likewise expired.

Tyr

Nordic god

The most daring

Tyr guaranteed right and justice.

Tyr was courageous and occasionally bold. He was ready for every fight, respected the rules of combat and usually decided who was to have the victory. He was invoked when men set off for war.

He was also a lawyer. He presided over the *thing*, the assembly where litigation was settled and where the rules of combat were established.

Tyr was one-armed. The Aesir had fearlessly raised Fenrir, a horrible wolf who was the son of Loki and the sorceress Angerboda. But Fenrir kept growing and growing, so the Aesir had a chain made by the dwarfs. The chain was as smooth and soft as a silk ribbon but was strong and sturdy. They asked Fenrir to allow himself to be tied up, as a joke, saying that he would have no difficulty breaking this fine thread.

Fenrir agreed, but, being suspicious, asked that an As should put his hand down his throat. Tyr agreed to do this. The thread held, and Tyr lost his hand as a result.

The precaution taken by Fenrir

'I am not of a mind to allow this cord to be passed round my neck. But [. . .] let one of your number put his hand down my throat as a pledge that everything will take place without any treachery.' (*Gylfaginning*, 24)

Vahagn
Armenian deity

The warrior

Vahagn was Visapaklal, the dragon-slayer, just like Indra Vrtrahan in India and Vrthragna in Persia.

Born of water and fire, Vahagn had the goddess of the stars, Astlik, as his wife. He had similar functions to the warrior in the tri-partite ideology of the Indo-Europeans. He was a 'destroyer of obstacles and the god of victory', as was the god Indra of the Veda and of the Avesta of Persia. The sovereign function was held by Aramazd, and the goddess of fertility and life was Anahit.

There was a certain similarity between Armenian mythology and Zoroastrian mythology: Anahita became Anahit and Ahura Mazda became Aramazd, 'the greatest and best of the gods, the creator of heaven and earth'.

The Milky Way

Vahagn was best known through myth. He was the creator of the Milky Way. One winter's night he was looking for straw for his horse. He stole some and fled in haste into the sky, leaving wisps of straw strewn across his path. This showed everyone the route he had taken, and these wisps of straw formed what is called the Milky Way.

Very little is known about the worship of Vahagn. We are left with only ten lines of a mythological poem telling of the birth of the god. A temple dedicated to Aramazd is located in the town of Ani, on the shores of the river Arpa in Turkey.

The birth of Vahagn

'Heaven and earth were engaged in the labour of childbirth; the purple-coloured sea was also in labour. The labour had snatched the tiny red reed from the sea. Smoke was trailing from the stem of the reed, and out of the flame a young man soared. He had fiery hair and his little eyes were suns.' (An ancient myth reported by Moise de Khorene, *Patmut 'iwn Hayoc'*, Venice, 1955)

Anahit

Anahit was regarded as being either the daughter or the wife of Aramazd. She was called Oskrhat, meaning 'sculpted in gold'. Her statue is made from this precious metal. The goddess of both life and fertility, she was likewise a healer. For the Armenians she was the sovereign goddess, 'the glory of our race and the dispenser of life, revered by all the kings and even by the king of Greece. She is the mother of all chastity, the benefactress of the human race.' (Quoted in Agat'Angelos, Patmut'iwn, Venice, 1930, IV).

During the spring festival, young maidens went up into the mountains to gather hyacinths and draw water from seven different springs. In the evening, an elixir of happiness was made. This was probably a health-giving love potion or a beverage like soma which gave immortality.

Great ceremonies were organized in honour of Anahit. The priests sacrificed many white cows to her. The young maidens from the upper classes were obliged, prior to their marriage, to prostitute themselves for a certain period in the temple of Anahit (*Strabo*, XI, 14–16). This practice made her into the goddess of love and established a parallel between her and Ishtar, Astarte and Aphrodite.

The Valkyries

Nordic goddesses

The angels of battle

As the female companions and messengers of Odin, the Valkyries selected those who were doomed to die.

The Valkyries were young, blonde, long-haired, blue-eyed maidens in the service of the god of war. They coursed over the battlefields amid lightning flashes and thunder. They wore breastplates, were armed with long lances and shields, and wore golden helmets on their heads. It was said that they were bird-like creatures.

Forty of them are listed in the whole of Nordic literature. Certain of them were combatant goddesses, such as Gunn ('battle'), Hild ('combat'), Hrist (the brandisher of weapons'), Baudihillie (the rule of battle), and Hladgunnr ('the battle involving the use of a trap'). Others tended to be sorceresses, such as Göndul ('skilled at handling the magic wand'), Göll ('she of the awful wailing'), Herfjoturr ('she who paralyzes her enemies by means of magic Links') and Mist ('torpor') They were queens and goddesses of fertility.

Glorious death

The Valkyries were experts in the matter of honour. They knew how to conduct a battle, how to cover themselves with glory, and how to gain a victory. They decided which side would be victorious. The name *Valkyries* was significant: *Kjora*, which produced 'kyries', means 'choice', and *Val* means 'death'. In the name of Odin they chose the brave who were destined to fall in battle.

It is not known whether the Valkyries were virgins wholly employed in the service of the god or lovers who selected their companions with pleasure from the fray. The fact remains that they apportioned death, not as a punishment but as a reward. They were more or less identified with the Norns, the goddesses of destiny. One of them, Skuld, was also known as the third Norn.

They carried off the soldiers who had been killed in glory and took them to *Valhalla*, the abode of the blessed, which was reserved for chosen heroes. There they became *einherjar* and spent their time fighting battles without being wounded or killed, in bacchanalian feasts and bouts of drinking. The Valkyries became their handmaidens. They presented them with dishes made from the flesh of the wild boar Saehrimnir and poured mead into their goblets.

Valhalla

Nordic peoples distinguished between two types of the dead: those who died a natural death found themselves in the gloomy empire of Hel, goddess of hell; the second type, who were chosen by the Valkyries, died in battle. After their death they were led into Valhalla, the dwelling place of Odin, a palace with 640 doors, beams made from lances and tiles made from shields. There they awaited the battle marking the end of the world, the so-called *ragna rök*, in which they would fight on the side of the gods.

The handmaidens of Odin

'She beheld the Valkyries who had come from afar, and who were prepared to ride right to the dwelling place of the gods. Skuld was holding the shield; the others were Skögul, Gunn, Hild, Göndul and Geirskökul. These are the names of the Valkyries, the wives of the lord of the armies, who were willing to ride through the plain.' (*Völupsa*, IV, 30)

Varuna

Indian god

World order

Varuna ruled over the world, gods as well as men.

With respect to sovereignty of the world, Varuna, one of the greatest Vedic gods, was associated with Mitra. He was its rigid inflexibility, the essential force, while Mitra was the world's benevolence, the aspect favourable to man. Varuna was depicted holding a rope in his hand: he was the binding force, the master of knots. His favourite animal was the tortoise, which implies both stability and solid foundations.

Varuna set limits on both heaven and earth. He placed air above the trees, shaped the mountain-tops, gave 'milk to cows, understanding to hearts, fire to the waters, the sun to the sky and positioned the soma on top of the mountain' (*Rig Veda*, V, 85, 1–2). He brought forth the rain and saw to it that water flowed away in the rivers. He was responsible for the fertility and fruitfulness of the soil.

His powers

Varuna was the guardian of *rta*. Rta was world order, with its rules and the regular occurrence of its phenomena. Rta was a universal form which imposed itself on all people and all things. It signified truth, the profound reality apart from which nothing existed.

Rta was also the whole body of sacrificial rites. Varuna saw to it that they were scrupulously carried out. The other gods took from sacrifices what conformed to the norm; Varuna took what did not conform and ensured that breaches of ritual were punished. Thus he held sway over spiritual matters as Indra did over temporal matters.

Varuna dwelt in the middle of the sky. His colour was black; black grain or black animals were sacrificed to him. His domain consisted of darkness and the waters. The stars were his thousand eyes, and he continuously viewed human activity. He was a dispenser of justice and was more inclined to see faults than kind actions. He punished any deviation from world order and any moral or ritual dissoluteness.

Varuna was master of the *maya*. The maya was the power to perform marvellous deed, or miracles. It was a creative power which went beyond human words. His action was sometimes unforeseen, and it provoked panic in an army or madness among sinners. The maya was often illusion, apparent change which had no actual reality, but a change which was deceptive, which could lead one into error and make one suffer. Varuna was a miracle-worker and magician.

Good and evil

Furious, violent and evil, Varuna caused earthquakes and sent disease. He produced evil and spread it throughout the world. He was terrible and to be feared. No one could hope to make him relent.

But, if he brought evil into the world, he could also set people free from it. He possessed all the remedies and all the benefits. He was the provider of both peace and prosperity, and he granted pardons and good health.

The substance of being

'Our being's many-roomed abode, contained within Varuna, must be ordered by Mitra into a precise harmony of its furnishings and usefulness. [. . .]. Mitra is the harmonizer, the builder, the founding light, and the god who effects this just unity. Varuna is the substance of it, the outside limit which becomes ever wider.' (Shri Aurobindo, *Hymns of the Atris*)

Vesta

Roman goddess

The hearth

Vesta's sanctuary was the city's central core, the unquenchable fire.

Vesta, an ancient goddess of Rome, was known particularly for the cult dedicated to her. Her temple was in the Forum. In contrast with the other temples, it was circular in shape like the huts of the former inhabitants of the region. It was served only by virgins who had been selected in their childhood from among the most perfect girls of the city. They were placed under the authority of the great pontiff and received many honours. If they failed to remain chaste, however, they were walled up alive at the Colline Gate.

The *Aedes Vestae* (Vesta's home) was the heart of the city. In it were kept the palladium, a mysterious object associated with the preservation of the city; King Priam's sceptre, a phallic symbol, and the city's penates (household gods). It was, as it were, the family home of the Romans, the city being regarded as the home of all (Cicero, *De legibus*, II, 29).

The fire was kept lit all year long and its flame was solemnly stirred up during the Vestalia on the first of March. This flame had to be obtained solely by rubbing two pieces of wood together. On that day Vesta's sacred animal, the ass, had the place of honour.

> **Address delivered to Vesta for the young Augustus**
> 'O gods from our past, o Romulus, o you, Vesta, queen of the Etruscan Tiber and of the Palatine Hill, permit, at least, permit that this young hero holds up a century which is in the process of crumbling away.' (Virgil, *The Georgics*, I, 498–502)

Viracocha

Incan god

The creator and civilizer

Viracocha, the supreme god, was the principle of heat and of generation.

Viracocha created the first men. But, disappointed by them, he changed certain of them into stone statues and destroyed the others by fire.

Viracocha re-created humanity, but he accompanied this creation by the creation of the sun and the moon. The new men thus lived in the light. He then began to travel all over the earth, fashioning mountains and plains on it, tracing out the course of rivers, and teaching the inhabitants farming, animal husbandry and all that was necessary to meet their needs and permit them to live in a civilized way.

After finishing his mission, Viracocha headed seaward and disappeared over the horizon. The people still await his return. There is a huge golden statue of him in the Cuzco temple. He was the special protector of the emperor of the Incas.

Vishnu

Indian god

The benevolent one

Vishnu gave the world its stability.

Vishnu made his appearance during the battle between the *devas* and the *asuras*. Both wanted to secure dominion over the world. The asuras hurled a challenge at their rivals: they (the asuras) would agree to leaving them (the devas) whatever territory one of the devas could measure out in three paces. Vishnu, who at this time was only a dwarf, put himself forward as champion of his fellow creatures and, in three paces, traversed the whole world—the earth and sky and all the intervening space (*Satapatha-brahmana*).

The three paces taken by Vishnu indicated the god's omnipresence and his vocation, which was to extend his influence indefinitely throughout the world. He was identified with *Brahman*, the totality of all existence. Vishnu was the god of space, while Shiva was the god of time.

Vishnu radiated like the sun, whose benefits sprang from the god. He was the origin of the fertility of both nature and man.

Vishnu became a supreme divinity. Icon-

ography depicts him as sleeping between two creations, on top of the thousand-headed serpent, Sesa. His sleep was not inactivity. It was a mystical sleep in which he was meditating on the world to come and preparing it in his mind. When he awakened again, a lotus flower was bursting forth from his navel. It bore Brahma, who was entrusted with bringing the new creation into being (*Mahabharata*, III, 272).

Vishnu's retinue was composed of Garuda, the eagle which served as his steed, and Hanuman, the king of the monkeys. Certain objects were linked with him: the disc, the conch, the club, the lotus flower, and sometimes the sword and the bow.

Occasionally Vishnu was confused with Prajapati. Both were compared with sacrifice or the place appointed for sacrifice, both were at the centre of the world, both were at the well-spring of the world's activity and both behaved benevolently towards men.

Lakhsmi was Vishnu's wife and was the model for every wife. She was the supreme beneficent goddess, the god's effective energy, his strength in action. Bhumi, the earth, was his second wife.

Under the name of Narayana, Vishnu appeared as a radiant being who was gazed upon by three individuals—Ekata, Dvita and Trita—after they had undergone a severe ascetic regime. They were blinded by the god's brilliance and at first heard only the prayers of 'white men' who were performing their devotions. At last a voice was heard, the voice of Vishnu. It said that only exclusive devotion to God (*bhakti*) would lead man to contemplate the Supreme Being; but for this bhakti, study of the Veda, non-violence and sacrifice were all in vain (*Mahabharata*, XII, 236).

Vishnu was omnipresent; he penetrated everything. He was the saviour. Whereas Shiva was the master, Vishnu was the friend who sided with men. He was the

---

Asuras and devas

The term 'asura' means the supreme mind. The term 'deva' indicates heavenly beings of luminous essence. Progressively, though, the deva monopolized the meaning of 'god' and the asuras became 'anti-gods'.

The protector

'In successive eras I come into existence for the protection of good and the destruction of evil, and to re-establish the dharma.'
(*Bhagavad-Gita*, IV, 8)

Vishnu, *the first principle of life, sitting in a large white lotus. All his attributes are there. In his hands he has the conch, the disc, the club and the lotus blossom; a long garland is around his neck. He is framed by an oval nimbus (an aureole of golden rays); this is the form of the Hiranyagarbha, the golden matrix, which is also the cosmic primordial egg. 'The glory of Vishnu'.*

Gouache of the Pahari School, beginning of the 19th century.

protector, and yet the immutability and inactivity which made up part of his being did not enable him to intervene directly in events. He therefore did so through many *avatars*, or reincarnations.

Each time the world needed him, he appeared in the form of a hero who not only represented him, but also identified with him or, in the case of secondary avatars, was imbued with the efficient strength of the god. The avatar showed Vishnu as the restorer of order and was the manifestation of the unity of the god in the multiplicity of creation.

The avatars

In the form of a fish, Vishnu saved Manu, the ancestor of mankind, from the flood. He then went to the bottom of the sea to look for the holy scripture, the Veda, which the demon Hayagriva had stolen from Brahma and put there when the waters rose (*Satapatha-brahmana*, I, 8,1).

In the form of a tortoise, he came to the aid of the devas and the asuras. They had undertaken to churn the sea of milk in order to obtain *amrta*, the assurance of immortality. To do this they used Mount Mandara as a beater, but it was sinking dangerously. Vishnu, as a tortoise, served as a solid and stable base for Mount Mandara (*Ramayana*, I).

In the form of a wild boar, Vishnu saved the world. It had become too heavy owing to the great number of demons on it, and the demon Hiranyaksa had sunk it in the sea. Vishnu plunged into the depths of the sea to catch the earth on his tusks. He then restored it to the place it should never have left (*Satapatha-brahmana*, XIV, 1, 2, 11).

In the form of a man-lion named Narasimha, he delivered the world from Hiranyakasipu, the brother of Hiranyaksa, who was threatening the gods. Hiranyakasipu had received from Brahma the privilege of not being able to be killed in daytime, or night-time, by any man, or animal, and neither inside nor outside the palace. Vishnu intervened, coming out from a pillar of the palace in the form of a creature which was half man and half lion. He appeared just at the moment when Hiranyakasipu had arrived to sacrifice his son, Prahlada, a devotee of Vishnu.

The fifth avatar concerned the dwarf who, in three paces, crossed the world. The sixth was Parasurama, who rid the world of the ksatriyas. The seventh was Rama, who put an end to the misdeeds of the Ravanas. The eighth was Krishna, who conquered cruel Kamsa. The ninth was Buddha, who came to forbid bloody sacrifices. Then tenth and final one was to be Kalkin, who would come at the end of the present age on a white horse to punish the wicked and reward the good.

This is the generally agreed list of the avatars of Vishnu. In reality, however, their number is incalculable (*Bhagavatapurana*), and no one knows what they all are.

In order to create, stabilize, lead, destroy and liberate the world, Vishnu had to divide himself. As manifestations which were less complete than the divinity's avatars, the *vyuhas* were, nonetheless, emanations. They were the brother, son, and grandson of Krishna and were called Samkarsana, Pradyumna and Aniruddha.

Vasudeva-Krishna possessed all six principal qualities of the deity: knowledge, might, power, efficiency, influence and vigour. Each vyuha, however, had only two. Samkarsana had knowledge and might; Pradyumna had power and vigour; and, finally, Aniruddha had efficiency and influence.

The avatars

'There are people who will say that there are ten avatars; others will say that there are twenty-four; and still others will say that they are innumerable. Everywhere where there is a special manifestation of the power of God, there is an avatar. This is what I believe.' (Ramakrishna, *The Teaching of Ramakrishna*, P.1047. Paris, 1980)

The avatar of the tortoise

' "Help us, o you who are powerful; lift up the mountain." At these words, Vishnu-Hrikesa, taking on the form of a tortoise, set the mountain on his back and lay down in the water, Hari. Then the soul of the worlds, Kesava, taking in his hand the summit of the mountain, the supreme Purusha [. . .] churned the sea of milk.' (*Ramayana*, I, 14, 29 – 31)

Visvamitra

Indian hero

The ascetic

As a ksatriya (warrior), Visvamitra wanted to make himself into a Brahman through an increasingly rigid asceticism.

Visvamitra understood that he could equal the Brahman Vasistha only by becoming a Brahman himself, so he withdrew to the forest and started to practise austerity. After a thousand years, Brahma gave him the title of royal *rsi*. But, since Visvamitra wanted to create a new sky, he used up all the merits accumulated in that time.

He returned to his austerity for a thousand years. Brahma again made him a rsi. But Visvamitra fell in love with the nymph, Mehaka, and lived with her for ten years. And so the fruit of his asceticism was irremediably destroyed.

Visvamitra persisted. He placed himself between the five fires in summer and in water in winter. Brahma made him a *maharsi* (super-rsi). But the gods sent him the nymph Rambha, and Visvamitra smelled a trap. He flew into a rage and lost all the benefits of his efforts.

Visvamitra then stopped eating and breathing for some years. He did not let himself be tempted, and he finally became a Brahman, and the equal of Vasistha (*Ramayana*, I).

Brahman and ksatriya
The Brahman was the priest who held religious power. Thr ksatriya was the warrior who held civil power. On a spiritual level, the ksatriya was subject to the Brahman; on a civil level, the Brahman depended on the ksatriya.

Wak

Ethiopian god

Creator

Wak was the supreme god who lived in the clouds.

Wak kept the vault of the heavens at a distance from the earth and covered it with stars. He was a benefactor and did not know how to punish.

When the earth was flat, Wak asked man to make his own coffin. Man did this and then Wak shut him up in it. Wak pushed the coffin into the ground. For seven years, he made fire rain down and the mountains were formed.

Then Wak trampled the place where the coffin was and man sprang forth, alive. He said he had slept only for a brief moment. This was said to be why man is awake for most of the day.

Man tired of living alone. Wak took some of his blood and after four days, the blood became a woman whom the man married. He had 30 children. However, he was ashamed at having had quite so many and so he hid 15 of them. Wak then made them into animals and demons.

Xipe Totec

Aztec god

Our flayed lord

Xipe Totec was the god of springtime renewal and nocturnal rain.

One of the great Mexican festivals was dedicated to the god Xipe Totec. It marked the return of blossom in springtime, which was attributed to the god.

The ceremonies began with human sacrifices. The victims were pierced with arrows so that their blood flooded the ground like a fertilizing rain. Then their hearts were torn out and, finally, they were flayed. People who had certain skin diseases asked to wear the skin of the tortured for 20 days in order to regain their health.

This was followed by a mock battle. Experienced fighters were set against young pupils who had also put on the still warm skin of the sacrificial victims. These young pupils were volunteers who wanted to perform an act of worship or to atone for some public misdemeanour.

Perhaps because of the yellow skins worn by the penitents, Xipe Totec was the god of goldsmiths.

Human sacrifices

Another culture, another mentality: the conquistadors were horrified by the blood shed in Aztec temples to 'feed' the gods; the Aztecs were terrified by the tortures imposed by the Inquisition.

Xipe Totec, with his impassive expression, observes the cruel ceremonies organized in his honour to mark the return of spring.

Polychromatic ceramic plaque, late post-classic Aztec civilization.

Xiuhtecuhtli

Aztec god

Fire

Xiuhtecuhtli (Otontecuhtli or Huehueteotl) was the old god.

Xiuhtecuhtli was an old, bearded man who carried on his head a brazier in which incense was burned. He was the god of the hearth. It was said that his colours were those of flames: red, yellow and blue.

Xiuhtecuhtli was honoured during the festival 'for the binding of the year'. The Aztec 'century' lasted 56 years. On the way from one century to the next, the gods could break their contract and the people were filled with terror at the prospect of the end of the world. But then the new fire was born. The priests gathered the precious fire and each took it to his own home.

The god of fire was also the god of the sun and of volcanoes. Dancers evoked the ghosts by smearing their bodies with soot and charcoal, products of fire.

Xiuhtecuhtli was associated with peppers, symbols of the life force. The pine, from which torches are made, was his tree.

> **The effect on opposites**
> Xiuhtecuhtli, the most ancient of the gods, had the power to act upon opposites. He was light in the darkness, heat in the cold, the male principle in the female elements and life in death.

Yama

The first Indian mortal

King of the dead

Yama was the first man. He was the son of Vivasvant, the sun. In Northern Europe he was called Ymir, and in Iran, Yima or Manu.

Yama had a sister, Yami. They mated in order to create humanity. In India, on the fifth day of the festival of the lamps, sisters invited their brothers as guests. They received them at lunch, prepared baths for them and worshipped them. Thus they commemorated the union of the first human couple. (*Rig Veda*, X, 10).

Yama, the first man, was also the first to know death. Thus he became the leader of the dead. It was he, or one of his servants, who came to look for those who had used up their lifetimes.

Nothing should have distracted Yama from this task. However, one day he became absorbed in sacrificial rites and did not make a single man die. The result of this was an excessive increase of the human race. Mankind was in competition with the gods. They had to wait for the end of the sacrifice before the situation returned to normal (*Mahabharata*, I, 1, 196).

Yu the Great

Chinese hero

The engineer

Yu was a demiurge who measured the world from east to west and from north to south in order to lay it out.

Yu, the son of K'un, the emperor of China, was a thin man who was ill and hopped about on one foot. Thus he invented the step of Yu, which was danced by sorcerers. He dug out the mountains and allowed waters to flow from a catastrophic flood, a tast which K'un had not managed to accomplish. He worked at it for 13 years without returning home.

When he became a god, Yu travelled the world in order to plan it. He stabilized the five sacred mountains at the four cardinal points and at the centre; then he summoned the deities of the great mountains and the great rivers.

Yu's wife was the daughter of T'u-chan, the mountain of the earth. One day, she saw her husband turning into a bear. She was turned into stone and, since she was pregnant, Yu had to split her open with his sabre in order to give birth to his son. Some say that he himself was born of stone. Yu was the first emperor of the Hsia Dynasty.

Zanahary

Supreme god of the Madagascans

The 'double' god

He was Zanahary, 'the creator god' and he was also Railanitra, 'father of heaven'.

Zanahary was a terrifying god who spoke in thunder and lightning. He was careless, however, and was deceived by his double, the Zanahary from down below.

Creation

In the beginning, there were two Zanaharys: one above, Andriamanitra, and one below. The Zanahary from below amused himself making clay figures representing men, women and animals. However, he could not bring them to life. Zanahary above asked him for some of these statuettes in exchange for sunlight. Zanahary from below then offered him fish; the other wanted women. They agreed and Zanahary above gave life, but Zanahary below refused to be separated from the women. The two gods became enemies, and that is how the worlds above and below came to be separated.

> **The origins of polygamy**
> Zanahary put clay figures into the hands of men saying: 'Move them around; they will start to live and be your companions.' Those who had several of these figures became polygamists.

Zeus/Jupiter

Greek and Roman god

The king of Olympus

God of all gods, Zeus won absolute power.

Zeus is depicted as a mature man who wears a large beard. He carries a sceptre in his hand as the insignia of his authority, or brandishes a thunderbolt, his favourite weapon. He is often accompanied by an eagle.

Zeus was the son of Cronos and Rhea. An oracle had warned Cronos that he would be deposed by one of his children, and so Cronos swallowed each of them at birth. Rhea then decided to bring a sixth one into the world secretly, in the middle of the night. She then gave Cronos a stone wrapped in swaddling clothes instead of a baby. He was fooled by it and Zeus was saved.

The conquest of power

The child was entrusted to the nymphs, the Curetes, and the goat-nymph Amaltheia. When Amaltheia died, Zeus used her hide as armour. He set out to seize power. Metis gave him a drug which, when taken by Cronos, would make him regurgitate his children. He freed the Cyclopes and the Hecatonchires, giants endowed with 100 hands and 50 heads, whom Cronos had imprisoned in Tartarus. They gave him thunder and lightning. And so, Zeus found himself at the head of a real army.

The war against Cronos lasted ten years. Zeus brought back victory, and the gods divided the power by drawing lots: Zeus got the heavens; Poseidon, the sea; and Hades the underworld, hell.

However, their supremacy was immediately challenged by the giants, creatures of invincible strength. They had the privilege of being able to be killed only by the joint action of a god and a man. Zeus appointed Heracles, who was only a mortal, to help him, and so finished off his enemies.

Now he had to confront internal conspiracies. Hera, Athena and Poseidon had quickly tired of being dominated by the king of Olympus. They decided to chain up Zeus. Thetis, however, who was still faithful, enlisted the help of the giant Briareus, who showed his strength and put the conspirators to flight.

The master

Zeus became the greatest of the Olympian gods and the undisputed master. As the god of light, he was the source of all heavenly manifestations: he caused rain, drought, good weather and bad weather; he commanded tempests and created storms.

Zeus also guaranteed order among the gods and among men. He was the arbiter in quarrels: between Apollo and Heracles over the ownership of the Delphic tripod; between Apollo and Idas for the possession of Marpessa; between Pallas and Athena when they fought; between Athena and Poseidon for the domination of Attica; between Aphrodite and Persephone for the love of Adonis. His decisions were just and well balanced, and he showed no favouritism.

His loves and his offspring

Zeus had many wives. Metis was the first, but since Gaea had predicted that the daughter who would be born to them would herself bring into the world a son who would take Zeus's power, he swallowed Metis before she could give birth. The child, Athena, sprang from her father's head, fully armed (Hesiod, *Theogony*, 924).

Themis was his second wife. By her he was the father of the Seasons, Eirene (Peace), Eunomia (Order), Dice (Justice) and the Moerae (the Fates).

By Dione, Zeus had Aphrodite; by Eurynome, the Graces; by Mnemosyne, the Muses; by Leto, Apollo and Artemis; by Demeter, Persephone. Then Zeus married his own sister, Hera. He shared his power with her, and their children were Hebe, Eileithyia and Ares.

Zeus also had affairs with mortal women. Alcmene, Danaë, Aegina, Pluto, Io, Callisto and many others all bore his children. In order to seduce them, he turned himself into another form—for example, a shower of gold, a bull or a swan—or put some other plan into action in order to hide his majesty, which could not otherwise be borne by a mortal. Many demigods and heroes were born of these unions, and there was scarcely a single important Greek family which did not claim such lofty ancestry.

Whether they were the result of debauchery or of a desire to interfere in the affairs of men, these passing love affairs infuriated his legitimate wife, Hera. She pursued her husband's mistresses and the children he had had by them. Squabbles were commonplace between the two spouses. Zeus was often angry with Hera, and he even went so far as to hang her from Olympus with an anvil fastened to each ankle.

Marpessa was the daughter of Evenus and Alcippe. She was betrothed to Idas but was kidnapped by Apollo.

Hebe, the daughter of Zeus and Hera, personified youth. On Olympus her role was that of Zeus's handmaiden.

Eileithyia, daughter of Zeus and Hera, worked on behalf of her jealous mother when faced with her father's escapades.

Alcmene was seduced by Zeus, who took on the appearance of her husband, Amphitryon.

Aegina was the daughter of the river-god Asopus. Zeus ran off with her, and Asopus travelled the whole of Greece in search of her. Zeus struck Asopus down with a thunderbolt.

Io was a young woman from Argus whom Zeus loved. Hera was jealous of her, so her lover changed her into an incredibly beautiful heifer. Hera then demanded her as a gift.

Callisto was a nymph and priestess of Artemis. Zeus took on the form of Artemis in order to seduce her. When the goddess found out what had happened, she turned Callisto into a bear.

His cult

The cult of Zeus Polieus was celebrated at the feast of the Dipolia. The main ceremony bore the name of Bouphonies. Cattle were set free, and as soon as one of them came near the barley or wheat which was set near the altar, a priest rushed forward to strike it down with an axe. The animal was then skinned, eaten and stuffed, and a dummy harnessed to a cart. The axe was accused of the murder and thrown into the sea.

Stoic philosophers made the Olympian king the symbol of the one and only god. As Cleanthus (232 BC) said: 'You are the supreme lord of the universe, and so nothing is produced on earth without you, nor in the ethereal heavens, nor in the sea.' (*Hymn to Zeus*)

Jupiter
Jupiter was the great god of the Roman Pantheon. He was assimilated to Zeus as the supreme god. He was called *Optimus Maximus*, 'The Greatest and the Best'. Romulus began his cult: during the battle of the Romans and the Sabines., Romulus raised his arms to heaven and promised to build a temple to Jupiter where he was standing if the enemy's progress was halted. The Romans won, and the temple of Jupiter Stator ('who halts') was built at the foot of the Capitol. Jupiter, having become the supreme master of the city, received the homage of the consul when he took office, and the emperors worshipped him particularly. Augustus claimed to have seen him in a dream.

Intermediary and Fantastical Beings

Many intermediary beings, such as angels, demons, monsters, giants and so on, often appear in mythology. They are set between gods and men by their natures, their modes of behaviour, their qualities or failings, and their powers.

There are other mythological beings, however, which do not play an active role, but which do have a place in people's imagination.

Intermediary beings

Islamic *djinns* were created by Allah from fire. They were invisible creatures, endowed with intelligence. They inhabited the wilderness, ruins and cemeteries. They were the true owners of the soil. Like men, they lived in tribes, married and had children, formed alliances and declared war on each other.

They were not, however, equal to men. They were not limited to one body, but had the gift of being able to move very quickly, and even to be everywhere at once, to 'listen at the gates of heaven' (*Koran*, XV, 18). They wandered abroad at night under cover of darkness and took on the appearance of different creatures: sometimes of hideous monsters, and sometimes that of more sympathetic creatures such as horses or dogs. However, their attachment to the earth meant that they preferred the form of creeping animals.

The djinns were close to men. They were capable of friendship and felt gratitude towards those who treated them well. Inexplicable deeds were attributed to them, and they gave inspiration to poets, talent to musicians and discernment to seers. They too had believers and unbelievers, for the prophet was also sent for them.

The *nats* of Burma or the *neq* of Pakistan were divided into 37 varieties, each having a strict hierarchy. This hierarchy, however, differed according to different regions and legends. Most of them were of unknown origin, but the commonly held view was that the nats were former human beings who had died unfairly and violently. Thus, some of them were men who had been made the guardians of a place by burying them alive on the spot. They were invisible but could appear in human or animal form. They could be good or bad and were worshipped in order to obtain their help or to ask protection from wrongdoing.

Trolls are part of Scandinavian mythology. They were evil spirits, dwarves or giants with fir trees on their heads. They lived in the mountains or the forest and usually stayed underground. They were the incarnation of the mysterious forces of nature.

Fantastical beings

There is also an infinite number of fantastical beings, whose adventures are told in legends and who were supposed to be present in certain places and circumstances. Big or small, beneficent or malevolent, sometimes alternating between both, they haunted the territory of men and inspired them with terror or tenderness. It is impossible to compile a list of them all since their habitat was often very localized. Some types, though, were more widespread and lived in many regions.

Ghosts are the manifestation of the dead to the living. They can take on very diverse appearances, from the exact form of the dead person, with his face and voice, to a shadow covered in a white sheet. They cause very many phenomena: haunted houses, spirit-rapping, poltergeists, noises without any apparent cause or showers of pebbles. Certain people, called mediums, say that they can communicate with them, make them appear and interpret their messages.

According to Allan Kardec (1804–1869), who closely studied this phenomenon, the ghost was the *périsprit*, a fluid covering forming the link between the body and the soul in life. When a person died, the soul slowly disengaged itself from matter and, during this period of change, the *périsprit* could appear and even move objects.

Spiritualism, the name given to Allan Kardec's theory, developed considerably during the 19th century. Large meetings were organized at which attempts were made to communicate with ghosts, tables were overturned or moved, revelations were made and messages were passed on. Well-known people such as Victor Hugo, Conan Doyle and the scholar Charles Henry practised it.

Fairies were mostly pretty young women, shining with light. They were long-haired, wore long dresses and carried magic wands, the instrument of their power.

The Fairy Stone, Fairy Rock, Fairy Bridge and other similar names indicate places fairies are supposed to have passed. They were sensitive and quick to take offence. They helped men and sometimes sent them great blessings; usually, though, there was a condition attached and, if it was not respected, the fairies disappeared.

We should particularly note, among the many fairies, Margot-la-Fée of Brittany, who had supernatural powers and brought dolmens to hide the entrances to their dwellings. Also notable were the Martes or Martines, who lived in the rocks of Berry and Bourbonnais. They were big, brown-haired women with enormous breasts who ran after passers-by in order to be suckled by them.

Sprites and *imps* were considered to be small creatures, but they could grow and take on the nature of an animal or even of a breeze. When they were beneficent they helped in the home, doing the washing-up and polishing the furniture. When they were

wicked, they followed passers-by and threw them into ditches, or scattered the grain at harvest time. They had many different names, according to which region they were found in: they were known as leprechauns in Ireland, as piskies in Cornwall (pixies in England) and as elves in Northern Europe. Robin Goodfellow, otherwise known as Puck or Hobgoblin, was a figure in English folklore in the 16th and 17th centuries. His characteristics were portrayed by Shakespeare in *A Midsummer Night's Dream*.

Werewolves were men with magical properties, who turned into wolves at night. They led a life of wandering, crossing hedges, ditches and ponds. They were not afraid of sticks, knives or fire, and they devoured the first person they met. During the day, they were perfectly ordinary people.

One became a werewolf by making a pact with the devil, by birth (especially illegitimate birth) or following an unconfessed crime. Werewolves have been around for a very long time. Virgil and Saint Augustine spoke of them, and the Slavs used to celebrate the cult of the wolf—a sign of the fear which the beasts inspired.

Succubi were female demons who came in the night to sleep with certain men, while *incubi* were male demons who raped women. It was said that the incubi used the semen which men had lost while asleep to fertilize their victims.

Vampires were dead people who came out of their tombs to attack living people. They drank their victims' blood and ate their flesh. A vampire could be recognized by his well-preserved skin and red lips. In order to kill one of them, a stake had to be driven into his or her skull or heart.

Pantheons

Genealogy of the Olympians

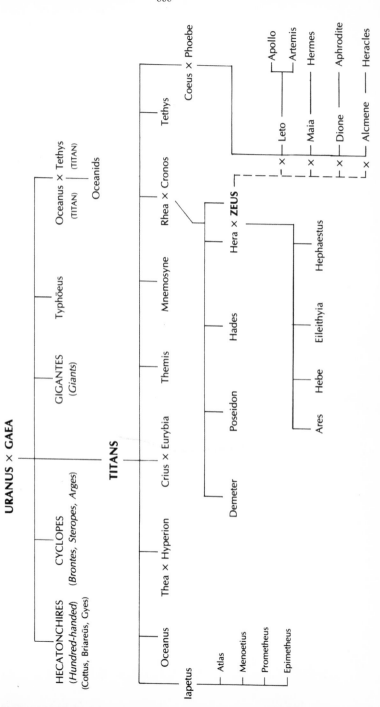

Gods of the Middle East

Name	Consort	Domain	Centre of Cult
Ahura Mazda		Supreme God	Herat (Iran)
An			Uruk
Anahita		fertility	Herat (Iran)
Angra Mainyu		darkness	Herat (Iran)
Anu	Antum	father of the gods	Sumer
Aramazd	Anahit	creation	Urartu (Armenia)
Astarte		war, love	Tyre
Baal	Anat	storm	Ugarit
Damuzi	Innana	vegetation	Uruk
Ea		wisdom	Akkad
Enki	Ningursag	wisdom	Eridu
Enlil	Ninlil	father of the gods	Nippur
Erra			
Hadad		storm	Assur
Inanna	Damuzi	war, love	Uruk
Ishtar	Tammuz	war, love	Assur
Kumarbi		war	Hurri
Marduk	Zerbanitu		Babylon
Mithras		sovereignty	Herat (Iran)
Mot		war, sterility	Ugarit
Nergal	Erishkigal	the underworld	Babylon
Ninurta	Gula	war, crafts	Sumer
Shamash	Aya	the sun	Babylon
			Assur
Sin		the moon	Babylon
			Assur
Tammuz	Ishtar	vegetation	Akkad
Tesub	Hebat	storms	Hurri
Tiamat	Apsu	the sea	Akkad
Vahagn	Astlik	war	Urartu (Armenia)

The Egyptian Gods

Name Consort	Domain	Symbol	Centre of Cult
Amun-Re (Mut)	universal god	ram	Thebes
Anubis	god of funerals	jackal	Cynopolis
Apis	fertility	bull	Memphis
Aten	only god	solar disc	Tell el-Amarna
Geb (Nut)	the earth	human form	the Delta
Hathor	joy and love	cow	Dendera
Horus (Hathor)	divinity of the pharoahs	falcon	the Delta
Isis (Osiris)	magic	human form	the Delta
Khnum	creation	ram	
Khons	son of Amen	falcon	Thebes
Maat	balance	ostrich feather	
Nephthys (Seth)	sterility	human form	the Delta
Nut (Geb)	sky	celestial vault	Heliopolis
Osiris (Isis)	vegetation	human form	the Delta
Ptah (Sekhmet)	creation	human form	Memphis
Sekhmet (Ptah)	power	lioness	Memphis
Seth (Nephthys)	evil	a composite animal	the Delta
Thoth	scribe	ibis	Hermopolis

The Hermopolitan Ogdoad

The eight pairs of elementary forces, the
personification of primitive chaos.

NUN $\longleftrightarrow$ NAUNET
primal water

HEH $\longleftrightarrow$ HEHET
spatial infinity

KEK $\longleftrightarrow$ KEKET
darkness

AMUN $\longleftrightarrow$ AMAUNET
the hidden

The Heliopolitan Ennead

The complementary deities, elements of the forces of nature which gave birth to the
two couples Isis-Osiris and Seth-Nephthys.

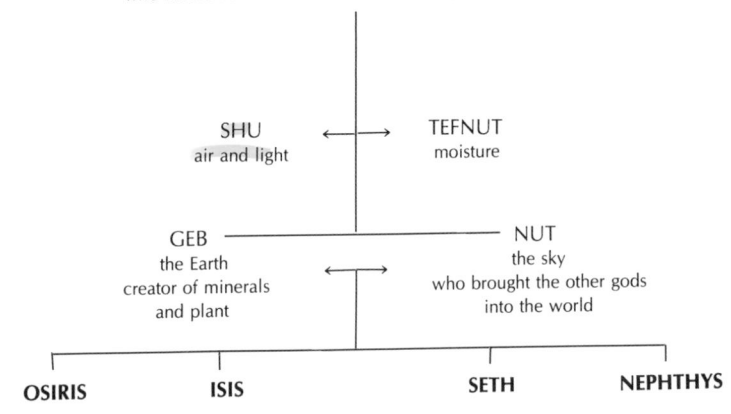

ATUM-RE
the solitary creator
who would become Amun-Re with the supremacy of Thebes

SHU   TEFNUT
air and light   moisture

GEB   NUT
the Earth   the sky
creator of minerals   who brought the other gods
and plant   into the world

OSIRIS   ISIS   SETH   NEPHTHYS

The entire Ennead is a manifestation of the demiurge.

The Gods of India

The Vedic Pantheon
The ancient gods of India

The sovereigns
MITRA, guarantor of the contract
VARUNA, organizer of the world

The fighters
INDRA, the exuberance of life ———
RUDRA, the destroyer ———

The gods of fertility
ADITI, the mother of the gods
AGNI, fire
PRAJAPATI, the primordial being
PURUSHA, the master of immortality
SARASVATI, the sacred river ———
SOMA, the drink of immortals
VISHNU, the master of space ———
YAMA, the first man

The Hindu Trimurti
The three great gods of
Hinduism

SHIVA-RUDRA, beneficent
and destructive
his wife: DURGA
his sons: GANESHA
SKANDA
his retinue:
KAMA and his wife RATI

VISHNU, the omnipresent
his wife: LAKHSMI
his avatars:
MATSYA, the fish
KURMA, the tortoise
VARAHA, the boar
NARASIMHA, the man-lion
VAMANA, the dwarf
PARASURAMA
RAMA, and his wife SITA,
      avatar of LAKSMI
KRISHNA and his wife RUKMINI
      avatar of LAKHSMI
BUDDHA
KALKIN
his retinue: INDRA
        HANUMAN
BRAHMA, the creator
his wife: SARASVATI

The Norse Gods

Name	Consort	Domain	Symbol
Balder		beauty and goodness	
Bragi	Idunn	poetry	
Freyja	Odh	love and sensual pleasure	the cat
Freyr	Gerd	fertility	the boar
Frigg	Odin	fertility	
Heimdallr		firstborn	
Idunn	Bragi	eternal youth	golden apples
Loki	Sigryn	evil	
Njord	Skadi	fertility	
Norns		fate	
Od	Freyja	holy fury	
Odin	Jord	knowledge of magic &	the raven
	Frigg	manual dexterity	the wolf
	Rind		
Thor	Sif	war and thunder	the goat
Tyr		war and justice	
Valkyries		angels of battle	

Index

Note: Entries in **bold type** refer to articles headed with the name shown.